Extreme Software Engineering

The Robert C. Martin Series

Robert C. Martin
Agile Software Development: Principles, Patterns, and Practices

Robert C. Martin
UML for Java Programmers

Ken Schwaber and Mike Beedle
Agile Software Development with SCRUM

Daniel H. Steinberg and Daniel W. Palmer
Extreme Software Engineering: A Hands-On Approach

Extreme Software Engineering

A Hands-On Approach

Daniel H. Steinberg
and
Daniel W. Palmer

Upper Saddle River, New Jersey 07458

Library of Congress Cataloging-in-Publication Data

Steinberg, Daniel H. (Daniel Howard), 1959-
Extreme software engineering : a hands on approach / Daniel H. Steinberg and Daniel W. Palmer.
p. cm.
Includes bibliographical references and index.
ISBN 0-13-047381-2
1. Computer software--Development. 2. eXtreme programming. 3. Software engineering.
I. Palmer, Daniel William. II. Title.

QA76.76.D47S732 2003
005.1'1--dc22

2003062232

Vice President and Editorial Director, ECS: *Marcia Horton*
Publisher: *Alan R. Apt*
Associate Editor: *Toni D. Holm*
Editorial Assistant: *Patrick R. Lindner*
Vice President and Director of Production and Manufacturing, ESM: *David W. Riccardi*
Executive Managing Editor: *Vince O'Brien*
Managing Editor: *Camille Trentacoste*
Production Editor: *Heather Meledin*
Director of Creative Services: *Paul Belfanti*
Art Director: *Jayne Conte*
Cover Designer: *Bruce Kenselaar*
Cover Image: *Spiral Galaxy NGC 4414 as photographed through the Hubble Space Telescope, Courtesy of NASA*
Art Editor: *Greg Dulles*
Manufacturing Manager: *Trudy Pisciotti*
Manufacturing Buyer: *Lynda Castillo*
Marketing Manager: *Pamela Hersperger*
Marketing Assistant: *Barrie Reinhold*

Pearson Education, Inc.
Upper Saddle River, NJ 07458

Printed in the United States of America
10 9 8 7 6 5 4 3 2

ISBN 0-13-047381-2

Pearson Education Ltd., *London*
Pearson Education Australia Pty. Ltd., *Sydney*
Pearson Education Singapore, Pte. Ltd.
Pearson Education North Asia Ltd., *Hong Kong*
Pearson Education Canada, Inc. *Toronto*
Pearson Educación de Mexico, S.A. de C.V.
Pearson Education Malaysia, Pte. Ltd.
Pearson Education, Inc., *Upper Saddle River, New Jersey*

To Dwight Olson for his friendship, encouragement, assistance, and support
Daniel H. Steinberg

To my Mom, for the blue suitcase and all it stands for
Daniel W. Palmer

Foreword

There is a difference between books written for a professional setting and books written for an academic setting. The importance of this difference was made abundantly clear to me as I read through the drafts of the book you are currently holding. As an author of professional books, I was humbled. I knew that my books reach and teach professionals, but *here* was a book that could reach and teach *students*.

The issue, of course, is context. When one professional writes books for other professionals, there is a massive amount of context that the author can take for granted. The author does not have to educate his readers about that context. The author can make statements without justification, can assert truths without proof, and can use words and terms without defining them. The author can depend upon a common base of knowledge and experience to help him communicate his ideas.

When I first read *this* book, I was assuming that it would follow the same pattern. I was incorrect. This book builds the context, defines the terms, justifies its statements, and demonstrates its assertions. What's more—wonder of wonders—it manages to do this without being boring. *This book teaches!*

The student who attempts to learn eXtreme Programming by reading the professional books is likely to find the reading a minefield of assumed context. But the student who reads *this* book will enjoy a step-by-step, goal-by-goal, exercise-by-exercise *education*. That student will also be entertained by the myriad anecdotes, stories, metaphors, and comparisons. Not only does this book teach, it's downright fun to read.

I have been a software professional since the early '70s. During this time I have been repeatedly discouraged at how unprepared CS graduates are to enter the workforce. Time and time again I have interviewed young men and women who held BSCS or MSCS degrees, and who could not write a line of code. During an interview I often ask the interviewee to write a program using the sieve of Eratosthenes to find prime numbers. I remain appalled at the number of graduates who cannot deal with the nested loop required to solve that problem.

It's not that these young graduates are uneducated, or even unintelligent. Most of them perform quite well in a question-and-answer mode. Most of them understand fundamental concepts of computer science, and know many of the current buzzwords and acronyms. However, many young CS graduates do not seem to know how to program computers.

Of those graduates that *do* know how to program computers, very few understand what it means to be a professional programmer. Very few have been instilled with the disciplines and values of the craft. Very few know how to distinguish bad code from good code. Very few understand that professional programming is more about crafting solid, well-tested, and well-structured code than it is about making programs work.

The book you are holding is part of the remedy for these ills. What CS students *need* is to get their fingers on their keyboards working in a team environment on real projects for real clients using real languages, real tools, and real methods. This book provides the instructor and the students with the tools and guidelines for doing just that.

An instructor can use this book to design a course that will have a real and positive impact upon their students. Such a course will be an adventure of learning for both the students and the instructor. It will be filled with milestones, successes, and defeats. It will give the students a feel for what a real project is like, and give them the skills to deal with real problems and real successes.

Most importantly, a course structured around this book gives the instructor the chance to work alongside the students and thereby to instill values and disciplines that simply cannot be learned in a traditional classroom setting. It allows the instructor to be a mentor to the students, teaching them by *doing*.

Imagine a course in which the instructors and students work together to produce a real software system for a real client. Imagine how much the students will learn as they pair program with each other and with the instructors. Imagine how much the instructors will learn about, and impart to, each student as they pair and work together. Imagine a teaching environment in which the instructors and students are part of the same team working to achieve the same goals. That's the kind of environment that this book will help you create.

Needless to say I am thrilled by the potential that this book offers. Not only is this book an excellent introduction to eXtreme Programming. Not only does it teach eXtreme Programming in a capable and competent manner. Not only does it teach solid values of software professionalism. In the end the promise of this book is that it will help prepare CS students to hit the workforce ground running, instead of stumbling.

Robert C. Martin

Preface

At some point in the process of learning the craft of software development, you need to work on a real project for a real client. The project must be large enough that you can't hold all of the details in your head. The duration of the project must be long enough that you don't remember what you were intending when you wrote the code that you later are trying to understand. The project must be complex enough that you need to clarify requirements that you thought you once understood.

Many colleges and universities offer a one- or two-term course in which the students learn about software engineering by working on a significant project for a real client. We don't claim to have invented this idea.

Our version of a hands-on software engineering class is derived from the course created by Fred Brooks at Chapel Hill. Students work on a real project for a real client while spending class time discussing readings on various software methodologies and on issues that can arise during the students' practical experience.

eXtreme Programming (XP) is well suited to the academic setting. Initially, and for several years, software teams in our course used the traditional approach. They worked their way from requirements' analysis to final delivery over the course of a semester. One semester half of the class continued with the traditional approach and half of the class used XP. The course now runs with all of the software teams using XP as their methodology for these practicums.

The pedagogical benefits of using XP were immediately clear. Students that work in small groups get consistent and useful feedback about their progress. This comes from other students they pair with, from seeing the unit-tests pass, from completing tasks, and from quick and frequent client reaction. All students communicate with clients, coaches, "bosses," and each other. No skill is as important as communication. The students are constantly required to communicate verbally and through their code and other writing. Students begin to see how various pieces fit together. Instead of working on toy programs intended to illustrate a particular point such as sorting, students see how they and others on the same project are dependent on the sorting code they've written.

HANDS-ON SOFTWARE ENGINEERING

There is a gap between the way students learn to program in an academic setting and the way software is written in professional practice. Some of the differences result from the differing goals of the two environments: computer science departments aim to teach the craft of programming, and professional software developers set out to create useful programs. Students are learning the craft, so they can focus on one thing at a time; professionals must deal with a myriad of factors simultaneously. The larger the gap grows the more additional training students need after graduation.

Academia is faced with the task of being more relevant to students without becoming a purely vocational venue. Certification programs exist, and do provide useful, short-term value, but because of the blazingly fast refresh rate of technology, students who choose this route sacrifice building a general, far-reaching foundation. The simple fact is that the specifics of a given platform, package, or language covered during the four years of college may very well be outdated by graduation. Today's language syntax or operating system (OS) features have little more staying power than a passing fad or a moderately popular sitcom. Instead, students must develop an understanding of the trade-offs, the issues, and the broader context that will shape "next thing" and "the thing after that."

This book describes a course that begins to bridge the gap between academic and professional software practices. It describes how to build an environment within the academic crucible that more closely mirrors the pressures, constraints, and interdependencies of a realistic software development effort. It uses methodologies that are flexible enough to meet the changing needs of clients within the rigid time constraints of an academic calendar. But eXtreme Programming is more than just a schedule management tool, it promotes good programming practices, it improves the quality of the produced code, and it helps integrate a group of individual programmers into a development team. In short, it's more than just a way to program, it's a great way to teach software engineering.

WHO IS THIS BOOK FOR?

This book is particularly well suited to be used in three settings.

1. A project-based class in computer science where the students work in groups on long-term (one quarter/one semester or more) projects for actual clients.
2. A team of developers interested in an immersive experience to investigate eXtreme Programming.
3. One or more developers planning a self-directed exploration of the principles and practices of eXtreme Programming.

Academic Settings

This book is primarily aimed at supporting an extended programming experience. The usual audience consists of established undergraduate computer science majors, with many semesters of computer science courses behind them. This course can serve as a capstone experience, and, as such, requires that students have a solid and varied collection of programming experience. Though it is not required for this course specifically or for software engineering in general, this book assumes an understanding of object-oriented programming, and in particular, the Java programming language.

This book is not intended to be a comprehensive introduction to software engineering. This book provides instruction, guidance, and examples in the experiential component of the class. Instructors will need to select a traditional software-engineering textbook or supplemental readings to cover methods from other Agile or traditional methodologies. As this landscape is always changing, we use supplemental readings as the basis for in-class discussions.

Professional Training Settings

A weeklong immersive experience using XP will give you the flavor of the methodology and enough experience to jump start an XP project in your work environment. In that setting, this book can be used as a valuable reference so that you can prepare for the training by reading the chapters in the Parts I and II to prepare for the training experience. You can then read the chapters in the Part III after the training week to supplement your understanding of the core practices.

Self-Study Groups or Individuals

For teams of software developers, the book provides you with a concrete look at the practices and of the life cycle of an iteration. In addition there are tutorial chapters designed to lead you step-by-step through the application of practices. The level of detail should support you and your group while studying this material on your own. Although pair programming is one of the central programming practices of XP, constraints may not allow you to explore XP with others. In this case you can still use this book as a study guide, but you should look for opportunities to try out pair programming.

FEATURES OF THE BOOK

Some of the book's features that support this interactive, project-oriented approach include: guidelines for setting up and presenting an XP software-engineering course (including an intense introduction to all the features of XP), a collection of tutorials on the core aspects of XP, a detailed description of what to expect each week when applying XP to a development project, and feedback from students, faculty, and clients who have been through the process.

The centerpiece of the book is the collection of practical tutorials that allow the reader to learn by doing the key XP practices. The tutorials provide step-by-step instruction on test-driven design, refactoring code, writing and running acceptance tests, interacting with the client, and using XP's planning game to determine where the development should focus its energy. Even if the reader unfamiliar with XP does nothing other than work through the tutorials, he or she will get the essence of what it is to work on an eXtreme Programming development effort.

For a fuller and more detailed portrait, the book offers a broader view of XP and how it integrates into a software-engineering course. In particular, the book provides a detailed description of what happens during a typical XP development effort. From the first interaction with the client, to ongoing meetings and programming sessions with fellow XP developers, through the conclusion of the project, this book describes in detail the activities, expectations, and responsibilities of all the participants in the process.

NOTE TO INSTRUCTORS

When a practical experience is the centerpiece to your course there are two basic approaches. In the first, you can take time to teach each of the practices or skills that the student will encounter before they encounter it. There are courses in traditional software engineering that do this. You lecture about creating a requirements document and then you have the students create one. A second approach is to get the students immersed in the programming experience as quickly as possible. The arguments for each of these approaches mirror the arguments for big up-front design versus the extreme just-in-time design.

We recognize the value in each of these approaches and have designed this book to meet some of the requirements of each. The fear that the up-front learning advocates have is that there are topics that may not be covered in the second approach. The extreme teaching crowd worries that the first approach spends a lot of time on concepts that the students don't know they need yet. This is not quite the you aren't going to need it (YAGNI) rule of XP. This is more that you don't know that you are going to need it. In teacher-training classes, future teachers are taught six different ways of asking questions and about different learning styles. They nod their heads and pass tests, but until they stand in front of their own class, they don't understand the relevance of the material.

You can cover the material in Part I to prepare the students for their practical experience. We suggest a Spike—a small practice project designed to get some of the kinks out before the actual project begins. Part II explains the shape of the iteration to the students. They need to read Part II before beginning their actual long-term project. Part III can be used in two ways, depending on whether you're taking the just-in-time or the up-front approach. You can either use these tutorials to cover and explain each of the practices before the students engage in them or you can leave them to the students to explore when they recognize the need. The remainder of the text contains information that doesn't need to be imparted to the student at any particular time.

NOTE TO STUDENTS

Most of the valuable learning from this book will come when you put it away for a while and work on exercises, step through tutorials, or try out a practice.

You can't learn Tai Chi sitting down, you can't learn to ski from the warmth of the lodge, and you can't learn to build large software systems using an Agile® methodology without booting up the computer. This book is designed for use in conjunction with an actual software development effort. The text *shows* you what to do instead of *telling* you what to do.

You will have a client. You'll find chapters that describe how to work with the client throughout the lifetime of the project. You'll work with a team. Much of the material in this book will help you negotiate with the team to figure out what is going to be done next and by whom. All of your code will be written in pairs. Pair programming may seem to fly in the face of how you've worked so far, but take this opportunity to give it a try. The biggest changes you will be asked to make are in how you actually write your code. You will be led through the process of writing test first code and looking for ways to improve it. As you need them, read and follow the tutorials on some of the more central practices.

Don't get too caught up in the details. XP is just a methodology. The goal in this course is to engage in all of the facets of software development. You will work with customers to elicit and focus requirements. You will design and build software. You will release your software and present your work to the customer. With XP you will pass through these steps many times during the semester. Each time, take a moment to note what you are learning and what you can do to make the next time through the XP process even better.

NOTE TO PROFESSIONALS

The advice in the "Note to Students" section applies to you too. In addition, you will find an outline in the second appendix of how you might organize the material depending on whether you are organizing a self-directed study group or a formal training workshop.

The easiest way to learn a new programming language, technique, or methodology is to choose a real project on which to experiment. With XP, it is even better to have an independent customer to interact with. It could be a real client, a friend, or relative. In a pinch you can be your own client—just be clear to keep separate when you are making decisions as the client and when you are making decisions as the developer.

The final request is that you give XP a fair trial. When you are a student in a formal course you will have to commit to XP for the duration of the course. With self-study or following a short-term immersion you can give up on XP before you realize the benefits. Writing code test first may feel like an added burden until the first time you have to perform a major refactoring and the unit tests protect you.

Contents

Acknowledgments

Daniel Steinberg would like to thank the following people:

Dan Palmer is a great sounding board, research partner, and friend. I came back from a conference where Bob Martin and Robert Koss led a hands-on XP workshop conference and convinced Dan Palmer that we had to learn XP. We played with it for a couple of months, ran a seminar on it, and then integrated it into Dan's software engineering course. Our "prime directive" in writing this book was that it shouldn't harm our friendship. It hasn't.

In addition to inspiring me, Bob Martin is always generous with his time and information. Bob invited me to participate in an XP Immersion at Object Mentor's offices in Chicago. I highly recommend this weeklong experience. I learn from Bob every time I have any contact with him. He has been a mentor and an inspiration.

Ken Auer is a wonderful combination of a deep thinker and a pragmatist, who is guided by a strong moral compass. Through his company, RoleModel Software, he has created an XP shop that has been a proving ground for this methodology. His staff has also been supportive and helpful. Ken has taken on apprentices and guided their education on their way to being craftsmen. I benefit from any conversation I have with Ken and appreciate his including me in the XP workshops held at OOPSLA in 2000 and 2001.

The XP community is full of helpful and caring individuals from whom I have gained much. Thanks to Ron Jeffries and Joshua Kerievsky for taking the time to explain things to me more than once in ways that I could understand. Thanks to Ward for groundbreaking ideas and to Kent for leading the charge. Thanks to the academic cohort that includes Joe Bergin, James Caristi, Robert Duvall, and Rick Mercer—your comments have been invaluable. Herb Schilling at NASA–Glenn in Cleveland carefully commented on an early draft of the tutorials. James Caristi classroom-tested this book at Valparaiso and has been a wonderful collaborator in workshops at various settings. The students in the XP seminar, software engineering class, and in the design patterns class at John Carroll University provided many helpful comments. Dwight Olson, the Mathematics and Computer Science department chair at John Carroll let me teach a course in Java when the language was barely a year old. He supported me both professionally and personally and provided a place for me to perch while working on this book. As if that weren't enough, he was our first XP client and let me use his name in describing the experience. I would like to thank the reviewers of our book: Kent Beck, James Caristi, Robert Martin, Peter McBreen, and Laurie Williams.

As always, thanks to Kimmy the wonderwife. These books take as much out of her as they do me. Raising our daughters, Maggie Rose and Elena, together has taught me more about pair programming than any XP project. Thanks to my in-laws, Tom and Geraldine Diemert for all the times they took care of our kids. Alan Apt is a great publisher and has been a joy to work with. I've wanted to write a book for him for a long time and it was an honor to do so. His team, in particular Patrick Lindner, has made this project quite pleasurable. Finally, thank you for being interested enough to read this book and try out these ideas.

Dan Palmer would like to thank the following people:

My friend, Daniel Steinberg is one of those modern-day renaissance people who refuse to limit themselves to only a handful of interests, ideas, or careers. Often when he returns from a conference he is so exuberant over the next "next" thing, that it's almost as if I had attended the event myself. I have learned much from these interactions and am grateful to him. This book is a result of one of these interactions.

I did much of my writing for this book under a Grauel fellowship from John Carroll University. It is a wonderful place to work and I am very appreciative of their support. Over the years, many people have been instrumental to the software engineering class, none more so than the faculty clients and student developers. I wish to thank and express deep appreciation to both groups for their efforts in making the course successful.

Faculty members who have been clients for the course are: Carl Anthony, Barbara D'Ambrosia (twice—in the same semester!), Marc Kirschenbaum, Dick Horwath, Sharon Kaye, Janet Larson, Jerry Moreno (twice), Paul Nietupski, Dwight Olson (three times!), Michael Setter, Wendy Shapiro (twice), Carl Spitznagel, and Mark Waner.

I have learned a lot from the students in the software engineering course—I hope that they have also benefited from our classroom experiences together. I want to thank these SE alumni: Tom Artale, Gyula Avshalumov, Nick Babik, J.J. Badri, Scott Barrett, Pat Barry, John Benander, Vince Benander, Michael Bertoni, Steve Blakeslee, Steve Blech, Mike Buck, Sam Calabrese, Leisa Campbell, Sam Capaldi, Pat Carey, Chris Casey, Mike Cavell, Mike Coletta, Aaron Craig, Margaret Czarney, Chris Dahms, Kristin Dudas, Derrick English, Victor Engoglia, Jeremy Esteves, Pat Fragle, Laura Freeman, Andrey Godes, Brian Graf, Gretchen Grubb, Chad Hantak, Doug Hayes, Christine Hawke, Ann Hricko, Jon Hunter, Kathy Jagodnik, Patty Jagodnik, Kevin Kappus, Trevor Kish, Matt Klus, Heather Korns, Mike Kovacina, Justin Lauer, Bill Lewins, Jim Lucko, Jamie May, Billy Meade, Tom Mis, Jon Murton, Jeff Neiner, Larry Nolte, Jeff Norris, Ann Ortega, Brian Palagyi, Tom Phillips, Gina Prodan, Pat Pulvino, Vadim Reydman, Mike Reynolds, Justin Robinson, Igor Roznik, Jerry Sabin, George Sample, Donnie Santos, Jeff Sawitke, Greg Schetter, Tim Schoenharl, Albert Sheynkman, Dave Swiatkowski, Maurice Vallentine, Chris Vasch, Jay Verba, Olga Vitlina, Jim Wetzel, Jen Wolke, Scott Wood, and Andy Wright. I am also grateful to Ernie Petti who listened to my plans, read articles, and discussed with me many of the concepts that are now integral parts of the course.

I would like to thank the reviewers of our book: Kent Beck, James Caristi, and Robert Martin, Peter McBreen, and Laurie Williams. Jake Warde has also provided very helpful assistance in putting together the instructor's resource CD. Kris Burm, inventor of the Gipf abstract strategy game project (www.gipf.com) has graciously allowed me to use his game as an example XP project, for which I am very grateful.

I want to thank the Palmers, the Wards, the Meagans, and the Seboks for all the family support and love they provide. Families, even when far away, are what really matter.

My wife Diane has been wonderfully understanding, caring, and helpful while I've been working on this book. My daughter Emily has been full of happiness, silliness, and not-so-subtle demands to let her use the computer during that same time. Both have made these efforts worthwhile. I wholeheartedly thank them.

Extreme Software Engineering

Introduction—

Previewing the Road Ahead

When you learn to program you read some material or listen to a lecture on a specific project. Then you work on a short-term project designed to ensure that you understand the topic being taught. If the topic of the week is recursion, then you know that your program will use some form of recursion. Maybe you work with others or maybe you work on your own. Often, by the end of the week you've come up with a program with a few classes that might total a few hundred lines. The program compiles and meets the specifications set by your instructor. While you are working on it, you can probably keep all of the details about the code in your head.

Your teachers have tried to instill good habits in you. They've asked you to include useful documentation with your source code. They've suggested that you draw some simple UML diagrams that help communicate the architecture of your solution. Some may have suggested that you include tests and test results to show that your program meets various requirements. This software-engineering course simulates the goals, pressures, and rewards that you might encounter in a professional software development environment. You'll be living with your project long enough to see the advantages of following advice on testing, documentation, source control, common coding standards, and others.

This course benefits from the synergies that arise from the combination of individually successful techniques. In this introduction we'll look at these individual components beginning with the notions of software engineering and how it has been traditionally taught. The most significant feature of this course is that students work on real long-term projects for real clients. We'll look at the benefits and origins of this hands-on approach. Many professional developers have successfully adopted eXtreme Programming or one of the other agile methodologies. We'll present an overview of the background and practices of eXtreme Programming (XP). Finally, we'll look at the advantages of integrating XP and a hands-on course in a capstone course on software development.

SOFTWARE ENGINEERING

To better understand the ideas of building large software systems, the process is often compared with constructing skyscrapers or building bridges. This metaphor is dated and may have been more appropriate when hardware had to be constructed or customized for a given programming task. In that case the discrete stages of analyzing the requirements and specifying the design of the software before building it to the specifications may have corresponded to designing a building, drawing up the blue prints, and then building it to these specifications. Other metaphors may better capture the idea of growing an organic system that must be maintained and can be changed to meet different needs over time.

Building Bridges

Software engineering is a very young field that is still growing and looking for new and better incarnations of itself. It's no wonder that there are so many open questions, so much room for conflicting ideas and so many different methodologies. On the other hand, bridge building goes back thousands of years. There continue to be innovations in the design and construction of bridges. The rate at which these changes are introduced is scales of magnitude less than in the field of software.

The first bridges were most likely trees knocked over creeks. One of the world's oldest bridges still standing today is the Martorell bridge located in Spain, near Barcelona. At one time it was the longest bridge in the world, spanning (a then mammoth) 37 meters. Built around 217 B.C., it is an early example of a semicircular stone arch bridge. We have more than two thousand years of experience in bridge building.

In contrast, the first computer program was written sometime between 1842 and 1952, depending on your definition of "computer program" and whether you care if it actually ran or not. In 1842, Ada Lovelace translated an article on Charles Babbage's proposed analytical engine. In her additions to the translation, she described the mechanics of how the machine could execute a program and purportedly supplied an example. The analytical engine was never built, yet she is often credited with writing the first computer program.

In 1945, John Von Neumann wrote a paper describing the principles of an electronic computer that stored its instructions like data. The paper included a program to sort values. The EDVAC, the first implementation of a stored-program computer, wasn't completed until 1952. During that 110 year stretch from Ada to EDVAC, there are many other contenders for the title of "first programmer" including teams of allied forces using Turing's decryption machines during World War II, those who worked on early electromechanical calculators and the teams of engineers that rewired the first computer, the ENIAC, every time a new program was run.

While the longest suspension bridge in the world as of this writing is 100 times longer than the Martorell bridge built two thousand years earlier, computer science has been moving at an insane rate. At bridge building's pace, software engineering wouldn't come up with a working screen saver for another several hundred years. So not only is the field young, it has been changing at a furious velocity. The combination makes one marvel that the situation isn't more chaotic.

There Is No "Software Physics" Supporting Software Engineering

"No Silver Bullet," Frederick Brooks' essay on the fundamental complexities of creating software systems, sums up the plight of the software developer as follows. "Software people are not alone in facing complexity. Physics deals with terribly complex objects even at the 'fundamental' particle level. The physicist labors on, however, in a firm faith that that there are unifying principles to be found … No such faith comforts the software engineer. Much of the complexity he must master is arbitrary complexity, forced without rhyme or reason by the many human institutions and systems to which his interfaces must conform."

Steve McConnell, author of *Code Complete*, echoes Dijkstra in attributing the complexity of software development to the incredible range that must be considered. As he puts it, "Computing is the only profession in which a single mind is obliged to span the distance from a bit to a few hundred megabytes, a ratio of 1 to 10^9, or nine orders of magnitude." When building a bridge, engineers can rely on other branches of study to provide formulaic understanding of different levels of consideration. Materials science encapsulates all the details and presents the behavior of concrete, steel or other materials in a macroscopic way to the bridge builder. The engineer doesn't have to know what's going on at a molecular level, he or she just needs to know the gross properties of a material in order to use them. Harmonics and aerodynamics are well understood and ignored at the peril of the disaster that befell the Tacoma Narrows Bridge over the Puget Sound. In 1940, it collapsed when high winds caused tortional waves that literally ripped the bridge apart. The flaw was calculable from the design.

There are no fundamental equations that can render lower levels of detail below consideration in software development. There are no metrics with which a software system's stability can be measured, before or *after* it is written. Though much of the development team can implement and deploy a system without knowledge or consideration of these issues, problems can occur at any level. Compilers do occasionally have bugs, "portable" software will behave differently on different platforms, and true optimization for speed can only be done with the utmost knowledge, care, and appropriate tools.

Tending Gardens

In *The Pragmatic Programmer,* Dave Thomas and Andrew Hunt argue that software is more like gardening than it is like construction. They explain that software "is more organic than concrete. You plant many things in a garden according to an initial plan and conditions. Some thrive, others are destined to end up as compost. You may move plantings relative to each other to take advantage of the interplay of light and shadow, wind and rain. Overgrown plants get split or pruned, and colors that clash may get moved to more aesthetically pleasing locations. You pull weeds, and you fertilize plantings that are in need of some extra help. You constantly monitor the health of the garden, and make adjustments (to the soil, the plants, the layout) as needed."

As this course progresses, you should return to this metaphor and see how your understanding of it changes. The methodology you'll use on your course-long project is iterative. You will see how often you return to tend to your existing code. You may want to introduce another plant to your garden and it requires changes to the location of your existing plants. You may introduce a plant that another of your team members later moves because it seems out of place.

In this course you are working as a team of gardeners tending someone else's garden. They may not know anything about the techniques of gardening. They may just say that the garden seems cluttered. It may be up to you to decide whether to move plants or cut them back or just to remove one here or there. You may suggest a certain bush that you know will be perfect for a particular spot. The customer may decide that, even though you're right, the cost is just too high for that bush right now.

Similarly, with software development, developers can design a little, and then build a little. The developers can then take stock of the project and check back with their client, redirecting it as necessary. By repeating this approach, incrementally building the system, the development time for each increment is small. The resulting system is therefore much closer to the client's evolving vision of that portion of the system.

The methods that use this approach are lightweight, flexible, and are collectively called "Agile methods." Agile methods embrace the inevitable changes to a developing system. Currently, eXtreme Programming (XP) is one of the most fully formed and widely used of the agile methods. It accepts as given that the requirements for a system will change and brings a customer onto the development team to make the quick decisions to react to the changes. The underlying concept is to pull everyone involved in the development onto the same side, and have each group address their appropriate issues. Business people make the business decisions and technical people make the technical decisions.

Surprisingly, erecting bridges can also be done in an Agile manner. In August of 1999, the U.S. Army announced the debut of the Wolverine heavy assault bridge. It is completely mobile, as it is carried on a tank. The bridge's two-person crew can deploy the bridge in under five minutes and they can get it back on the tank in less than ten. The resulting span can cross a gap of 24 meters and can support crossing vehicles weighing 70 tons traveling at 10 miles per hour. Each bridge is digitally linked to military commanders, allowing interactive deployment from centralized locations [Army Release #99-60 www.dtic.mil/army/link/news/Aug1999/r19990831newsrel99-60.html]

A "HANDS-ON" SOFTWARE-ENGINEERING COURSE

For professional software developers working together in large teams, no activity (including designing, coding and testing) takes on a more important role than communicating. Developers must exchange information with three separate entities: their fellow developers, a paying client, and a manager or boss. The first important feature of this course is that it provides representations of all three entities. You will be grouped into teams of four or five, the instructor will act as the boss, and someone will play the role of the client. When possible the client is a real customer with a real software need. The client role can also be filled by a former student, teaching assistant, fellow faculty member, or your instructor. The second important feature of the course is that it revolves around a fairly significant software problem. The project should be sufficiently involved that it will keep four to five students actively engaged for the entire course. The third critical feature is that the teams have only one primary focus for the course: developing and delivering the software product. Typical distractions of an academic environment must be kept to a minimum and all the efforts of the students must go into the project and the development methodology. The team must adhere to a defined methodology that is followed throughout the semester. In this context, it is not necessary for the instructor to contrive situations to illustrate specific points. These situations will inevitably arise on their own, requiring innovative solutions, additional research or reasonable renegotiation. Real problems illustrate their own points.

Course-Long Project

In this course you will work on a project that lasts a long time. This allows time for mistakes to expose themselves and for you to actually reap the benefits of good practices. This may differ from your experience in an introductory course where you typically had many short-lived assignments. Now, you will live with your program long enough to realize the implications of decisions made by you and your team members.

Short assignments are used to test your mastery of specific skills in targeted problems. Small programs hide the benefits of modularity and readability because only programs of increased size and complexity offset the up-front costs of these ideals. Small programs do not generally interact with other programs, making documented interfaces avoidable. You probably have written most of your assignments on your own or in groups of two or three. This eliminates interdeveloper communication and removes the primary entry point of conceptual bugs in the program. With only one developer, multiple scheduling constraints do not exist and the programmer's responsibilities do not extend to anyone else.

Program assignments in introductory courses tend to have just the developers and instructor or grader as users. This allows a cumbersome interface to be ignored, overlooked, or tolerated. Unexpected inputs are never attempted because the programmer-user, perhaps unknowingly, self-censors the ones that won't work. Subtle bugs may never show themselves. Minimal use also means that the requirements are very unlikely to change and that the software will not have to be ported to other systems. In essence, this type of project ends at delivery; there is no maintenance phase of the project.

Outside Independent Client

Simply having a larger project is necessary, but not sufficient to fulfill a more realistic simulated programming environment. To complete the picture, the project needs someone who is counting on the project. That person will be the real user of the system. If your instructor is the client in this course it will be clear when he or she is acting as the customer. The client will have request user interfaces to make your application more accessible, he or she will rely on the user's manual to understand systems features, and he or she will think of new, unexpected uses for the system. Just knowing that the software will actually be used has a dramatic impact on the attitude of the developers. The client will express actual needs and reject simplifying compromises that you might think reasonable. The client presents issues that cannot be ignored or argued away.

The outside independent client provides expertise in what is referred to as the business domain. In some cases the client will be outside of the field of computer science. A less-technical client does not mean an unknowledgeable client. In fact, the client will be the expert on the application—not on how it works, but on what it does.

For the team's programming abilities, it is the client who determines what the program will do. Implementation issues will be resolved within the team. But the client determines the program's interfaces to the user, all the processing the program will do, and the formats of its inputs and the outputs. The client's vested interest in the software becomes the driving problem for the development team—software development is a tool, no different from a hammer. Using a hammer to simply pound nails is a self-serving activity. Using a hammer to build a birdhouse is worthwhile. Without the client's driving problem, the software development in this course reduces to pounding nails for no purpose.

ORIGIN OF THE HANDS-ON SOFTWARE-ENGINEERING COURSE

The hands-on software-engineering course has a genealogy that dates back to the earliest computer science degree programs in this country. Frederick Brooks Jr., author of *The Mythical Man-Month* and "father" of the IBM 360 operating system, also developed and, starting in the 1970s, taught for 15 years a hands-on software-engineering course at UNC-Chapel Hill. Brooks, who expounds the benefits of external collaborations to keep his own research focused and pertinent, sought outside clients with real programming problems for the software-engineering course for similar reasons. Instructors of the UNC course take pains to provide a real live client, who might be as fickle and arbitrary as real paying clients. In this way, graduates of the course are better prepared for what they might find in the programming world outside of academic institutions.

Traditional Software Development

At a wide variety of schools, instructors have taught this software-engineering course using a traditional model of the software development process. Based on the waterfall and modified waterfall models, students work through requirements analysis with their clients, design a system to meet those requirements, code the design, test, and then deliver the system. At each step of the process the development team produces a document chronicling the work done and agreements made. The teams meet with their clients early in the semester and discuss the work the clients wants done. As the students begin to understand the needs and expectations of the client, they write a requirements document, translating their understandings into terse, hierarchically numbered statements that fully describe the characteristics of the software they will develop. The numbering scheme allows the requirements to be tracked throughout the lifetime of the development and referenced in all subsequent documents. The requirements document serves as both description of the work to do and a contract between the development team and the client to do that work. Both parties and the instructor of the course sign the document. At this point, contact with the client drops off, only necessary for clarification of unclear points in the requirements document or for renegotiation of the agreement.

The team then develops a design for the software system that meets the now "frozen" requirements. Realistically, frozen requirements do change, but that is also an important lesson of the process. It is also important that the design phase overlap the requirements phase so that the designers can provide input to the requirements process. Even so, there will be requirements issues that arise during the design process. Missing or unclear requirements must be filled in and conflicting requirements must be resolved. Every change identified must be rolled back into the requirements document and major changes require re-evaluation by the client. The culminating result of the design phase is a design document that is only viewed by the team and the instructor. Every numbered requirement must be addressed. The level of detail in a design document varies. Some organizations require two separate design phases: high-level and detailed. In any case, the designs must match up directly with the requirements and the entire system could be developed from the design document. Often in industry this is exactly what happens. One team or contractor does the requirements analysis and design, but another does the coding and development. The development team may know nothing of the system except for what they find in the design document.

Once the requirements document is complete, a separate, parallel development of the testing plan can begin. The testing plan is the assurance that the software developed meets the requirements agreed upon. The plan uses the same hierarchical-numbering scheme of the requirements document to make certain that all the requirements have at least one corresponding test. It is not only reasonable, but also desirable for the testers to create the plan independently of the design and coding efforts. This prevents any unintended knowledge of the internals of the program to affect the verification of the code. In addition to the testing plan document, the testers also develop any necessary software to support the tests. This might include programs to generate input files of various size and content including ones with error conditions. It could also include simplified programs to simulate the basic functions of other portions of the system that won't be available when the testing needs to begin. The testing plan is also internal to the development team and not intended for outside scrutiny. Once the software is complete enough to begin testing, the testers and the developers enter feedback cycles. As the testers find problems with the software, specifically a case in which the system fails in some way to meet a requirement, they report it to the developers. They, in turn, fix the bug, note the fix on the bug report and give the new code back to the testing team with the next internal delivery. This process completes when the testing team signs off on the full compliance with their testing plan.

In parallel with the testing, another team (or sub-team) writes the user's guide. This final document, along with the software itself is the delivered product to the client. The user's guide must include all information necessary to install and use the system. As mentioned earlier, there is no maintenance phase in a software-engineering course, so the user's guide in conjunction with the requirements and design documents should embody a starting point for any subsequent programmers who attempt to fix, modify, or expand the system.

In addition to grappling with a larger program and the associated issues, students in this course learn to work in groups. Programming, often perceived as an isolated activity, is in fact highly communal, requiring both professional communication abilities and social skills. Achieving the common goal of creating a successful software project requires an understood protocol of interaction among the team members.

Organization of the Team

Brooks advocates in the original *Mythical Man-Month* and reiterates in the follow-up 20th anniversary edition that a design coming from one mind is the best way to create software systems with conceptual integrity. He argues that systems designed by committee are not interesting or intuitive and that systems with one creator (or at most two who work very closely together) attract a large following of dedicated users. As examples of committee products, he offers Cobol, MS-DOS, and Windows. As single-mind creations he presents Fortran, C, and UNIX. Though the product list is a bit dated, the point is well made and can be extended to further variants of Windows on one side and Linux on the other. Brook's presents his approach of how to keep the single-mind vision in a project that requires the efforts of many programmers. In *Mythical Man-Month*, he advocates Harlan Mill's metaphor of a surgical team for software development. Each member has specialized duties: surgical nurse, anesthesiologist, specialists and so on, but the surgeon has the final say on everything. Much work can be done, but a single vision is maintained. In software development, the lead developer or system architect is the surgeon and the support roles include coder, tester, tool smith, librarian, researcher, and secretary. Completing the team and complementing the lead designer is the project manager. In the surgical analogy, this person would be the hospital administrator. He or she has no authority in the operating room, but handles all the administrative issues to insulate the surgeon from distractions.

In the hands-on software-engineering course that uses the traditional software development methodology, teams are often structured to reflect the different course requirements. Often, one student is solely responsible for all design and technical decisions: the system designer. Another student fulfills the role of project manager in charge of all administrative tasks and project scheduling. Other students fill other roles and almost everyone will be a programmer during the course. But the final decision on anything technical comes from the designer. The project manager is the primary contact for both the instructor and the client. They are responsible for developing and administering the project's schedule. With that responsibility comes the authority to designate tasks for the other members of the team. This approach to team organization is highly centralized, with all critical design decisions made by a single person.

This book and the associated course does not teach the traditional software development methodology. Instead, it makes good use of the hands-on features of the earlier versions of the course—student autonomy, outside clients, course-long projects—and applies them to eXtreme Programming.

EXTREME PROGRAMMING

The fathers of eXtreme Programming are often listed as Ward Cunningham, the inventor, Kent Beck, the articulator, and Ron Jeffries, the realizer. Beck credits Cunningham with being the source of what has become XP. In *Extreme Programming Explained*, Kent Beck describes XP as "a lightweight, efficient, low-risk, flexible, predictable, scientific, and fun way to develop software." Ron Jeffries worked with Beck at Chrysler on the first large project to use XP and spends much of his time teaching and writing about XP. On his web site, www.xprogramming.com, Jeffries describes XP as "a discipline of software development based on values of simplicity, communication, feedback and courage. It works by bringing the whole team together in the presence of simple practices, with enough feedback to enable the team to see where they are and to tune the practices to their unique situation."

These descriptions will mean more to you as you learn more about XP. The only way to really learn XP is by doing it. Using this text, you will do just that. In the meantime, you can get a feeling for what XP is by taking a closer look at the definitions given by Jeffries and Beck. Both clearly underscore that XP is a methodology for developing software. Both also imply that it is a departure from traditional approaches, perhaps a reaction to perceived deficiencies with existing methodologies. Jefferies highlights XP's "all for one, and one for all" philosophy, which makes working in XP teams enjoyable and rewarding. He also mentions the four principles that permeate eXtreme Programming and the simple practices that form its foundation. The practices *are* simple and with experience, comfortable to follow. Yet, their interrelationships create a powerful process exhibiting all the characteristics that Beck enumerates in his definition. Some of the important flavors of extreme programming not captured in these definitions are its incremental nature of development, its collaborative relationship with the client, and its decentralized approach.

Learning XP

Everything in XP is done in small steps. Small steps are easy to plan, easy to perform, and easy to evaluate. And, perhaps most importantly, small steps are easy to undo. The small step philosophy supports simplicity, feedback, lowered risks, predictability, and flexibility. Each small step taken is completely resolved before taking the next small step. As a result, the system always compiles, always runs, and always correctly performs its processing. The "always" philosophy supports efficiency, lowered risks, flexibility, and fun. The fun comes from the morale-building property of always having a working product.

Enough professional software development projects have ended up in litigation to perpetuate the image of an ugly, adversarial relationship between the paying customer and the software development team. The roots of this conflict rise from the difficulties in predicting software development schedules (which can lead to hiding the truth) and the fallacy of frozen requirements (which can lead to unreasonable expectations and promises). Extreme programming moves the clients from the other side of the table and places them squarely at the center of the development team. They become keenly aware of the problems and issues that plague software development and dictate how the existing resources should be applied to the address them. Instead of pulling on opposite sides of a legal battle that no one can win, the client and the software team pull in the same direction from the beginning. There are no late schedule surprises. Having the client on the development team supports communication, flexibility, feedback, and camaraderie.

Finally, the developers all have the same responsibility and authority with respect to the software and the methodology. Whoever notices a problem, fixes it. Whoever is working on a particular piece of the system, designs it and writes it. Whoever discovers a better way of doing something, implements it. Yet no one does anything alone. There is no hierarchy among the developers. Thus the team forms a cohesive group, each member performing important tasks, but not in a way that creates single points of failure. Any member of the team could have done the task, one particular pair just happened to. With no primary designer, and with each member performing his or her limited portion of the task, the system itself dictates an emerging, growing design that is always appropriate as the system expands in functionality. The decentralized organization of the team supports communication, simplicity, team cohesion, flexibility, and lowered risk.

The Practices of Extreme Programming

In *Extreme Programming Explained*, Kent Beck presents twelve eXtreme Programming practices. Beck also discusses the underlying values of communication, simplicity, feedback, and courage as well as a list of basic principles. As XP has been used and applied, the methodology continues to evolve. Some of the practices have been refined, expanded, refocused, or split. The key point is that although the practices are individually straightforward, when taken together they interact in complex ways, forming a fundamentally new approach to producing software. Below is the list of XP practices; hopefully, each one makes sense on its own, but their interaction is rich and complex.

Think back to when you first began learning how to drive. The function and use of the gas pedal were obvious, same with the brakes. It's hard to imagine a more intuitive user interface than the steering wheel. The meanings of traffic signs, such as STOP, DO NOT ENTER, and ONE WAY, were equally straightforward. Even traffic lights presented no fundamental mysteries. Yet full intellectual understanding of the driving laws and the controls of an automobile does not provide a picture of the intricacies of traffic flow one would see in a time-compressed video of a busy intersection. So, as you read about the practices of XP, bear in mind that there will be a lot more going on when you get behind the wheel.

Kent Beck's twelve XP practices were: the planning game, small releases, metaphor, simple design, testing, refactoring, pair programming, collective code ownership, continuous integration, 40-hour week, on-site customer, and coding standards. The evolution of XP has changed four of these practices to date. Testing has split into two separate testing-related practices: customer tests and test-driven development. Refactoring has been renamed "design improvement" to emphasize the efforts put towards system design in XP. The 40-hour week has been renamed "sustainable pace." The intent is the same—don't burn yourself out—but the new practice recognizes that XP can be applied in many scenarios, not just a typical working week. Finally, the on-site customer practice has been expanded to include characteristics of the "whole team." Part of that team is the on-site customer, but it also includes coaches, developers with different specialties, a manager, and so on. So, after a dose of practicality and a round of evolution, here are the current thirteen practices of eXtreme Programming.

Whole team. XP removes the artificial barrier between the customer and the rest of the development team. The client becomes a part of the team with the responsibility and authority to make critical decisions on the direction of the development. The rest of the team includes developers, testers, a manager, and other roles, all filled at various times by different members of the team.

Metaphor. Everyone on the development team should use the language of a common analogy for the system. The common terminology helps express concepts between group members from different domains and supports the conceptual integrity of the system. The greatest example in modern programming is the "desktop metaphor."

The planning game. The planning process in XP specifies the next step of development, and as the project goes on, provides a better and better picture of what can and will be accomplished by the deadline. The clients express their goals for the software through *user stories* that specify overall behaviors of the software. The development team takes these stories and estimates costs. The client prioritizes the stories and thereby drives the direction of the project. After delivery, the team evaluates their estimates, and incorporates that data into the next round of estimation.

Simple design. The design of the system is always as simple as the current level of functionality allows. There is no extraneous complexity needed or allowed. To keep the incremental design simple, the design must extend only far enough to encompass the next iteration's added features. When the code becomes cumbersome or unwieldy, it's time for refactoring (see design improvement).

Small releases. XP development teams release tested, working code, whose functionality is specified by the client, very frequently. By necessity, these deliveries are small. Every development cycle (iteration—typically two weeks), the client gets new software. The client then evaluates it and uses the current status to dictate the content of the next delivery, one iteration in the future.

Customer tests. The customer develops acceptance tests to determine whether the regularly delivered software meets the user stories they previously developed. These tests are automated and used frequently by the development team to determine whether they have completed a current user story.

Pair programming. Programmers working in pairs write every line of code delivered to the client. Two programmers and one computer represent the indivisible unit of XP code development. One person at the keyboard writes the code, the other supports in whatever role is appropriate at a given time. They may track and correct typos, make implementation suggestions, or take over at any time.

Test-driven development. Once the developers have established their next mini-goal, instead of writing code, they write an automated test first. The test must verify that the code they will write shortly satisfies the mini-goal that they are working on. The test becomes part of an ever-increasing test suite that is constantly run, providing feedback on the developing system.

Design improvement. As the team notices deficiencies in the software, it refactors the code, making it incrementally better. By starting with a simple design, and always making small improvements, by induction, XP produces code with good design characteristics.

Collective code ownership. The team, as a whole, owns the system software. Who originally wrote a particular section of code is immaterial and most likely not even remembered. Anyone can modify any code at any time without asking anyone for permission. Obviously a revision control system is necessary when two pairs are working on the same code, but otherwise XP code is like the contents of a refrigerator at a frat house—you shouldn't expect anything you put in it to be in the same shape the next time you look at it, and anything you find in there is fair game.

Continuous integration. At all times, regardless of the level of functionality, the system compiles, runs, and passes all the tests. Any code written must, before being added to the system, compile, run, and pass all the tests. When new code is integrated back into the system, the system must again meet all those criteria. Continuous integration means making new system builds multiple times per day.

Sustainable pace. The team should put about the same amount of work and effort into every iteration. Overtime leads to burnout, mistakes and more overtime. By maintaining a sustainable pace throughout the development, the team can create better software in shorter amounts of time in the long run.

Coding standards: The developed code should not look like an amalgam of differing styles. The team will adopt and follow *some* coding standard to be used throughout the development. The particular standard is not nearly as important as consistently adhering to that standard.

Many organizations that try XP pick and choose among the practices, deciding ahead of time which ones are appropriate for their development efforts. While no methodology is pristine and there is an exception to every rule, there is also a synergy among the XP practices that should be experienced before making modifications.

INTEGRATING XP AND A HANDS-ON SOFTWARE-ENGINEERING COURSE

At one point during the evolution of the hands-on software-engineering course, Brooks shifted the efforts of the students away from late, full-system integration. Paraphrasing Brooks from his article "No Silver Bullet," "Harlan Mills proposed that any software system should be grown by incremental development ... I have seen the most dramatic results since I began urging this technique on the project builders in my software engineering laboratory class." Extreme programming is based on incremental development and continuous integration. Other improvements to the traditional software engineering methodology over the years include recognition and acceptance of feedback cycles within the waterfall model, valuing the benefits of user input from rapidly built prototypes, and evolutionary deliveries to the client. These features or analogs are also central to extreme programming, not as add-ons, but built into the methodology from the beginning. So integrating extreme programming into a hands-on software-engineering course is a natural next step being implemented at many colleges and universities.

There are differing views of how to create a well-designed system. In "No Silver Bullet," Brooks supports Harlan Mills' claim that incrementally grown systems require a top-down design. XP takes the opposite stance, basing its development model on the idea that incrementally grown systems require incrementally grown designs. So XP advocates a bottom-up design that addresses only those features currently about to be added to the system. Effectively, the design is the same size as the system at all times. The trade-off comes when the XP approach encounters a new feature that requires major changes in the existing design. XP says, "Up until this point the system has worked at all times, and by not doing up-front design the project has maintained flexibility and realized more functionality. It was entirely possible that the need for this feature has just arisen, or if known about ahead of time, might have gone away. The cost of reworking the design for this new feature is the price XP willingly pays for its flexibility." Top-down design advocates would say, "The time investments and efforts put forth planning ahead for this (and all) features are worthwhile compared with the cost of reworking the design multiple times." In today's world of short shipping schedules and volatile market forces, it's hard to imagine not dealing with unstable requirements, it's just a question of whether you expect them or not.

Part I

The Spike—

Getting Up to Speed

There is too much to learn at the beginning of the course. It would be difficult to try to understand all of the practices of eXtreme Programming (XP) at the same time that you are meeting with a client and starting to work on a long involved project. Just getting used to some of the core practices will take time. With pair programming, you will need to write code as one of two actively involved people at the same computer. Next, test-first programming requires that you write your tests before you write the methods they are testing. You do this knowing that your tests will result in the program not compiling. You will be reminded to take very small steps. In XP you always try the simplest thing that could work, and then you return to the code to see if you can improve the design by refactoring. Refactoring means that you are rewriting working code instead of adding more functionality. If you see code that needs improving, you need to improve it. You know you aren't breaking anything because you have the tests that you wrote protecting your code. All of the XP practices support each other.

Just getting used to the basics of XP is enough for now. Customer interaction is also central to XP, but if you start working on a project with a real customer right away, there is too much to understand at once. The solution is to take a couple of weeks to work on a practice problem while you try to get used to XP. You get to learn a bit about how you work and how your team works. This understanding will be critical to your success on the course-long project. This directed experiment is called a spike.

Chapter 1, *The Metaphor,* introduces XP through descriptions of familiar experiences. It contrasts XP with a traditional software approach and places XP in the context of concepts you already understand. Chapter 2, *Getting Started,* describes how to get going on an XP project. You will practice this during the spike in preparation for the real client with the real project. Part III of this book provides tutorials for the core practices. You can refer to them at any time. Chapter 3, *Pair Programming,* and Chapter 4, *First Test, Then Code* describe the two practices that will occupy most of your time. The problem with teaching a course built on interdependent practices is knowing where to start. Pair programming and testing first are the cornerstones of developer activity throughout the course, so they will be introduced first. These practices each benefit from other activities, but they can be used to bootstrap the XP process.

Chapter 1

The Metaphor—

Developing a Sense of Where We're Headed

Think back to a college course that you took that didn't go exactly as planned. The first day of class you were probably handed a syllabus that looked pretty good. The exams were nicely spaced out and the final was already scheduled for ten to fifteen weeks away. The material and scheduled assignments seemed evenly distributed. All in all, the professor seemed to have done a nice job with the schedule.

The semester (or quarter) began at a reasonable pace and continued until one day the professor notices what day it is and how little of the material has been covered. Suddenly the beautifully constructed lectures are cut short with a comment that "it's all in the text anyway." Although your instructor is no longer returning assignments to you, you find yourself putting in more and more time on this course. In the weeks before the final you are spending way too much time on this course at the same time that the same situation is occurring in the three other courses you're taking this semester. You load up on sugar and caffeine and make it through finals week, then go home and take it out on your family.

WRITING THE SYLLABUS

So how does this happen? Imagine, for a minute, that you are the instructor of this ill-fated class. You sit down during the weeks before the semester begins with your textbook, a pretty good idea of what you want to cover, and an academic calendar. You already know when the final exam is scheduled. The registrar often schedules the time and place of the final before the semester even starts. You also know when midsemester grades are due. You're going to need some data before then. On the other hand, it takes a while to get through enough material to actually write an interesting exam. This pretty much fixes when the first exam must be given. You notice that the holidays fall a little oddly this year and so your second exam has to be scheduled around them.

At this point you have a rough structure for your semester. Because this is just a fictional account, you can stand back and laugh at yourself for having made these decisions for no pedagogically sound reasons. Now you do a quick count of how many classroom hours remain once you deduct the time for the two exams. You start scheduling the material. Maybe you look at the chapters in the text that you intend to cover and decide about how much classtime each section should take. Oh, you think, that's pretty easy. It should only take a day. Hmmm, that's tricky. Better schedule two days. Maybe you think in terms of the labs that accompany the course. The students need to know *that* before they are asked to do *this*.

Depending on how detailed a syllabus you intend to provide, you create a week-by-week or a day-by-day schedule. You write the dates of the exams in stone and you create a pretty version with a short paragraph on how the grade will be computed. Finally, you make enough copies for your students, the department, your office door, graders, and the dean's office.

Sometimes there is nothing you can do about it. Sometimes you teach one or two sections of a multisection class for which the final, and possibly the midterms, are scheduled ahead of time. In addition, some department committee may be setting the material that is to be tested on the exams in stone. On given dates, your students will be tested on a body of material, and it is your job to get them ready. This usually occurs in an introductory course that you have taught many times. You actually do have a feel for how long the material takes and year after year you have refined your estimates, perhaps without knowing you are doing so.

You probably know faculty members who year after year find themselves behind. They may complain that their students aren't as good as they used to be, but for some reason they need to cover a disproportionately high amount of the course in the last few weeks. They dump large amounts of just graded homework in a box outside of their door hours on either side of the final exam. They don't know how they got this far behind. Perhaps it was the graders' fault.

FIRST THINGS FIRST

Not surprisingly, this discussion of a typical college semester has everything to do with software engineering. When Bob Martin of Object Mentor gives an introductory talk on XP he likes to set the scene by asking, "What's the first thing that a developer knows about a software project?" Most of the audience nod their heads as Uncle Bob answers, "the Deadline." Before you know what features are required or what constraints will be imposed, you know the due date. Although many of Martin's points are summarized in this chapter, his account is much more entertaining and complete. It can be found in a series of articles he wrote for the *C++ Report* beginning with his February 1999 article, "Iterative and Incremental Development." You can also find it in his Prentice Hall book, *Agile Software Development: Principles, Patterns, and Practices*, as Appendix D, "A Satire of Two Companies."

Getting back to our story, there may be a good reason for this deadline. Maybe there's a big tradeshow coming up where the marketing folks want to show off your new offering. Maybe the sales staff had to make this commitment to close a big sale. Maybe your company only has enough money to survive until then. In any case, somebody has made a decision about *when* the project will be finished and that date has now been set.

The college professor worked backwards from the deadline of the final exam to come up with dates for the exams. We'll see how the software team can similarly divide up their task. There are, however, other ways to tackle this problem, both in the world of software development and in the world of academia. One alternative would be for the professor to just start teaching and, when the students feel ready, give a test, and when the students are really ready, give a final exam. This is too unstructured. What if the professor doesn't finish until midway through the next semester? The school isn't set up to accommodate this. What if the professor finishes early? What if some of the class finishes at one time and the rest of the class finishes later? After all, the goal really isn't for the professor to finish presenting the material. The goal is for the students to have some mastery of the material. We'll look at an alternative in a moment.

THE WATERFALL METHOD

We don't just want to tell the software team to start coding without thinking about the problem first any more than we want the professor to just start teaching. How much thinking should they do and what should they think about? You saw in the previous section that the professor did quite a bit of thinking about the course before teaching it and the reality still didn't match the ideal.

In 1970 Winston Royce wrote about what is referred to as the "waterfall method" of software development. Simplistically, you can think of this method as consisting of Requirements Analysis, Design, and Implementation. It also includes the three additional stages of Testing, Integration, and Maintenance, but we won't consider these for now. Royce understood that when you begin to design, you will find problems with your initial analysis and, similarly, when you begin to implement the design you will find problems with the design and, therefore, possibly more problems with the analysis. If you have been at organizations that implement the waterfall method, it may surprise you to discover that Royce understood the value of feedback from the downstream processes.

In many organizations the three activities of analysis, design, and implementation are seen as three discrete steps that must occur sequentially. It may be more courteous to Royce to refer to this process as a *modified* waterfall method to make it clear that this misinterpretation is not his fault. You complete the analysis phase and then move on to the design phase. You complete the design phase and then move on to the implementation phase. There are advantages to this approach. A manager can chart the software team's progress through this process. "Look," the manager proudly says, "my team is done with analysis. All they have left is design and implementation."

LIMITATIONS OF THE MODIFIED WATERFALL

So let's look at what may be wrong with this discrete phase interpretation of the waterfall method. Fundamentally the problem is the lack of hard data on which assumptions can be made. Whether your department is a Computer Science department or a Computer Engineering department, your background as a scientist or engineer compels you to build your conjectures on as much data as you can gather or to label them as fantasy. You should be uncomfortable making statements and predictions unless you can offer evidence to support these statements and predictions.

Unanswerable Questions

The implementation phase is when the code is actually written, the design phase comes right before it and is when the design of the application (sometimes all the way down to descriptions of each method) is hammered out. Suppose you are asked to estimate the time needed for the implementation phase or the design phase before you begin the analysis phase. How would you come up with this number? You don't know *what* you are building (analysis) or *how* (design) but you are expected to know *how long* it will take.

Maybe we're asking too hard a question. Back up a minute. Imagine you are beginning the analysis phase. When will you be done with analysis? This is like deciding to write a story. So first you need to come up with a really cool idea. How long is it going to take you to come up with that idea? Suppose, at least in the software case, you can actually complete the analysis phase. Now, picture that magic day when you are done with analysis and your manager has crossed that off of the list of tasks to be done. What happens *if* the customer changes the requirements? Actually, the real question is what happens *when* the customer changes the requirements.

Building Estimates on No Data

Here's Martin's characterization of the process. Suppose that on the first of June there is a big kickoff meeting for a new software project that must be delivered in six months. This project absolutely must be completed by the first of December. As scientists and engineers, we know the track record for software projects. We know there is a very low likelihood that the project will be on time or complete when it is released.

First you are asked how much time you'll need for analysis. You don't know. The actual requirements haven't yet been set in stone by the customer or by your company's marketing team or by whoever is responsible for coming up with the complete set of requirements. Let's call that entity RP for requirements producer. So you are asked if, assuming that you have this mythical document, two months sounds reasonable for the analysis phase.

You certainly have no information that this estimate isn't correct. You try to explain that you can't possibly create an estimate based on no data. Management asks you for a more reasonable number. You can't come up with one. "Well," they explain, "you can't take more than two months on analysis and still deliver December 1 so we'll go with that." It's settled then. The analysis phase will be complete on the first of August.

The next step is to estimate the time needed for design. Forget for a minute that you don't know what you're designing because you haven't done the analysis. You can even forget that you can't do the analysis because you don't have the requirements. Find your inner manager and come up with a number for how long the design will take. There's a part of you that says, "Two months was an acceptable answer for analysis, it's probably a good answer for design." There's another part of you saying, "That only leaves two months to write the code. There's no way we can do that." You need to ignore this second part of you if you ever want to be a manager. Because you don't know what you're building, how can this part of you *really* know that it can't be done in two months?

The management team is only half listening to you anyway. They realize there's only four months left in the project once analysis is complete. Design has to be finished by October 1 if you are to keep on schedule. Once you bought into this fantasy world, you had to come up with the same number, so you nod your head in agreement and it's settled. The design phase will be complete on October 1.

In a way, you have constructed your own syllabus. The midterms and finals have been replaced by nicely spaced out delivery dates. It looks pretty on a chart and everybody knows what activity is supposed to be going on at each moment. Raise your hand if you see a disaster coming. Put your head down on your desk if you know what to do about it.

The Life of the Project

In the school setting there are regular points at which feedback is provided. This doesn't mean that everyone gets access to an accurate assessment of what's going on. Picture a first year student who is struggling in some course their first semester at college. The student did great in high school but now there's trouble. One day the student's parents call to see how their pride and joy is doing. Junior thinks, "I got a D on the first two exams. If I get an A on the final I'll get a B in the class." What Junior says out loud is, "I'm getting a B." The end of the story isn't pretty. Junior gets a D on the final and a D in the class. The parents are surprised because that's the first they've heard about it. They say, "But you were doing so well. What happened?" Junior says, "I didn't do very well on the final." The parents' expectations may have been different if they had been told the actual results of each of the exams as soon as Junior knew them.

Meanwhile, back at our software development project, during June and July the team works on analysis. A few weeks into this stage they get a complete set of requirements from the RP and the analysis work begins in earnest. Actually it doesn't happen that way. Really the RP doesn't know much about requirements as developers see them. The RP knows how to vaguely explain the desired outcome. The RP might say, "We want to totally automate the payroll system." Many meetings later the analysts have worked with the RP to translate the requirements into system inputs, processes, and outputs. What the RP considers requirements and what the engineers consider requirements differ. The requirements document tries to capture the official requirements that the engineering team is agreeing to produce. A couple of weeks later they get an update to the requirements document. Some features that weren't anticipated are now necessary. Maybe, if RP is the sales staff, they've figured that if this particular feature is added then more people will buy the product. For whatever reason, the requirements have changed. Your team accommodates this change and alters the analysis.

This process goes on until you are summoned into a meeting with management. They remind you that analysis was to have been completed on August 1. You see that it's August first and you've probably done enough analysis for now so you agree that you're done with analysis and turn over all of your analysis documents.

Time now to work on design. This will require producing more documents and using really cool GUI tools that produce diagrams and cross listings. In your shop you want to create a design that is developer proof. All they have to do is follow your design and the application will just work. Now and then RP drops off additional requirements, but you're pretty busy designing. You're done designing on October 1.

So far you haven't written a line of code. How are you doing? Are you going to meet your target? How reliable will the software be? You are playing the same game as Junior. You're ignoring what you haven't done and depending on that big push at the end to get the project completed on time. This software project looks like the problematic syllabus we saw before. You have just looked up on October 1 and realized how much you have to get done and how little time you have to do it.

On the other hand, your manager is delighted. Two out of your three activities are now completed. Meanwhile, RP is continuing to deliver little changes to the requirements. Your team starts coding. After a month of coding you realize that you are not going to make the deadline. To return to the course analogy, this is where the professor looks up and says, "There are only four weeks left in the semester and I've only covered six of the twenty-four design patterns." In your case, before you go to your manager with the bad news, you take another week to gather some data so that you can explain just how bad things are. It's November 1 and this will be the first indication the manager has had that the project is in trouble.

What Happened?

In one sense you weren't fair to your manager. You didn't provide the manager with any information that could have been used to make decisions. The manager wasn't allowed to manage. On the other hand, you weren't allowed to provide the manager with any useful information because you weren't allowed to gather any. You didn't want to spend two months on analysis and two months on design.

This whole process has been based on little or no information being used to produce dates that other people depend on. What does it mean to successfully complete the analysis phase when the requirements continue to change? This isn't an argument that analysis isn't important—it is. The point is that analysis can be distributed throughout the process. You can do a little analysis, a little design, and then begin to code. Soon you'll need to do a little more analysis, a little more design, and then more coding. This is the way the waterfall method was originally designed to be implemented.

Let's look at yet another metaphor that illustrates the dangers in frontloading the analysis and design steps. Suppose you are a meteorologist and you spend one hour a day predicting the weather. One day an efficiency expert follows you through your routine and notices that twenty minutes each day are spent setting up your equipment and ten minutes are spent to generate the maps for each of the next four days. This means that on Monday you spend twenty minutes setting up and ten minutes on Monday's map, ten minutes on Tuesday's map, ten minutes on Wednesday's map, and ten minutes on Thursday's map. On Tuesday you spend twenty minutes setting up and ten minutes on Tuesday's map, ten minutes on Wednesday's map, ten minutes on Thursday's map, and ten minutes on Friday's map.

The efficiency expert reports that you spend too much time repeating your efforts. On Tuesday you have wasted all but ten minutes. The twenty minutes spent setting up again is wasted and you've wasted half an hour generating the maps for Tuesday, Wednesday, and Thursday again. You make some lame argument about how a weather map for Tuesday generated on Tuesday is more accurate than the one generated on Monday. Your boss realizes that your protestations are an indication of your unwillingness to change. The boss mandates that you predict the entire weather for the month on the first day of each month. The efficiency expert agrees that it will take you the twenty minutes of setting up plus, at the most, thirty-one times ten minutes. This total of six and a half hours saves the station around twenty hours a month.

Now back to creating software. What if you'd done a little analysis, a little design, and started to code back in June. Now after a week you could say to your manager, "Here's what we got done this week." Now when the RP shows up with additional requirements you could say, "Here's what we did last week. Suppose we could do about that much this week. What would you like us to do next?" You can also add, "By the way, if we continue working at this pace we'll be done next April 20, give or take a month."

Another week goes by. You can now say, "Here's what we did this past week. Based on these two pieces of data we'll be done next April 3, give or take two weeks." You can then ask the RP what they'd like you to work on next. The difference here is that you're basing every estimate except the first one on real data and you are giving the customer quick feedback. The customer can use this real information to make solid decisions they can depend on.

In XP the customer is very involved in this process. At this point in our story all we care about is that your estimates are based on real data. As your project progresses, the margin of error should decrease because the number of data points on which it is based is increasing.

BACK TO THE CLASSROOM

This same XP approach can work in a classroom as well. The professor will have constraints the same way a software project manager has constraints. The professor wants to cover a certain amount of material in the semester and the exams must fall when they fall. The professor can then produce a syllabus as fine grained as is desired. But each day the professor can see where the class is and make adjustments. Early in the semester the professor can announce that not all material will be covered in lecture.

To be effective, the professor needs to know where the students' knowledge is on a regular basis. The professor can not constantly make measurements. Giving an in-class quiz or exam eats up class time when material could be presented. There is a balance between taking too many measurements and not taking enough. In most cases, not enough measurements are taken. You hear professors say "I taught that," and you wonder if the students can say, "I learned that."

In software engineering you've seen that ineffective measurements don't allow problems to be identified or fixed. You can't constantly stop developers from coding so that you can measure their progress, but you also can't ignore determining where a project really is until it is too late. XP is full of tiny steps. The fear of many who champion big up-front analysis and design is that without these phases you may be building the wrong system. But after each tiny step is a moment to look around and ask, "Where are we?" During this moment, we can chart our progress climbing the tree and we can give the RP a chance to say, "Hey, that's the wrong tree!" before it's too late.

SOFTWARE ENGINEERING APPROACHES

In traditional software, the requirements document exists as a way to protect clients and developers. If the client doesn't get features that are in the document, the client can point to the relevant portion and say "But you promised." If the client wants to change requirements in midstream, the developer can try to explain that it isn't in the document. Often a developer will know better than to agree to additional requirements, but the client will be very persuasive about a particular requirement or two. The developer agrees to add this feature and the developer and client pretend that this additional feature is free. The truth is that something has to give. The client has just added a requirement to a software project that is probably already running behind.

XP customers tend to be happier than non-XP customers. XP customers are involved in decisions and have reasonable expectations because they are continuously apprised of the state of the project. If halfway into an XP project a customer comes up with a new feature that must be included, the XP team would agree. The difference is that they would be able to tell the customer with certainty the amount of work that is getting done each week. The team could then show the customer the estimates for the remaining user stories (requirements in XP). The discussion is pretty simple. The team says, "You want this much additional work and we can do only this much work a week. Would you like the schedule to slip or are there some requirements that aren't as important as this new one you gave us?"

There's really nothing to fight about. The developers are saying yes to the customer. The developers are just being up front with the cost. The XP team is aware of the amount of work they can produce in a week and so they can explain with data what the cost of this new feature is. What can the customer say? Work longer. Work faster. The team can't work faster and working longer doesn't help in the long run. With the customer located on-site working with the development team, there's no room for back biting and assigning blame. Issues aren't given a chance to fester because they are dealt with immediately. There should be no surprises the week before the software is scheduled to ship.

LAST THINGS FIRST

Of all the XP practices, metaphor is the hardest to teach or explain. We can't give you the right metaphor for the project you're working on. We will, however, suggest metaphors for some of the example projects we present later in this text. In some sense, metaphor is the practice we used throughout this chapter. We needed to explain to you the software process we're asking you to abandon, so we have tried to provide several metaphors for understanding the problems and appreciating the alternative approaches.

In this chapter you've been a software engineer, professor, meteorologist, and student. The experiences you've had will help you understand the dangers ahead. When you are engaged in a software engineering project with an actual client, it can help you to say, "This is kind of like . . ." A metaphor helps everyone get the same fuzzy picture of the system. It will become clearer as the system evolves. No one metaphor worked entirely. We didn't argue about what role in a professor's life corresponded to design and what corresponded to implementation. In some ways, metaphor is a tool more than it is a practice. It is a tool that helps developers and customers communicate with each other.

Chapter 2

Getting Started—

Introducing the Core XP Practices

Think of an application you've written with a complicated GUI frontend. Once the application is up and running, buttons respond correctly to clicks, check boxes know what to do when they're checked, and text fields know where to send the information entered into them. Anthropomorphism aside, the application knows how to respond to user input. After the application is up and running, it is the picture of object-oriented programming. Objects respond to messages from other objects.

There is, however, another part of the life cycle. Some part of the program is responsible for getting these objects up and running and wired together so they can communicate. The "big bang" part of this application's life is contained in the main() method. The static keyword modifying main() allows a method to be called before any objects exist. In Java™, having to explain the role of main() presents many challenges.

So it is with starting an eXtreme Programming (XP) project. Once an XP project is up and running, each step feels very small. A programmer signs up for a task that shouldn't take very long to complete. As a member of a pair, the programmer suggests a test that needs to be written and then writes the code to make it pass. Each step is small. Refactoring allows the programmer to view a piece of functioning code as modifiable. You are only able to refactor with abandon because you have a full set of unit tests. Not only is each step small, but many decisions can be changed without huge consequences.

There are places where the steps are not so small. Getting started is one place where your decisions have more weight. Choosing one technology over another is a situation in which the decisions may appear large. Sometimes the process will stall when the programmers don't want to do what the client wants them to. Even though XP says the customer determines what the programmers work on, you may convince yourself that you can't perform your task until some other task is performed. When faced with large steps in each of these situations, you may be unwilling or even feel unable to move.

Some of what makes the initial steps seem so large is that all at once many things you are handling are unfamiliar. A team might be struggling to figure out how to parse XML or manipulate a JPEG file at the same time they are trying to figure out how all of the XP practices fit together. It is helpful to have a short mini project that can be used to get a feel for the noncustomer-centered practices of XP. During this time, the team can work out some of the kinks in estimating, pairing, testing first, and refactoring. The programmers will then begin to understand the importance of communication to the process.

This chapter looks at these situations. You'll explore the issues raised here, but the crux of the chapter is the suggestion that you take a week or two to explore some of the practices of XP before you tackle the real project with your real client. When you need to learn about an unfamiliar technique or technology in XP, you need to spend some fixed amount of time exploring alternatives. When you have learned enough, you can throw your experiment away and return to writing code for the client. Imagine the freedom and benefits of throwing code away and starting over on projects you've faced in the past. It is too difficult to learn the new process of XP at the same time that you are first meeting with a client and trying to become familiar with the requirements of your actual project. The advice is simple:

Sage advice: Experiment with some of the core practices of XP before you are engaged in a project for an actual client.

In other words, engage in an XP *spike*. As you'll see in a moment, a spike is a quick investigation designed to help you learn about something you don't have much experience with. In this case, the goal of the spike is to learn XP. You need to experiment with the core practices of XP before using them in your course-long project in the same way that your instructor experimented with them before teaching them to your class. You need to pair program with someone and write test first code and refactor.

MAIN()

There are many versions of the *Stone Soup* story. The idea is that a hungry man arrives at the door of a miserly woman and convinces her that he can make a fine soup out of just a stone. So she puts on a pot of water and he adds in the stone. He tells her that it will be good soup but it could be even better with some celery and carrots. She gives in and lets him add some of her celery and carrots to the soup because, after all, he's making the entire soup from a stone. The story continues as she agrees to add one ingredient after another until he has made a rich and meaty soup out of standard ingredients. The stone that started the whole process has nothing to do with the end result and should, in fact, be discarded.

The same is true when you start your XP project. You have user stories from your customer. You and your team have estimated these stories. This will necessarily involve a lot of guessing the first time you do it. You probably don't know how fast you code. You probably are being asked to write code in many areas that are new to you. Each task somehow seems to depend on the others. In the story, the hungry man was shrewd enough not to present his whole grocery list in the beginning. It would have overwhelmed the woman, and she would have refused to let him make the soup. You need to fool yourself in the same way.

What concerns many people about beginning to work in XP is the lack of up-front design. If you have five people coding without coordinating with each other, isn't this similar to having five people work on the design of a house that each one sees differently? Wouldn't a house built on such an ad hoc collection of plans be unstable? Of course, you wouldn't want to design a house this way. The good news is that you aren't. Maybe the first thing you're choosing is a door. You and a partner design a door that opens and closes and place a frosted glass pane in the center of the upper half and select a door handle with a simple lock. The customer says no, they meant for the door to be solid oak with a deadlock bolt. You and your partner make the simple adjustment and soon you're finished with that door. Meanwhile, another pair is working on laying out the kitchen according to user stories. Your group's end product is the design of the house. Things can be changed along the way and, because no one owns any piece of the design, the kitchen team can later refine the door design.

Even so, it still may be daunting to begin testing without an up-front design. It's okay to design a little. Using XP doesn't mean you can't or even that you don't ever do any design. XP doesn't want you to spend an inordinate amount of time on design—that's fine. The XP teams certainly do not spend the time to put these quick diagrams into any archival form. Your goal is to write code that meets your client's needs. If you need to spend a little time discussing some of the overall structure of the application or sketching a quick UML diagram that gets everyone headed off in the same direction, that's fine. You can't get a customer to sign off on a design and later tell them, when the application is crawling at a painful pace, that this is the design they approved. You don't want to spend two months on design, two on analysis, and then in the fifth month start to produce something the customer can actually touch and understand. You want the customer to see the evolving product immediately. The customer has described the house they want to live in—build a door.

SPIKES—A QUICK INVESTIGATION

You have just met with your customer and found out that they want you to provide an application that communicates with data they have stored in a database. Unfortunately, no one on your team has done much work with connecting to a database using JDBC®, and you've never worked with this particular database. Although the details may change, the point is that on every project you will encounter some piece of technology that is new to you. Most of the time, the customer won't understand what the problem is. They figure that you'll be able to work things out.

You may avoid the problem for a while, but eventually some user story (those tasks that the user tells you are most important in the next iteration) will depend on this bit of unknown technology. This makes it difficult for you to estimate how long it will take to complete the task. One solution is to drive a spike.

A spike is a short exploration of the area where you don't feel confident that you know enough. Imagine you are building a piece of furniture and the method you are using to join edges is unfamiliar to you. A spike would involve taking two lengths of inexpensive wood and performing the technique to join them. You would then throw this experiment out and proceed confidently to work on your actual project. The key features of the spike are the same that you use software. When you used the scrap lumber, you stopped when you understood what it was that you were trying to learn. The pieces of wood that you worked on were discarded. There was no temptation for you to bring that project to some sort of completion. You also allowed yourself to make mistakes on this project that didn't count.

Be wary of the temptation to engage in too many spikes or to spend too long on them. Some teams like to know everything they might possibly need up front. One pair on a team may have a notion that they need to parse some XML so they learn about SAX, DOM, JAXP, JDOM, and any other initials they can think of that relate to XML and Java. They argue about the right way to structure their data and how best to process it. They can spend weeks in this process and learn quite a bit. Meanwhile, another pair realizes that in this case the task can be completed simply with a comma-separated list. None of the XML knowledge is ever used on this project.

There are core XP principles being violated in the behavior of the first team. First, the customer is supposed to decide which requirement has the most value at this time and the team should be working on those tasks. Sure, taking an afternoon to investigate a technology may not have been on the customer's priority list, but it will help you better respond to the customer's needs by giving you the experience to better estimate and accomplish the tasks required by the user stories. Keeping the investigations brief and infrequent can benefit the client. The second problem in the behavior of the renegade pair in the previous paragraph is the violation of the short feedback loop. All of the XP practices conspire to make sure you have good information about where you are all the time. You should quickly return to the code so you know where you stand. Finally, XP encourages you to think of the simplest way to accomplish a task and cautions you not to do something if You Aren't Going To Need It (YAGNI). Unfortunately, you may not know the simplest way to accomplish a task. It is possible that a short investigation will greatly benefit the development effort.

AN XP SPIKE TO LEARN THE BASIC XP PRACTICES

You will encounter the problems described in the last two sections when you are learning XP. How do you figure out pair programming, testing first, refactoring, user stories, and all the rest of the practices while you are busy trying to meet the customer's requirements? It's overwhelming. Drive a spike.

You are now going to take some time to learn the ideas behind XP on a project that doesn't matter. Instead of a spike to learn a technique or technology, this spike is driven to help you learn XP. Pick a project that you plan to throw away. You will play two roles in this activity: the client and the programmer. Once you've gained confidence with a core set of XP practices, you can stop working on this XP spike and start working on your actual software-engineering project. The experiment will last less than two weeks but you'll have a better feel for what you're doing.

Start with a sample project. Several are suggested at the end of this chapter. You are not expected to finish it. As in the example above, you are using low quality wood; throw the project away. You won't be an XP expert when you finish your spike, but you'll know enough to start on your real project. You'll have enough experience with the programming tasks so you are ready to learn some of the customer tasks and begin to integrate them. Here are facets of XP that you are trying to get a feel for: user stories, estimating, working for the customer, pairing, testing first, refactoring, and the synergies of these XP practices.

User Stories

A user story is a short description of some piece of desired functionality for the application. It must fit easily on a 3" × 5" note card. It doesn't need to contain anything more than a name and a short description. It's not intended to be a written in stone. A user story contains just enough text to explain what is to be done so that the customer and the developers can look at this card and understand it the same way.

Usually the stories evolve. The customer writes something and then the developer asks questions or makes suggestions to help clarify what is being expressed. The developer makes sure that the customer has an idea of how to test for the successful completion of this story.

Once you begin your actual project, the customer will write the user stories. During the XP spike, the team will write the user stories, refine them, and then estimate them. This part of the exercise will provide you with experience in receiving and working with user stories so that you develop a sense of what user stories have to look like. This sense will help you work with the customer after receiving a set of user stories. In addition, your customer will probably not be experienced in the role of customer. You can help your customer write stories in the first place. It may seem odd, but part of your role this semester may involve coaching the customer.

Estimates

It is important that you develop a sense of self-awareness as you program. You do this by making estimates, out loud, in front of other people. You say things like, "I could do that in about two hours." Initially, you'll be really, really bad at this. The way you improve is to continue to make estimates and note the difference between your estimates and your actual times.

After making your estimate, go away with a partner and work on your task. You'll need to come back to the group and say something like, "Well, I've spent ten hours on the task and I'm almost done." Don't worry that you guessed two hours. Your next guess will now use this additional data. You may even overestimate how much time is required.

At the end of the semester, you'll have made more than a dozen estimates and you'll be getting a little better at it. Use the first two weeks to learn a little about yourself. What is it you'll be estimating? You'll take the user stories and break each one into tasks. You'll then estimate each task. The user story explains the customer's needs and is the customer's domain. The tasks are how the story is to be accomplished and are the developers' domain.

Living with Set Priorities

During your XP spike you take on more than one role. Once you have estimated tasks, (taking into account that all the code will be written by a pair) you have to switch roles and put on your customer hat. Decide which user stories are the most important from the end user's point of view. Swap hats again, take on your programmer persona and decide how many of those user stories (prioritized by the customer) you can do this week. Then become the customer again and choose the most important stories that fit within the time estimates the programmer gave you.

You, as the programmer, must then work on these tasks. The hardest thing to learn during the spike is that you are playing both roles, so you may be tempted to make decisions on the fly. You may say, "Oops, I'm falling behind on this task, I'll just eliminate this other task." You need to consciously change roles. As the developer, you should identify that you are slipping a deadline. In that role, you need to meet with your group and see how everyone's doing. Once you have a full assessment, adopt the customer role, tell yourself how disappointed in you you are, then reprioritize what you want to achieve next. Have fun with this. You might bring different hats to these sessions and physically change them so that you and your group members are conscious of the role you are currently playing.

This separation is important because you need to be aware when you are making decisions that aren't yours to make. In an XP project, there are decisions that the customer makes and decisions that the developer makes. As with other practices, you will find it freeing to worry about just those issues under your control. In this XP spike exercise, not only will you gain experience in the developer side of the role before you begin your real course-long project, but you will also gain an understanding of the customer's role. You will probably welcome being only one person and letting someone else make those hard decisions.

Pairing

Pairing—working with others is hard. After trying pair programming for the next three months, you can decide if you like it or not. Your challenge in the first two weeks of the course is to learn how you can best benefit from pairing with others. You should try to pair with at least three other people during this XP spike. If you always pair with the same person, you may risk falling into a rut and saying, "Oh, that's what pairing is." As you pair with different people, your idea of what pairing is will change.

One of the benefits of pairing with multiple partners is that ideas and techniques spread throughout the group. When you're working on an actual project it may mean that use of a particular design pattern or a refactoring may spread throughout the group. For example, two people who used a particular technique one day are now paired with two others, and they spread the ideas they learned from the day before. During your XP spike, you're less concerned with the technical information that gets spread; but you'll notice that techniques of pairing become distributed. Even so, the way you pair with individuals will be particularly useful to you both.

Testing First

At first, the practice of testing first may feel awkward. It doesn't seem logical, but using it will help you to clarify the problem you are trying to solve. Testing often suggests an appropriate algorithm. Suppose your task is to take several items on a bill and calculate the subtotal, the sales tax, and the total due. Why not just start writing the code? With testing first you start by asking, "How do I check that the sales tax is correct and that I get the right final amount?" You find the answer by writing the test for it. The code doesn't compile because the objects you're referencing and the methods you're calling don't exist yet. That feels so wrong. Why not just create the objects and the methods first?

You need to trust the practice a bit. It won't make sense to you until you experience it. The next step is to create the objects and methods that the test requires. Once you've done this, the code compiles. Then you run the tests. They don't work. They can't work yet. The tests work when you write the methods to make the test pass and it feels great. Maybe you could write the code correctly without the test. But now you know when changes you make to your code later break your test. If you introduce code that results in an incorrect total, you know you need to fix it. This area of the code is protected before the code was ever written.

Continuous Design Improvement

There are many little ways that your program could be improved. You may wish you'd named a variable or a method differently. Change it. This is called refactoring. You notice that a method is a little long and that part of it is used to calculate the subtotal, part of it is used to calculate the tax, and part of it is used to calculate the total. Separate them into three methods called calculateSubTotal(), calculateSalesTax(), and calculateTotal(). Now your code is both more readable and more modular. There are larger refactorings that can also improve the design of your code.

During the first two weeks, you and all your pairing partners should be aggressively and continuously refactoring. At first you won't see enough opportunities for refactoring while just working in pairs as you would with more eyes looking at your code. You may find it helpful to schedule a code review with your whole group during the first week. More eyes looking at the code will produce more suggestions of how to improve it. What makes code improvement possible is having unit tests for all of your code. You know that you aren't breaking anything when you refactor because all of the tests continue to run. You may need to go back to refactor your test code as well. When you change the name of a method, you will have to change what the corresponding test calls the method.

Synergies

You will be tempted to pick and choose among the XP practices. Don't do it, at least not yet. There are magic synergies that arise when you combine practices. For example, one of the advantages of pair programming during the XP spike is that it reinforces the commitment to testing first. You might be tempted to write just a little bit of code without a test, but your partner can ask, "What's the test for that?" and keep you honest. Once you have tried as much of XP as you possibly can, then you can tailor it to yourself and your situation. One of the purposes of the XP spike is to get you up to speed on XP practices so that, during your project for an actual customer, you use all of them all of the time.

Certain practices are central to XP. You may find times when you are tempted to adapt one or another. The danger is that you may end up doing XPb. This is "XP but." Industrial teams that say they use XP will say, "We do XP, but we don't really believe in having the customer involved." Alternatively, they say, "We do XP, but we have a design team scope out the project and give it to the analysts before we give it to our developers." Before you do XPb at least give XP a fair try.

A spike is very freeing. You are going to throw the code away. Be as free with the code as you like. Try some ideas that you might not try on production code. Pay attention to the communication that happens in the pairs and in the larger group. At its heart, XP is a social methodology. Everyone is communicating with everyone. Don't hold back. In a polite, helpful way, make your opinions known.

WE NEED TO DO THIS BEFORE THAT

One of the hard things about estimating stories is that there are dependencies. Often if a particular story can be completed first, it smoothes the way for implementing others quickly and easily. Unfortunately, your stories can't be estimated in this way because you don't get to choose the order. You estimate each story by assuming it is in isolation. As the project progresses you will be able to revisit and reestimate your tasks. Remember that your original estimates will be off because you didn't know your own pace. You're really making guesses of relative speed. You're saying, "This task will take twice as long as that one," and not "This one will take four hours and that one will take eight hours."

Once you find out that the first task took six hours you have a better estimate of the second story . You also have a notion of dependencies. You can see that after some tasks are finished, others will go much more quickly. Often one task is a variation of another. Your estimates will tend to work out. Your estimate for the first task was probably too low and your estimates for the similar tasks are now too high. It seems to work out.

Even if you see dependencies, you can't depend on the customer choosing the stories in an order that supports your efforts. You can go to the customer and describe the savings you anticipate if the ordering is as you suggest. The bottom line is that the customer makes that decision.

THE CUSTOMER MAKES THE BUSINESS DECISIONS

One thing that you'll learn in your XP spike is that it is hard to be an XP customer. You need to stay involved and make decisions. When you go back to the role of the developer, remember what it felt like to be the customer. It was very empowering for you, as a customer, to decide what was worked on next. Remember when you looked over a set of options and thought to yourself, "Oh, that's more important to have than this one." That is completely the customer's right. You are building software for the customer, so the customer gets to make the decisions of what is the most important item left on the list.

But what if the customer is wrong? What if the customer asks for the wrong thing next? Take a minute and think of what this means. Do you mean that the customer asked for something out of order? You've already seen how to handle that. Either make an argument of why the order needs to change or accept the customer's order. Do you mean that the customer doesn't see why some other feature isn't much more valuable than the one selected? On the one hand, the customer determines value. The customer is paying for the product of your labors. The customer decides what is most valuable to have if the support for the project ends at the end of the current iteration. On the other hand, the customer may be arguing for a pretty GUI and you realize that getting the database working correctly is more important to the success of the project. Make your case but let the customer decide. The customer may have to show marketing what the GUI looks like and that may be a more pressing need then actually getting functionality.

You are (or are training to be) a professional developer. As you deliver features to the customers on a regular basis, they will begin to have more trust in you and in your judgment. You will have the opportunity to express your opinions and have them listened to. Once you've programmed a while you will know that there are many ways to attack a problem. Often there are better ways and worse ways but you will seldom come across absolutely right or absolutely wrong ways. The customer decides non-technical issues.

CHOOSING AN XP SPIKE

You need to choose a project to experiment with XP before you do "the one that counts." Because you will be your own customer, you need to choose a project that you can scope out well enough. Here are a few quick suggestions. Remember, you are not expecting to finish this project. Take a look at the time you have available for pairing. In this first week or so, it is important for you and your partners to schedule plenty of time together. It's going to take you a while to get going. You'll have problems installing software or getting the hang of testing first. Choose a project that allows you to quickly write down the user stories and get right to work. Here are a few suggestions.

1. *The bowling scoring problem.* You will design an application that correctly scores a bowling game and then add a GUI front-end to it. This is a well-traveled example because of the article written by Robert Martin and Robert Koss, which is available online at www.objectmentor.com/resources/articles/xpepisode.htm. Read their description of the problem and then quickly write up a bunch of user stories. Write down some tasks and start working. This is a short application. For maximal effect do not develop the GUI until you have all of the logic working correctly.
2. *Tetris or another video game.* The advantage of choosing a video game is that the research is fun. You generally know the game you are trying to recreate so your team can get together and write user stories. You can see if the user stories adequately communicate customer needs. Note that you don't want to test the program by playing the game. You still want automated tests. Again, the hint is to create the GUI last. GUIs tend to be hard to test. You want to include as little logic in the GUI as possible. This way the logic is well tested and the GUI doesn't have to have many tests.
3. *If there's ever time . . .* There must be an application you've been meaning to write for a long time. The problem is that you never have enough time, and you never end up getting very far when writing this application. Choose it for your spike. You probably won't finish the application but what you learn by playing with it may give you the confidence and incentive to return to it someday.

Chapter 3

Pair Programming—Learning to Work Together

In eXtreme Programming (XP), every line of code is written by two people working together at the same keyboard. This relationship between the two programmers is not a hierarchical relationship, yet one person leads and the other person plays a supporting role, directly aiding the leader's actions. At any time, the supporting person can question any of the leader's ideas or actions or even take over. The former leader reacts to this by assuming the supporting role. This switching of roles happens so frequently that it becomes natural. Throughout the course of a project, each member of the pair will form similar partnerships with other programmers.

While pair programming does become natural, it is an unusual professional relationship. We are used to bosses, managers, and project leaders. Try to envision Tiger Wood's caddy grabbing a pitching wedge out of Tiger's hands and making the shot himself. Imagine, in the middle of a card trick, a magician's assistant reminding the Great Mysterio to have the audience member return the card to the deck *before* shuffling it. Or picture a two-man bobsled team somehow stopping halfway down the track to have the brakeman jump off, the driver shift back to work the brakes, and a new person jump onboard to steer. Pairing is impractical and ridiculous in these contexts, but it works extremely well for programming.

One reason pairing is successful in programming is that outside of the hierarchies of professional life, it is very common and familiar. Pairing occurs naturally in many aspects of our lives. Relationships, friendships, and families often interact this way. You may drive to a restaurant (concert, movie, etc.) and your significant other might drive home. Sometimes you let your friends choose the activity; sometimes you decide. If you've ever witnessed multiple amateur plumbers working together on a leaky drainpipe, then you know whoever has the wrench makes all the decisions and everyone else helps. That is, until it's clear that no progress is being made. Then one of the helpers has earned the unspoken right to be the "wrench-bearer," and try a different approach. This is also the way it works when several students try to talk through a difficult math problem with only one pencil or one piece of chalk. In any case, at first it probably will seem a very strange way to program, but it can quickly become the only way you want to code.

ROLES IN PAIRING

Pairing means that other programmers are going to be intimately familiar with the way that you code. They will see how much you know and don't know about the language you're using. They will see your abilities and limitations as a programmer. This can be very scary. Whether you are confident of your own abilities or not, it is very different when you show someone your complete working code and let them see all the mistakes you've made along the way.

The most important criterion for successful pairing is that the pair work comfortably together. XP requires communication and successful communication requires an atmosphere of trust, comfort, and security. Much of your time in pair programming is going to be spent pointing out each other's mistakes or asking to take over the keyboard to try things your way. All other considerations (who controls the keyboard, how often you give the keyboard to your partner, whose ideas translate into code, etc.) are secondary to working well together. As you pair, you'll develop a comfort zone with each different partner. You will most likely pair differently with different people.

There are two distinct roles in a pair. The *driver* is responsible for creating the code the pair is currently working on. If they are writing a method, then the driver types in the method signature and starts working on the body. The *copilot* watches what the driver is doing and often makes syntactical corrections and suggestions. The copilot also has less of an investment in the code being written and can, therefore, ask broader questions about whether this is the way to address the problem.

What makes the dynamic of pairing work is that two different people are playing the two different roles. In creative writing the author embodies the two roles of creator and the editor. As the author begins to write a new paragraph he or she must stifle the urge to go back and fix previous work. As soon as the editor enters the process, it is hard to encourage the creator to continue working. In XP the creator is driving while the copilot is responsible for all of the editorial duties. As you'll see, having the copilot watch for dropped semicolons or misspelled method calls allows the driver to concentrate on driving.

So which should you be, the driver or the copilot? The answer is that you will be both. There will be times when it is natural for you to drive and times when it is natural for you to copilot. You will see possibilities when you are copiloting that will lead you to ask to drive. Once you are given the keyboard, your view changes. It seems to narrow in on the solution you saw before and now your partner has the broader view and may suggest a refinement or ask for the keyboard back. The XP model is that the roles switch frequently. This should be the goal that you strive for. However, in some pairs the same person may tend to drive for long stretches of time. You will find that you pair differently with different people in the same way that you converse differently with different people. Ultimately, the goal is for both members of the partnership to be comfortable working together.

The Driver

The driver is the person who controls the keyboard and the mouse. The driver is engaged in the task of writing tests and then writing the code that passes the tests. The person driving may change during the writing of any given test or in the middle of a method designed to pass a particular test. Even so, at any given moment the pair knows who is driving. The person driving is engaged in the activity you think of as coding.

At the same time, the driver is actively talking to the copilot. The copilot is pointing out small typos that would be caught by a compiler. The driver is explaining the intent of the code and talking with the copilot, so they can both be aware of the direction of the development. Knowing that the copilot is watching every move, one might expect that the driver would feel stifled or "under a microscope." Instead, after an initial adjustment period, the driver derives great freedom from the scrutiny. The driver can concentrate on algorithmic concepts because the copilot is helping with the minute details of keywords and variable types. The activity of coding is less tiring and the driver is able to write tighter code for longer stretches of time than before.

The Copilot

The copilot is not a passenger. Passengers are merely along for the ride. They may be bored and a distraction to the driver. Neither is the copilot simply a navigator (the term frequently used for the nondriving partner in a pair). Navigators focus only on the task of plotting the course. The copilot is someone who is paying attention to everything that is going on around; he or she notices and advises the driver whenever anything important escapes the driver's attention. At a moment's notice, the copilot can take over and perform equally well. Being able to take over is what makes the copilot's role more than that of a sidekick. In many ways being a driver is a more familiar role to programmers. It's what you do when you're coding. Being an engaged copilot is difficult and must be learned.

The copilot has several roles. The first role is to assume the duties of a navigator, taking on the larger questions: "Is the code is headed in the right direction?", "Is there a simpler way of looking at the problem?", and "When we finish this, what is the next step?" By looking a few paces down the path, when the pair arrives at the next point, some of the issues have already been considered and evaluated.

Another role for the copilot is to monitor details. By not having the controls, the copilot is also free from the onus of creating. The copilot can watch as the tests and the code appears on the screen. It is the copilot's job to continually process and evaluate the information passing before them and evaluate it. Where is that variable declared? Did we allocate enough storage for that array? What if the value passed in is negative? Has that method been written yet? How can we tell which panel we are listening to? Any question without an immediate, satisfactory answer is a blip on the radar screen that should be communicated to the driver.

Perhaps the most important role for the copilot is that of alternate driver. When the situation dictates, the copilot and driver swap roles. Unlike relief pitchers in baseball, this does not occur only when the team is in trouble. Switching roles is a fundamental and necessary part of pairing. It stimulates the flow of ideas and it keeps the pairs mentally fresher by changing their activities. So, when you are copiloting, listen for that vague nagging in the back of your head that suggests it's time take over for a while and try out some other ideas.

GOOD THINGS HAPPEN IN PAIRS

This unusual relationship between programmers creates a working environment that is part development effort, part tutoring session, and part a system of checks and balances. It emphasizes the strengths of both programmers and reduces the effects of their weaknesses. It helps keep the pair focused and, as a result, they produce better code than they would individually.

A Tale of Two Pairings

In XP each programmer signs up for his or her tasks for the week. Imagine that you and your classmate Ima Whiz both signed up for tasks and estimated them. Think of how much faster your work would go if you could get Ima to put everything aside and help you with your tasks. So you ask Ima for help and she says yes. Actually you knew she'd say yes because it's understood that: *If someone asks you to pair with him or her and you can, then you must say yes.*

There aren't a lot of XP rules so this one is pretty important. The next few sections will talk about how you and Ima work together, but assume for now that with Ima's help you were able to complete your tasks within the time that you estimated.

Collectively this doesn't seem so efficient. Suppose you estimated the task would take you six hours and that together you and Ima accomplished it in four hours. This means that a six-hour task for the group actually cost the group eight hours. You'll soon see that there are enough other benefits to pair programming that pay off in the end that this simple measurement does not tell the whole story.

Just because you've finished your tasks for the week doesn't mean that you can catch up on your e-mail and start surfing the net. Now Ima needs to get her tasks completed and she ends up pairing with another student who has experience in that area. Meanwhile, Lester Clews asks you to pair with him on his tasks. You remember the rule and tell him you'll be happy to pair. You find that some of his tasks require techniques similar to the ones that you and Ima just worked on. The work goes surprisingly quickly and you are pleased to notice that now three members of your team know this helpful technique. You and Lester actually find a slightly nicer way to accomplish the task so you and he go back to your task and apply the changes there as well.

Couldn't you, Les, and Ima have worked individually on your own tasks? Could you have finished sooner? Possibly, perhaps probably, but a really important facet of XP is that *every delivered line of code is written by two people sitting at the same keyboard working together.* No code written by one programmer gets delivered to the client. The remainder of this chapter explains what this really means and offers suggestions as to how to best make it work for you.

Two Heads Are 1.7 Times Better than One

In the example above, Ima and her partner encounter the troubling notion that pair programming takes more resources than solo efforts (eight total hours vs. six). It is a common and incorrect impression that pair programming reduces productivity. Martin

Fowler, author of *Refactoring, Improving the Design of Existing Code*, answers this criticism on the Wiki with "That would be true if the most time consuming part of programming was typing."

Taking a closer look at these issues, some research has shown (e.g., *The Costs and Benefits of Pair Programming* by Cockburn and Williams) that for an additional cost of 15% in terms of development time, pair programming provides a wealth of benefits to both the team and the software. These benefits include: improved quality of design, fewer software defects, reduced dependency on individual team members, enhanced technical skills, improved team communications, and measurably more enjoyment. The extra cost in terms of development time is more than made up for in a corresponding 15% reduction in software defects.

The time spent and resources applied may be greater, but two programmers working together on the same code, at the same time, are more productive and provide a greater benefit to the development team than independent efforts by the same people. Synergies between the programmers are invaluable and opportunities for cross-pollination of ideas negate any perceived under use of resources. Pair programming is definitely a case where well, . . . the sum *is* greater than the parts.

BENEFITS OF PAIR PROGRAMMING

If pair programming is simply two people writing one big program together instead of writing two smaller ones separately, it shouldn't warrant much attention. If, even worse, pair programming uses twice the resources to produce the same result, then it clearly wouldn't be useful at all. Yet despite these perceptions, pair programming provides tangible advantages that individual programming cannot. Pairing does four things: it reduces the number of mistakes that programmers introduce into their code; it helps avoid everyday programming distractions; it forces thought and evaluation of possible solutions; and it provides an opportunity for team members to exchange programming knowledge and project-specific information.

Real-Time Code Reviews

Some people think that they make more mistakes when typing with an audience; others argue that you make the same number of mistakes, you're just more acutely aware of them when someone is watching. In either case, a second person makes the mistakes easier to spot and correct. The goal of pair programming is to form a single working unit so that any feeling of performer and audience diminishes and the advantages of four eyes and two brains are manifest. The driver can concentrate on producing and the copilot can focus on catching mistakes. Pairing catches three kinds of frequent mistakes: typos, cognitive dropouts, and invalid assumptions.

When one works individually, the compiler identifies a large number of your mistypings. At the time you made the error, you were concentrating on writing code. The logic portion of your brain was engaged and filtering out minor distractions. Maybe you typed `whole (x!=0)` when you meant to type `while (x!=0)`. It's common to make this sort of mistake; it's like writing a sentence and leaving out a word. To everyone else the missing word is obvious, but to you, since you meant to type `while` you may continue to misread `whole` as `while` until you read the code very carefully or out loud. Typos slip by and once forgotten can be quite challenging to find and correct. In this case, the compiler caught the mistake and it is trivial. However, other typos can be much more subtle and aggravating, for example: `a = b = 1` instead of `a = b - 1`. When pairing, the copilot watches the screen with a brain that is not engaged in creating, but one that is trying to understand what is being created. The copilot is fully aware of the driver's intentions but not of the details, so when either of the examples above appears, they jolt the copilot who catches them immediately.

Cognitive dropouts can occur in any development of a nontrivial program. Every programmer has satisfyingly "finished" a module only to realize after stepping back that an entire class of inputs wasn't addressed or a boundary condition needs additional handling. The driver can only focus on so much of a program at one time—the copilot provides additional capacity. Because the copilot isn't as close to the code, he or she can see the larger picture and easily realize the missing feature. Once cued by the copilot, the driver invariably recognizes the problem. Often it isn't outside the pilot's grasp, but rather outside the current sphere of consideration. It's the copilot's job to be constantly adjusting the extent and boundaries of the driver's focus. After being redirected, the driver can begin to incorporate the additional code to handle whatever was left out.

The very nature of invalid assumptions makes them difficult to avoid and correct. They are kept in the part of the mind labeled "I Know These Things Are True," and you look everywhere else for problems before going back there. In the original edition of David R. Palmer's novel, *Emergence,* he wrote that polar bears are members of the mink family. In the afterward to the signature edition of the novel, Palmer explained that this was something that he simply knew for a fact, so there was no reason to question or research it. He writes that he has no idea where that erroneous "fact" came from, but someone outside of his incorrect assumption had to point it out to him so he could make the correction. The copilot has a different set of assumptions than the driver and provides the necessary outside viewpoint to identify invalid ones. Examples of common invalid assumptions are broadening the class of inputs that existing code can handle, eliminating a class of conditions from consideration, and relying on nonexistent code. These pitfalls are of a more concrete nature, but it is also the responsibility of the copilot to watch out for less tangible problems. The driver may be entering a bug-free and computationally efficient implementation of a radix sort, but if the radix sort is inappropriate for the current problem, it is not helping the cause. The copilot should also consider these issues and, if he or she cannot offer alternatives, at least argue against the dead-end approach.

Avoiding Distractions

Time is precious for pair programmers. As a student many things vie for your attention: other classes, homework, and extracurricular activities (not to mention commuting issues, jobs, fraternity obligations, and friends and family). The time you've set aside for pairing is a valuable commodity. In the past, when working on non-XP programs, you could justify getting distracted or putting off getting started because you could always pull an all-nighter to get the program written. This is not true in XP. Programmers must work at a sustainable pace and individually written code cannot be incorporated into the project. So time for pairing is not something that can be wasted without consequence. Hence, both members of the pair must come to the pairing session with a mindset to get work done. If not, both will have to find another time to do it. Early on in the XP process, you'll learn to put your scheduled pairing time to good use.

When pairing, you have a responsibility to the trust that your partner has given you. Without discussing it, without planning it, suddenly one person's inattention, laxity, or goofing off directly and negatively impacts someone else. So when you're pairing, there is a strong tendency to "be on your best behavior." The software engineering class has a tendency to bring out the best is some students. Bad habits like waiting until the last second to write programs and giving up too soon get replaced simply because it is unacceptable not to correct them. You and your peers work harder at becoming good XP citizens because if not, nobody will want to pair with you. In short, you'll be shunned; social trust and social expectations can be very strong forces.

Team spirit sounds like something cheerleaders produce as a by-product of their enthusiasm. That's actually not too far off in the case of pairing. When two people work together with a serious purpose to reach a common goal, they get caught up in the process. The dynamics of the situation become you and your partner against a particularly recalcitrant test case. When one of you comes up with the key that gets you past the current problem, the other cheers. As your program grows and its capabilities increase, confidence in your partnership grows. Working together to overcome adversity builds team spirit. Once a team is formed, you want to perform well for each other. You want to be the one to slay the next dragon. This is the exact opposite of shunning; by becoming a champion of the social contract you'll be sought out as a partner. You'll be labeled a "team player" and a "contributor"—strong medicine against distractions.

All four of these factors work together to create an environment in which staying focused is expected and rewarded, and, therefore, easier to do.

Managing for Two

If two people express an opinion on how to approach a problem, the resulting course of action either becomes unanimously clear or nothing gets resolved. Pairing will help you realize how many decisions you are used to making unconsciously when programming by yourself. Again, this can be jarring at first, having your actions, which are "the obvious things to do," questioned. But if you keep an open mind, questioning these actions has only two possible results: the question can be answered, which reinforces the practice or the question uncovers a flawed practice, which can be improved or removed. Everyone likes to think that their way is a good way or the right way, but when one is presented with clear evidence to the contrary, it's foolish not to adopt the better way.

The important point here is that when two programmers working together on the same problem agree on the same approach, it increases their confidence that the approach is reasonable. If they disagree on how to tackle a problem, it naturally forces discussion. This method is an incredibly simple, yet resilient failsafe mechanism. When both agree, full steam ahead. When there's dissent, stop briefly, discuss, and move forward. It is important to remember that these are small steps and everything is reversible. The decision-making process in pairing is an exercise in balance.

Imagine that you are one of two runners out for your morning's exercise. The primary goal is a good workout. It doesn't really matter where you and your partner run as long as you keep moving. The concept of pairs programming is similar. Which branch to take at a fork in the path can be decided nonverbally by a simple nod of the head or by drifting to one side of the path. Imagine how pointless it would be for the runners to stop at every intersection and argue the relative merits of each option for several minutes. Even taking a somewhat less ideal path is better than a prolonged interruption. On the other hand, if both runners drift to opposite sides of the path as they approach a fork, and follow with two opposing tilts of the head, a momentary pause and brief conversation might be necessary. Every so often, the differences in the paths might result in a more extended discussion. One runner might not be aware that one path tends to be very muddy after a rainstorm. But then the other argues that the remaining path is too steep for this late in the run. If both feel strongly about their choice, it is still small compared to their overall feeling about the importance of continuing. Pick one, neither wet shoes nor weary muscles is that big of a deal.

In the context of pair programming, the interdependencies among the XP practices of simple design, testing first, refactoring, and collective code ownership help to keep decision making easy. By maintaining simple designs, and working in baby steps, the depth of a design disagreement cannot be too severe. Usually a few minutes of discourse can resolve any conflict. Once paused, there is a strong impetus to get moving again for all the reasons given on avoiding distractions. So if the disagreement is minor, the pair usually won't invest a lot of time into overanalyzing it. Even if the suggested approach falls flat, it can be fixed during refactoring by someone else with a different perspective. (This could happen even if your idea prevails, so it's not worth investing too much in an either/or option in the first place.)

If there is a strong disagreement, then the level of discussion increases. From a very simple arrangement adaptive strategy appears that applies the greatest amount of effort where and when it is needed. Again, even these more striking disagreements can usually be resolved without ongoing arguments. But if they can't, if the pair cannot agree on which of two possible courses to follow, like the runners, they should simply pick one. Take turns. Let the driver decide, or let the copilot decide. Let your partner decide. Use a random number generator. If you can't reach a consensus after a reasonable period of spirited discussion, stop and try a different approach. Chances are that the reason no approach emerges as a "clearly superior one" is that there are advantages and drawbacks to all approaches. Make use of the interdependent XP practices. Even if you make the completely wrong choice, the penalties are small and the problem is correctable. Who knows, maybe there's something you're not seeing in your partner's approach and you could learn something by trying it out.

Some veteran XP practitioners note that when they pair with a long-time partner, they can become too comfortable. They are so aware of the other's thoughts and work patterns that they come close to working with one mind. Ironically, this brings about the exact problem that pair programming hopes to avoid—programming from a single perspective. So, if you find yourself pairing with the same person a lot and you start missing the same types of problems, regardless of who's driving, make an effort to take a break and pair with others for a while.

Knowledge and Information Migration

A more subtle and, in the long term, more important, benefit of pairing emerges as you begin to witness others on your team picking up your good programming habits. You suddenly realize that you are using a technique that only one person on your team knew when the project started. This benefit is much more pronounced when a variable-skilled team of five or six work together on a larger project and mix up the pairings well, but even a team of two will observe the phenomenon.

It is an example of cultural or societal evolution. Unlike biological evolution, in which all traits—good and bad—of the fittest members are passed on, societies are able to pick and choose characteristics to propagate. In the context of eXtreme Programming, programmers are constantly, and without fanfare, being shown better mousetraps by their partners. The truly beautiful consequence of this is that the groups' overall level of software skills doesn't sink to the lowest common denominator, nor does it somehow average out. Instead, the level rises to a composite of the best characteristics of the team. Ironically, the person passing along the technique, trick, or short cut doesn't consider the incidental gift significant. To that person, it is a known quantity that "everyone must already know about." They are simply programming the way they normally work. So even if the team sat down beforehand and agreed to share their programming knowledge, these useful pearls would not even come up. Thus working in pairs, especially in groups of pairs, can make one better at programming, both at that moment and in the long run.

However, it's not only good programming practices and little known commands that one learns as different pairings take place. Knowledge of the developing software also spreads across the team. Knowledge spreading is part of the XP practice of collective code ownership, and it fosters developers who are well versed in the software. This attribute is invaluable in an academic setting in which students have demanding schedules. When working on a software project that is evolving quickly, it's important that at least one of the programmers available for each day's pairings is familiar with what's been going on.

Consider an alternative, non-XP approach in which a single team member has all the knowledge of a particular subsystem or technology for the project. This is the "strategy" often employed by software engineering teams using a traditional developmental methodology. Often the code created by the closeted specialist would benefit from examination by other team members. In addition to discouraging the others from understanding or even looking at that subsystem, it also renders the project vulnerable to better job opportunities or an unforeseen calamity. Less dramatically, it increases the interdependency of the team and lowers productivity whenever life intervenes and disrupts that interdependency. Maintaining the full team's knowledge of a system cannot possibly scale to very large systems. But for smaller projects and self-contained subsystems, it provides both system robustness and programmer confidence.

PAIRING IN PRACTICE—DEALING WITH PRACTICAL ISSUES

All the students who have taken eXtreme Programming classes from us have come to enjoy, and in many cases, preach the benefits of pair programming. Those initially resistant to the idea and even those who ultimately decided that eXtreme Programming was not right for them have unequivocally supported pairing. However, even the strongest supporters of the extreme programming methodology took some time to find their pairing comfort zone. What follows are some pointers on how to reach the pairing comfort zone; these are things that you need to be aware of when pairing. Again, every pair finds their own way to work together, but the issues discussed here can impact everyone, so take them under consideration and apply as needed. A more comprehensive treatment of pairing, including motivations for adoption, programmer personalities, and ergonomic issues can be found in Laurie Williams and Robert Kessler's book, *Pair Programming Illuminated*.

The Third Alternative

A third role for the pair is a combination of four parts: designer, negotiator, advocate, and manager. When pairing, whether you are currently wearing the driver's or the copilot's cap, you also have an individual responsibility to the quality of the system. Over and over again, pairs encounter small issues that require a judgment call. Sometimes the driver handles it as a matter of course. At other times the copilot may take over and bring the development in another direction. But, when the issue requires a discussion, the typing stops, the roles temporarily fade, and together the two *developers* work out an attempt to overcome the obstacle. This can occur when the next step is not obvious to both members, the "simplest" way to pass the test might be one of several options, or they disagree on whether another test case is necessary. The pair stops coding and selects their course of action. While stopped, they may be designing a little, thinking through the necessary details to make a test work, or considering a potential refactoring. After getting back together on the same page, the pair continues on, either resuming their roles from before the consultation or switching.

The Pair

Think of a couple you know. Each member of the couple has an identity and then the couple as a whole has its own identity. So it is with pairs. Although your role may be changing between driver and copilot, throughout you are part of this integrated whole. Your responsibilities change, while the responsibilities of the pair remain fairly stable. The pair is responsible for creating tests and then creating code for passing the collection of tests. Each individual needs to communicate ideas, suggest approaches, and, most importantly, keep the code simple. Pairing requires lively, ongoing discussion about the code. Once you've committed yourself to the prospect of writing code in tandem, you don't care who had which insight. The key observation in pairing is that the driver and the copilot together form a single entity that writes the code. Any action that furthers this result is a positive for the development effort.

Groups of Pairs

In an ideal setting in industry, an XP team works in the same room. Just as pairing leads to unexpected benefits, another level of synergy occurs when multiple pairs from a single team work together in the same location. In such a crucible, intrapair conversations impinge on everyone's awareness and sometimes the teammate who knows the answer may have overheard you asking your partner the question. You may remember overhearing another pair struggle with the same issue that you're wrestling with today. This proximity also fosters development of team camaraderie. Time after time, someone on the team has the answer. Everyone cheers the successes and, when they are faced together, the obstacles don't seem as daunting.

It isn't always possible to pair everyone up. There may, for example, be an odd number of group members. This situation often resolves itself into a rotating trio. Two members of a group of three will pair in the standard driver/copilot combination, while the third member does something else independently. This could be anything from homework for other classes to a bathroom break to reading e-mail. When one member of the pair needs a break, they switch places with the extra person. Practitioners of this approach say that it provided all the benefits of pairing and kept everyone fresher for longer periods of time. Often the third member can be seen listening in and contributing as well. As long as each member of the trio is engaged and any one of them could drive at any time, this seems to be an acceptable arrangement.

Learning by Watching and Doing

One way to become comfortable with pair programming is observing an experienced pair in action and then pairing with one of them. If the instructor doesn't provide such an opportunity in class, ask to pair with the coach or seek out former XP students. By watching and working with an experienced pair, you can observe good habits and try them out. Avoid pairing for the first time with another novice; you'll both be looking to each other for guidance and not progressing. On the other hand, don't wait too long before pairing with others at your experience level so you can avoid developing dependencies on having a veteran partner. It's always a good idea to pair with different team members to see different perspectives and avoid getting into mental ruts, especially when first starting out.

Reading Each Other's Signals

When two programmers pair up, they need to find the pairing comfort zone mentioned earlier. One of the quickest ways to achieve that is to be aware of each other's needs. Pairs that work well together know when the copilot wants to takeover. They know when the driver isn't ready to release control. They know when they need to take a break. They acquire this knowledge by pairing together and learning the signals. The less consciously the transitions can take place, the less impact they'll have on a pair's production.

Giving Up the "Wheel"

Whenever you drive, listen to your copilot. If the copilot asks to drive, try to accommodate. Generally, the copilot won't initiate a switch in roles without a good reason. Likewise, the driver shouldn't veto a switch without good reason. If you're on a roll and about to implement something significant, ask the copilot to wait, but don't let them forget their intent. Be careful, because at this point the copilot isn't paying as close attention to you as you drive because the copilot is thinking about the alternative code. Another issue arises when you've been driving for a while and the copilot doesn't ask to drive. Sometimes you have to initiate the switch. It might be as simple as saying, "Why don't you drive for a while."

Font Size and Eyesight

A practical issue that extreme programmers rarely consider before pairing is font size. When one member of a pair has eyesight that is significantly worse than that of the other, an increase in the font size can easily resolve an otherwise problematic issue. This is especially true if the pair tends to switch roles frequently. As an aside, some of our most interesting pairings came during a demonstration when we projected the computer screen on the wall and allowed anyone to participate. Talk about your large font sizes!

Code Formatting

Arguing the merits of different coding formats (amount of indentation, bracket placement, etc.) is the largest and most time-consuming nonissue since the ongoing vi vs. emacs editor debate. However, consistently maintaining *some* coding format *is* a very big deal, especially when pair programming. XP emphasizes this importance through the coding standards practice. Whether the XP team resolves this "religious" issue among themselves or a coding standard is mandated by their organization, it is critical that the formatting be consistent throughout the program. The danger of having inconsistent code is strong enough that the team must resolve this issue before programming begins. When working with existing code, the team must maintain the agreed upon standard, regardless of which programmer is driving. The scenario to avoid is participating in a vicious cycle of *formatting-refactoring*—using collective code ownership to champion a particular style over another. Pick one style, stick to it, and forget about it.

Revision Control

For two-person projects, this is a complete nonissue, because only one piece of code changes at a time. But for larger teams, the practice of collective code ownership makes it critical that sure pairs don't impinge on each other's changes. Unlike in the professional environment, this might be less of a problem in academia due to scheduling constraints. During some semesters it is very rare that two different pairs from the same team program at the same time. But an equally important issue is making the most up-to-date version of the system available to all team members. A third revision control issue is the ability to easily back out of a pairing session that went down the wrong direction. There are many commercially available revision control systems, including free ones such as CVS, available for both Unix-based and Windows systems. Many if not most IDEs now have integrated systems that prevent unintentional overwriting. One by-product is that there are incentives to the programmers to keep the code checked out for as short a time as possible. Whoever checks the code in last must resolve any conflicts between the two versions. It is important for larger teams to use a revision control system that addresses all three issues. And while two person groups don't require mutually exclusive access, they can still benefit from the archival and backing-out features of the system.

Mixing and Matching

When working in a multiperson team, there will invariably be people with whom you prefer pairing When those people reciprocate and tend to want to pair with you, that's an indication that you work well together and that you probably make an effective team. But don't let that degenerate into an exclusive subgroup. We have discussed the importance of ideas flowing through the group in a pair-by-pair fashion. An exclusive pair will create separate spheres of information flow and detract from the overall betterment of the team. There's nothing wrong with frequent pairing, just don't stop pairing with other team members.

Scheduling Time to Pair

Professional programmers will have some issues coordinating pairing, but only to a limited extent, after all programming is their primary activity. In an academic setting, many different classes vie for student attention. In an extreme programming software-engineering class, students find that scheduling weekly times to pair, and treating that time as a commitment as strong as a class, works well. It reduces conflicts, doesn't require any recurring effort to schedule, and provides the whole team with a snapshot of their work times during the week. With such a rigid schedule, other team members can drop-in at the last minute and participate. It also makes estimations more accurate because the number of working hours per week remains basically constant.

A FINAL WORD ON PAIRING

In a lot of ways pair programming is like skiing. You can read as much about it as you want to, but until you get out on the slopes, you really don't have a feel for it. Go; try pair programming with an opened mind. Next we have a number of programming and nonprogramming exercises designed to introduce you to pair programming and its associated styles of communication. These exercises will help you get used to the ideas of pair thinking and pair working.

PAIR PROGRAMMING EXERCISES

PAIR COMMUNICATION AND COOPERATION BUILDING EXERCISES

1. Working with a partner, one pencil, and one sheet of paper, write out the instructions for someone caring for a pet while the owner is away for a week.
2. Working with a partner, one pencil, one sheet of paper, and no external reference, draw, to the best of your recollection, a universally recognizable image, for example:

   a. A map of the United States of America
   b. The Monopoly game board
   c. The layout of a standard keyboard

3. Independently write a half page or so describing the largest metropolitan area closest to your current location. Get together with another person in your class who has done the

same thing. Combine your two descriptions into a single, seamless composition that includes all the things mentioned in either account.

4. Form pairs, and in each pair have one person (the artist), out of sight of the other, draw a simple line drawing on a sheet of paper. The drawing should be an arbitrary collection of shapes, lines, and points and take no more than a minute or two to draw. The other partner (the "copier") is then shown the drawing for no more than two seconds. The pair then attempts to recreate the drawing as closely as possible with some restrictions. The original artist can continue to look at the drawing but may only participate verbally. The "copier" controls the pencil and another sheet of paper but may not see the original picture again.
5. Find a partner and cut a crossword puzzle out of the newspaper. Make three separate clippings: the puzzle itself, the across clues, and the down clues. Each person gets one set of clues and is not allowed to look at the other set. Working together, solve the puzzle.

PAIR PROGRAMMING EXERCISES

1. Write a test for a piece of code that is supposed to find the largest element in a list. With a partner, using the pair programming techniques described in this chapter, write code to make the test pass.
2. The code provided below displays nine panels of different colors in a 3 × 3 grid. Whenever the mouse enters a panel, it turns magenta; when the mouse leaves, the color reverts back to its original color. Add the following user story: "When the user clicks on the center panel, the colors of the eight surrounding panels rotate to the next panel in a clockwise direction." Find a partner to augment the code to pass the additional test. Before beginning, select one person to be the driver for the entire test case. When complete, add this user story: "When the user consecutively clicks on two of the outer panels, the colors of these panels are swapped." The copilot for the first half of the exercise will be the driver for the entire second half of the exercise.

```
import java.awt.*;
import javax.swing.*;

public class Init {

    public JFrame jFrame;
    private MyJPanel panels[];
    public Color colors[] ={Color.blue, Color.green, Color.red,
         Color.white,Color.yellow, Color.black, Color.orange, Color.cyan,
         Color.gray};

    public Init() {
       panels = new MyJPanel[9];

       jFrame = new JFrame("NINE SQUARES PROGRAM");
       jFrame.setSize(500,500);

jFrame.setDefaultCloseOperation(JFrame.EXIT_ON_CLOSE);
       jFrame.getContentPane().setLayout( new GridLayout(3,3) );

       for(int i=0;i<9;i++){
          panels[i] = new MyJPanel(colors[i]);
          jFrame.getContentPane().add(panels[i]);
       }
```

```
            jFrame.setVisible(true);
        }

        public static void main(String args[]){
            Init init = new Init();
        }
}

import javax.swing.*;
import java.awt.*;
import java.awt.event.*;

public class MyJPanel extends JPanel {

    private Color myColor;

    public MyJPanel(Color myColor) {
        this.myColor = myColor;
        setBackground(myColor);
        addMouseListener(new MouseWatcher());
    }

    public void setSelectedColor(){
        setBackground(Color.magenta);
    }

    public void setOriginalColor(){
        setBackground(myColor);
    }

    class MouseWatcher extends MouseAdapter{
        public void mouseEntered(MouseEvent me){
            setSelectedColor();
        }
        public void mouseExited(MouseEvent me){
            setOriginalColor();
        }
    }
}
```

3. With a partner, write from scratch (i.e., write tests first) a program that plays tic-tac-toe against a human opponent. As you write the code try out different pairing techniques and keep track of those that work and those that do not. Be sure to swap pairing roles frequently.
4. On the ExtremeTeaching website(www.extremeteaching.com) there is a growing list of suggested projects of different sizes and scales. Look here for additional exercises in pair programming.

Chapter 4

First Test, Then Code—

Understanding Why We Test First

Before the building inspector at city hall gives the go-ahead to a general contractor to build a new garage, the inspector provides a copy of the local building codes. These are standards against which the inspector will judge the completed garage. Think how risky it would be for the contractor to first build the garage, and then go to the inspector and say, "It's time for you to tell me what the building codes in this town are." For an eXtreme Programming (XP) pair, testing first means that once they decide on their next task, they write a test to verify successful completion of the task before writing the code to perform the task. The tests must be more specific, more dynamic, and narrower in scope than a generic set of building codes, but the concept is the same: first create a definition for a successful conclusion, then work toward achieving it. Note that getting the building codes is vastly different from being handed blueprints. The contractor can't build the garage from the code and the codes in no way specify what the garage will look like. As with test-first programming, a successful garage must, at a minimum, pass the tests set out in the building codes.

Testing first requires you to think differently. No other XP practice jolts your ingrained programming habits as much, and no other practice has more of a cascading effect on the rest of the software development process. Simply put, if you are not testing first, you are not doing eXtreme Programming. If you follow no other XP practices, but you do test first, then you are at least getting a flavor of this different way of doing things. Because of its unfamiliar concept, testing first is one of the more difficult practices to embrace; however, because of its wide-ranging impact, it is also the most important.

Anytime someone asks you to "Think differently" the question "Why?" should immediately come to mind. When, (and if) the "why" has been satisfied, the next question, "How?" should follow. Before attempting to convince you why testing first is a good idea, take a temporary leap of faith while you see how it's done. Once you have a feel for the concept, it will be easier to justify the "why." If you don't want to take it on faith, you can first read the section "Testing First Helps You Write Better Code" and then look into how to test first afterwards.

HOW CAN YOU TEST FIRST? THERE'S NOTHING TO TEST

Generally, when you think of any kind of testing (government automobile crash tests, final examinations, checking a swimming pool's chlorine level, the road portion of a driver's test, or throwing a piece of pasta against a wall to see if it sticks) you think of a test administrator (a professor, a pool maintenance person, a chef) putting someone (a student) or something (pasta) through an experiment or series of experiments to evaluate the resulting performance. There needs to be someone or something to test before you can test it. The same is true for software. Another definition of software testing is taking existing code and evaluating it. So the seemingly obvious, seemingly necessary order is to first write the code and then perform tests on it. Say you've decided that pasta is done when you can take a noodle out of a pot of boiling water and throw it at the wall and it sticks. By designing that test, you have specified what the process should be. You know you'll need a pot of boiling water and some pasta. You'll need a way to get a piece of pasta out of the water, and you'll need a wall. The process for testing software is the same. Before you write your next piece of code, think about how you might test it. Look at everything the test implies about the code that you're going to write.

eXtreme Programming sidesteps the apparent sequential dependency of "code, then test" and requires that programmers think first about the testing and only afterwards address the actual code. It is still true that you cannot evaluate something before it exists, but like the building inspector, we can explicitly lay out the necessary criteria for passing a test before having the object to test.

To test first in XP, you write a small piece of code—called the test case—that runs another, as yet unwritten, portion of code. The test case should return true when the nonexistent code runs successfully and false when it does not. So all programming efforts at this stage go into determining and expressing these two sets of conditions. Once you've written the test case, you then write the code that passes the test. This is one of the keys to successful extreme programming. By writing the test before the code, you are forcing yourself into a simple, bottom-up design. In maintaining that order (test, then code) you cannot get ahead of yourself on the design.

Writing a Test Case

After deciding on the next subtask to accomplish, you and your partner write the test case that will determine when that subtask is successfully completed. The subtask should be small, and the test case should be simple. For example, suppose you decide that the next task for your pair is to find the largest of three given integers. First you write a test case that indicates the success or failure of the code that you will write.

```
if (maxOfThreeInts(1,7,3) == 7){
   System.out.println("Passed Test");
}
else {
   System.out.println("Failed Test");
}
```

The test case example here is simplistic, but it captures the essence of the practice. It does have the disadvantage of requiring you and your partner to look at output and find the words "Passed Test." You would like your tests to be automated and they will be soon. For now this syntax is more familiar and will allow you to concentrate on what is being tested.

Notice what occurred in this simple example. In writing the test, you decided to use a method and also determined that the method takes three integers as input parameters and produces one integer output. You gave the method a descriptive name. All of this information is directly useful in writing the code to perform the task. By writing this test before writing the code, you have forced yourself to consider how the code will be invoked: its inputs and its outputs are both things that *should* be considered before writing the code. Without further effort, you have all the necessary information to write the signature of this method.

```
public int maxOfThreeInts(int num1, int num2, int num3)
```

Certainly, you could have written a signature without writing the test case first, but, as the code gets more complex, the act of writing the test case really does help you focus your efforts and address issues that can be otherwise overlooked.

Passing the Test

With the signature for a method in hand, writing the method becomes the formalization of the algorithm to produce the output from the input. The goal here is to write the simplest code possible to pass the test.

```
public int maxOfThreeInts(int num1, int num2, int num3){
      int max = num1;
      if (num2 >= num1 && num2 >= num3) max = num2;
      if (num3 >= num1 && num3 >= num2) max = num3;
      return max;
}
```

Yes, there are other ways of returning the largest of three values, some of those ways use else clauses, some don't require the logical operations, and some are wrong (see exercises 1, 2, and 3). Why look for something smaller or slicker when you might end up with something that doesn't work? What is important now is to implement something simple and straightforward that passes the test. Better solutions can be refactored later if needed. In our experience in many cases refactoring isn't necessary. The easy, explicit solution is sometimes never replaced.

If simplicity is important, there is a much simpler way to get the test to pass. Because the example in the test case happens to have the largest element in the second position, you could write a method that just returns the second parameter.

```
public int maxOfThreeInts(int num1, int num2, int num3){
      return num2;
}
```

This code will pass the test, but it is insufficient. This implementation is useful as a starting point, but it immediately requires another representative test case with the max in a different position. The second test forces a refactoring of the insufficient solution, and pushes the code towards a more general solution. As an XP developer, you will find a comfort level for writing your test cases and coding solutions. You need to balance the number of representative test cases against the degree of simplicity of your solutions.

What's an Alternative to *Exhaustive* Testing?

Why not write enough test cases to handle all the possible scenarios? In the example there are six different combinations of three integers that could be tried as inputs. If we had written out all six cases, then "cheating" to pass the test would not be possible. The set of tests would be larger, so it would be harder for additional errors to slip through. Finally, we'd also have an increased level of confidence in the code, because it passed a more rigorous set of probing. Indeed then, why not do exhaustive testing?

Despite appearances and programming instincts, there really is not much to be gained. Dijkstra proclaimed in his *Humble Programmer* speech, "Program testing can **be** a very effective way to show the presence of bugs, but it is hopelessly inadequate for showing their absence." This claim is another way of saying that it is not possible to prove a program is correct through testing. So even after extraordinary efforts, no claim of defect-free software can be made. Second, simple test cases are easier to write correctly. Exhaustive test cases are difficult and time consuming. When code is written in a cooperative, responsible manner, then the time spent writing additional test cases is not worth the effort. Third, generating complicated test cases is just as likely to introduce bugs into the system as writing code. Thus a test case should be no more complex than the code it is intended to test. In every scenario exhaustive testing is much more complicated than the code itself. If exhaustive testing is not used, what is the alternative?

One practical alternative to exhaustive testing is representative testing. Representative testing demonstrates the primary, expected behavior of a segment of code. For example, suppose the goal is to write a test case for code that will find the largest of three single digit integers. An exhaustive test (shown in code segment 1 below) must check all 1,000 combinations of the digits 0 through 9, and verify that the largest is always found. A representative test (code segment 2) picks some triple set of integers and verifies that the maximum is correctly found.

```
int result;                                                      (1)
boolean error = false;
for (int i=0; i<10; i++){
    for (int j=0; j<10; j++){
        for (int k=0;k<10;k++){
          result = maxOfThreeInts(i,j,k);
          if ( result < i || result < j || result < k){
             error = true;
          }
        }
    }
}
if (!error) System.out.println("Test Passes");
if (error) System.out.println("Test Fails");
```

```
if (maxOfThreeInts(9,2,7) == 9){                                 (2)
     System.out.println("Test Passes");
}
else {
     System.out.println("Test Fails");
}
```

Clearly, the exhaustive case in code segment (1) introduces many more opportunities for bugs in the test case than does the representative one. Since you're writing both the code and the test cases, and you are undertaking the task in a serious manner, the difference in benefit between the two test cases is minimal. Many first-timers have trouble letting go of the idea of exhaustive testing. So as you are starting out, stick to representative testing and only consider adding more tests as the need arises. There will be a great difference between adding the tests you need and exhaustive testing.

It also makes sense to include test cases that cover any boundary conditions and extreme cases. Having a few other tests in addition to the test in code segment (2) will improve the coverage of the tests and potentially uncover hidden bugs. For this example, possible additional tests might include test cases (3), (4), and/or (5).

```
if (maxOfThreeInts(1,1,5) == 5){                                 (3)
     System.out.println("Test Passes");
}
else {
     System.out.println("Test Fails");
}
```

```
if (maxOfThreeInts(8,2,8) == 8){                                 (4)
     System.out.println("Test Passes");
}
else {
     System.out.println("Test Fails");
}
```

```
if (maxOfThreeInts(3,3,3) == 3){                                    (5)
     System.out.println("Test Passes");
}
else {
     System.out.println("Test Fails");
}
```

In version 1.4 of Java, Sun introduced assertions into the language. Using the keyword `assert`, you can embed test cases more easily into your code. Instead of test case (2) above, you can write the same predicate inside an assert clause as shown in test case (6).

```
assert (maxOfThreeInts(9,2,7)==9) : "Test Fails";                   (6)
```

If the Boolean expression evaluates to `false`, the program aborts and the message will be printed as part of the stack trace. If the assertion evaluates to `true`, then nothing occurs and the execution continues. This approach has the added advantage of allowing the programmer to globally turn the test cases on or off with a compiler option. However, using either of these approaches can be cumbersome. In the following chapter a testing support tool is introduced that automatically runs all the test cases and provides visual feedback.

"Test First" Really Does Mean "Code Afterwards"

The technique of testing first can be so uncomfortable initially that some programmers reinterpret this practice by writing the test immediately after writing the code. Or perhaps you have decided to embrace this practice, but you unexpectedly find yourself writing code that doesn't have a test. How did that happen? No question, testing first is difficult, but like any mold-breaking behavior, the more you do it the easier it becomes. Eventually, it can become second nature. But early on, the novelty of writing test cases at all, combined with "almost-adhering" to the practice by writing the test before moving on and writing more code, can lead the programmer to overlook the apparently minor infraction. Whether by accident or through reinterpretation, writing code before writing the test is fundamentally opposed to the intent of extreme programming. So when you catch yourself unintentionally writing code without a test, stop, write the test, and continue. Work harder to think of testing as the first step when tackling a subtask. On the other hand, if you don't really think there's a difference whether you test first or not, you probably haven't given it enough of a try. As we'll see later, the act of writing the test case first drives the design and then forces programmers to focus on the immediate subtask. It helps eliminate ancillary issues and gives a very different perspective on writing code.

Developing a Test Suite

The overall goal of a software development project is to create a usable, reliable system that works. It's easy to focus on the software as the goal and treat everything else as secondary. In an eXtreme Programming project, creating tests—collectively known as the *test suite*—is equally important. As the development progresses, the number of test cases and the breadth of the test suite increase, making it more useful and valuable. The value of the test suite is clear if you think of it as a custom-made, project-specific tool for probing the developing system. It immediately provides a system status report and can be used as a roadmap through the software to locate problems and help correct them. Many project leaders would pay outrageous amounts for such a valuable tool, especially late in the schedule of a software development effort that is missing its milestones. In XP, this tool is a natural by-product of the methodology, arising from the short cycle of writing a test and then writing code. So without a separate development effort, the test suite grows incrementally both in breadth and completeness with the software. However, to be useful, as well as complete, the test suite must be extremely easy to run. It needs to become another step in the edit-compile-execute cycle. It needs to be automated.

Automated Testing

Testing first is only half the story; the other benefit is the ongoing testing. Once a test case has been written and passed, it becomes part of the test suite. The real advantage to the development team is that they can now run all the tests over and over again, getting repeated feedback on the state of the system. To be effective, the test suite must have software support to do the following: be fully automated (all the tests run at the click of a GUI button), write test cases easily (simple, expressive syntax), interpret results (visual feedback and descriptive error messages), and be fast (visual feedback begins displaying immediately, results completed shortly thereafter).

JUnit, developed by Kent Beck and Erich Gamma, contains all these attributes and is the de facto standard for XP automated testing in Java. JUnit belongs to a family of automated testing systems that are tailored for different languages. Collectively known as xUnit, the family includes CppUnit (C++), VBUnit (Visual Basic), PyUnit (Python), and many others including the original SUnit for Smalltalk. By virtue of its community-wide acceptance we will use it for all future examples in the text. Chapter 10 provides an introduction to JUnit and a step-by-step tutorial on testing first.

TESTING FIRST HELPS YOU WRITE BETTER CODE

Simply inverting the traditional order of coding then testing has dramatic effects on the entire software-development process. Testing first provides a context in which programmers must think about the smallest piece of code before writing it and, by extension, guides the design of the overall system. It gives immediate, useful feedback on the development of the current piece of software and, as a by-product, produces an invaluable, custom-designed tool to gauge the health of the entire development project. This section is a laundry list of the positive aspects of adopting this XP practice.

Testing First Forces Simplicity

You will find yourself taking a split-personality approach to testing first. After you begin to get the hang of it, you'll discover that you treat a test very differently before and after you write it. Before you write it, your goal is to state the test case as completely as possible, and then to find enough distinct representative tests to sufficiently cover your task without being redundant. Even after you get used to the idea of representative testing and embrace the concept of taking baby steps, you will still strive to ensure that your test completely covers the case in question. However, once the test is written, your goal is now to write code that passes the test. At this point in the software development there *is no goal other than making the test pass*. All notions of elegant solutions, complex data structures, or even laying the groundwork for future enhancements are moot. You have the freedom, and indeed the obligation, to do the least amount possible to reasonably make the test pass. Having a nonworking test narrowly focuses all of your programming efforts onto a single, simple problem. This technique forces simple, bottom-up code development. So what if you produced ugly code if you know you're going to change it later anyway? It passes the test now. Mission accomplished. Besides, "changing ugly code" is just another way of saying "refactoring." XP expressly separates these two activities so you can focus on one at a time.

Simplicity Drives the Design

In *Essential XP: Design*, Ron Jeffries argues that by following a simple set of rules, a bottom-up development leads to a good high-level design (see www.xprogramming.org). Erich Gamma and Kent Beck point out that defining a "good design" is notoriously difficult and argue instead that a programmer's goal should be a system that exhibits good design features such as modularity, lack of redundancy, loose coupling, and high cohesion. Writing bottom-up code and taking baby steps creates a system that contains these desirable traits.

So is all the time spent designing programs wasted? Is XP saying that design is unnecessary? The answers are no and no. First, XP is only one of many different software-development methodologies. Some of them advocate an up-front design phase, others, like XP, do not. Whether XP can scale to very large systems remains to be seen. It certainly does not fit into development environments requiring long-term predictive scheduling. This most emphatically does *not* say that XP dismisses system design, instead XP promotes designing and building the system in tandem. Designing and building in tandem is not appropriate for building garages, but it can be and has been successfully applied to software development. XP advocates testing a little and coding a little—taking baby steps. Part of that cycle is designing a little.

Designing in XP is a reaction to the tests. Robotics researcher Rodney Brooks of MIT, in "Planning is Just a Way of Avoiding Figuring Out What to Do Next," argues that reacting quickly to immediate conditions leads to better behaved robots than trying to plan out the robot's actions ahead of time. Ron Jeffries and the Agile software community echo this concept, believing that the cumulative effect of making lots of good, but small, design decisions leads to a good overall design.

How can this be? It seems counterintuitive that the sum of lots of small, local choices can have globally effective results. If none of the decisions made take global issues into account, how can the resulting system address them? Where does the second law of thermodynamics—that systems tend toward more disorder—come into play? Isn't this process destined to produce a hodgepodge system of cobbled-together pieces that won't work well together? Again, the answer is no. The phenomenon is called emergent behavior and prevents this type of system from heading towards chaos. Consider a swarm of wasps building a nest. No wasp knows the global design of what they are building. Each one makes small decisions based on their local situation. The sum of all their efforts produces the nest. In addition to insect societies, you can also observe emergent behavior in many contexts from traffic patterns to economic trends to embryonic formation of body organs to growth patterns of cities. An excellent resource of the subject is Steve Johnson's book, *Emergence*.

So, testing first forces you to keep it simple and if you do a good job at the simple level, the overall effect will be that you're doing a good job at the higher levels too.

Testing First Clarifies the Task at Hand

Writing code to meet a particular problem specification can be a large, somewhat open-ended activity that potentially covers multiple methods, classes, or even subsystems depending on the specifications. Writing a test is a small, self-contained action; think of it as an example to help understand what the code needs to do. For all extreme programmers, but especially the novices, the effort spent writing a test—the necessary critical thinking about the problem before writing the code—helps with both the understanding of the problem and laying the foundation for the solution. Put another way, writing a test acts as a checkpoint; if you don't understand the problem well enough to write a test case, you certainly are not ready to begin writing the code. In order to get beyond the checkpoint, you must wrestle with the problem enough to break off and fully express a small piece. These actions improve your understanding of the task at hand and begin the process of defining a solution. To write a test case, you often must postulate a new class or a new method in an existing class. So once written, the test also provides a starting point for coding: create that new class or add that new method. When you have a better grasp of the problem, moving forward becomes easier.

Testing First Frees You from On-the-Fly Editing

Often when you are at the end of writing some code you've been working on for a while, you suddenly see a different, perhaps better way of implementing it. This isn't a very surprising occurrence because writing the code forces you to think in a more detailed way about a problem. Now comes the decision—do you scrap what you've done and take the new approach or do you leave the code as is and wonder if it should be redone? Either way, you are taking a hit on your effectiveness as a programmer. In the first case, you've lost some time and in the second case you've lost some concentration. As long as on-the-fly editing is a possibility, whether you do it or not, it distracts.

One of the most gratifying facets of testing first is that you don't have to sweat those kinds of decisions as you're writing the code. Instead of trying to balance a myriad of trade-offs between efficiency, readability, maintainability, along with speed, size, and cleverness, testing first eliminates the balancing act. By aiming for the simplest correct solution, testing first frees you (at least temporarily) from second guessing your code. Later in the process, all the code can be reexamined. "Later" for some programmers can mean immediately after writing the code. As soon as the code is written, it is fair game and subject to change. More experienced XP programmers tout the value of very short refactoring cycles. For others, a longer refactoring cycle might be more comfortable. They wait until the "bad smelling" code has reached its full bouquet and make larger changes less frequently. In either case, by forcing a psychological split between writing and editing the code, XP lets programmers focus on the subtask immediately at hand. In essence, XP takes the question of trade-offs and on-the-fly decisionmaking out of your hands and makes a sweeping, project-wide decision ahead of time. It simply makes the code work.

Once it works, then you can look at better alternatives and more consistent solutions, but first and foremost, pass the test.

Test Suites Make Refactoring Possible

There is a limit to the amount of code we can comfortably fit in our heads. The comfort zone can range from as little as an expression or a statement to a method or perhaps a small object. Regardless of where the limit is for the individual, to go upwards, we must abstract away details. For more complex entities (i.e., large objects, subsystems, and systems), we no longer can think directly about code. The student referred to earlier also points out that no other field requires the extreme range of size that programming demands. There is no other way to handle such orders of magnitude without abstraction. All changes still have to be made in the code, even when the changes are conceived at a higher level. Details can be lost and bugs introduced into the program. So programmers tend to be more comfortable making changes at or about the size of the code they can fit in their heads.

Having a test suite provides a safety net for making changes and effectively increases the size of the comfort zone. This help comes in two forms: catching subtle or overlooked mistakes in small, simple changes and providing confidence through safeguards for making large, complex changes. Even when we're absolutely sure that there are no unexpected side effects from a code change, we welcome objective, external confirmation of that certainty. On those infrequent occasions when our sureness is lacking, the test suite fills in the gaps. Also, knowing that we have a test suite safety net in place, we are willing to overextend our reach when making larger changes to the code. We can even experimentally probe the structure and dependencies of the software by making tentative changes and observing their consequences. Both of these effects make our system more flexible. We will explore these concepts in more detail when refactoring is discussed.

Testing First Makes Sense

In addition to all the direct advantages of testing first, there are many secondary benefits. The test cases provide extremely useful documentation of the system. Some extreme programmers claim it's the best documentation they have ever worked with, because it also encapsulates the developers' intent when writing the code. In this sense, the documentation is also very useful in tracking the project. The test suite is an electronic diary of the development of the system. At any point, someone outside the team (an administrator or a client) can look at the test cases and get a very clear picture of the status of the system development. Finally, it provides future maintainers of the code not only with the chronology of the development, but also with the most useful tool they could desire. Imagine again the entry-level developer, only this time instead of being handed a 4-inch thick, sparsely documented stack of code, they are handed the code, along with an entire test suite that not only provides the developers' intent, but also can be used to guide any future changes made to the code. Clearly, testing first is a win-win-win scenario.

TEST SUITE MAINTENANCE

As you become more comfortable with the cycle of selecting a task, writing tests, and then writing code, there are two situations that will occasionally force you to break the cycle. In each instance, the task results in performing maintenance on the test suite. Instead of selecting a new task, an old task or the current task needs additional work before you can proceed. Test suites grow large. As they interact with a developing software system, they require maintenance.

This is similar to child rearing. Parents make rules for their children. Some rules cease to apply as the children grow and change. High school students may not be allowed to drive after 9:00 P.M., but they can cross the street by themselves. You will do the same with your test suite. As your code changes you may need to go back and modify some of your existing tests. Consider also how parents come up with rules. They try to anticipate dangerous situations or destructive behavior and make rules accordingly. They tell their children not to use crayons on the walls and come home one day to see that the creative imps have followed the rules and used paint instead. It's time for a new rule. Similarly, as you code you find the program misbehaves in a way the test suite doesn't anticipate. You'll add a new test to cover this new case. Just like the code that you've written for the project, your test suite will need refactoring from time to time.

Fixing Broken Test Cases

As you modify your code, it is possible to break some of the tests. Not in the sense of introducing a bug to the code, but changing the way the code does something that prevents the test from running correctly. You may have changed the return type of a method, renamed a class, or changed an inheritance hierarchy. Whatever the cause, tests that used to work don't work anymore because of an incompatibility. A typical symptom of an incompatibility problem is that many of the tests that were working successfully suddenly stop working. As with all XP development, if a test case won't pass, the next goal of the developers is to make it pass. In this case, you must refactor the tests to reflect the new signature, name, or structure. Often, once you compensate for the incompatibility in one test, all the tests start working again. The important thing here is that the tests continue to exercise the same conceptual feature. Suppose the original test checked to see if a positive integer passed into a method returns a positive integer result. You had to change the method from using `int` primitives to using `Integer` objects. The modified test must check the same characteristics (positive in means positive out) but accessing the integer value must now be done through the Integer class's `getValue()` method.

Adding Missing Tests

If at some point during the development of your software, you find a bug that the test suite did not, then you must write a test that exposes that deficiency before fixing the code. In other words, if running the test suite reports back with 100% success, but you know there's something wrong with the code, then the test suite needs at least one more test. As always, you should write the test case first. Perhaps the calculated results are off; perhaps the program was given erroneous data, but it still produced results without any warnings. Before the development team takes any other action, a test must be written that will fail because of the error. This serves two purposes. One, it causes the tests to reflect the erroneous condition of the software; and two, it prevents missing the problem in the future if it creeps back into the code through old versions or continued incorrect assumptions. Having a test fail prevents the code from being incorporated into the system and requires that the next level of effort be focused on passing the test.

TEST SUITES CONSIDERED HELPFUL—TO THE TEAM'S FRAME OF MIND

It is a very exciting moment when an XP programmer comes to truly embrace the implications of testing first and the benefits of having a growing test suite. It may happen like this. One member of your pair suddenly has an insight that perhaps a large chunk of code is no longer necessary. It seems that the new code your pair recently added handles a more general case and now the large chunk that used to handle a special case is useless. The code is complex enough that it might take about twenty minutes using a standard approach to ensure that it can be removed safely. So, if you had not been using XP, the temptation to say, "Better safe than sorry," and just leave the code in place would probably have prevailed (it's a small program). Instead, because it's an XP project, you grab the keyboard from your partner, comment out the code, and run the tests. They pass! Your coding insight has been verified, you delete the offending code and, a minute or two later, you can move on to the next problem.

In addition to improving your code, the change provides several levels of mental satisfaction. First, it makes it possible to verify your insight. That it was a correct insight strokes your inner programmer. Second, the resulting code is tighter and therefore easier to work with. Altering the code gives you a better understanding of the code and more confidence in future modifications. Third, you can see the process working, which reinforces your commitment and expectations. These are all examples of the mental boosts to an XP team's frame of mind that come from having fast, accurate feedback on the current status of the code.

The Psychological Benefits of Green

JUnit has a friendly green progress bar that extends with every successfully passed test. If all the tests pass, the developers are rewarded with visual feedback to "go" forward because all is still right with the existing code. Every test case you write during an XP development stays with the project throughout its lifetime. When you run tests in the final week of the project, every test case you wrote (or an updated, refactored version of it) is run again. Every time the bar turns green, it gives you an extra boost of confidence in the code. You immediately know that everything that ever worked continues to work. You know that the most recently added code not only works in its own context, but that it has not broken anything else in the process.

The Psychological Benefits of Red

Like a traffic light, JUnit's progress bar turns red when it is not safe to move forward. The red warning indicates that at least one test failed or an error occurred during execution of the test suite. But failing test cases are also good for morale. When you run a test that is supposed to fail and it does, it validates your internal model of the program. Likewise, when you run the test suite between writing a test case and writing the code for it, having the bar turn red validates the relevance of the new test case. (If the bar turns green at this point, you know there is something wrong with the test case.) The other major benefit of getting a red test bar is that you know exactly where to look for the problem. There is no mystery. Even in very large systems, a red test bar means that there is a problem in the most recently added code. Everything was green last time. You made one change and now its red. Clearly there is something wrong with the new code. Knowing where to look for problems drastically reduces development time, and it gives you confidence in your abilities to correct problems in a timely manner. In the worst possible scenario—when even knowing where to look does not turn up the problem—it's no big deal. Simply remove the new test and the new code and the system returns to full working order again.

TESTING FIRST EXERCISES

1. Decide whether each of the following implementations of `maxOfThree` work correctly. If they do not, write a test case that exposes the flaw.

```
public int maxOfThreeInts(int num1, int num2, int num3){
      int max = num1;

      if (num2 >= num1) max = num2;
      if (num3 >= num2) max = num3;
      return max;
}
```

```
public int maxOfThreeInts(int num1, int num2, int num3){

      if (num1 >= num2 && num2 >= num3) return num1;
      if (num2 >= num1 && num1 >= num3) return num2;
      if (num3 >= num2 && num2 >= num1) return num3;
}
```

```
public int maxOfThreeInts(int num1, int num2, int num3){

      if (num1 < num2) num1 = num2;
      if (num1 < num3) num1 = num3;
      return num1;
}
```

```
public int maxOfThreeInts(int num1, int num2, int num3){
     int max = 0;

     if (num1 > max) max = num1;
     if (num2 > max) max = num2;
     if (num3 > max) max = num3;
     return max;
}
```

```
public int maxOfThreeInts(int num1, int num2, int num3){
     int large1;

     if (num2 > num1){
          large1 = num1;
     }
     else {
          large1 = num2;
     }

     if (large1 > num3) return large1;
     if (num3 > large1) return num3;
}
```

2. The section entitled, "What's an Alternative to Exhaustive Testing?" states that there are thirteen different combinations of three integer inputs. This is true with the assumption that repeated values are allowed and the only criteria for differentiating values are their relative sizes. Using A, B, and C to represent integers whose relationship is A > B > C, write out the thirteen test cases.
3. Continuing with the same example, if we allow the sign of the inputs to also be a distinguishing characteristic (i.e., explicitly include positive and negative integers as well as zero), compute how many different inputs there are. (Note: Would this cause you to rethink your answer to Exercise 1?)
4. You and your partner decide that your next task is to write code that accepts and verifies a four-letter password. Assume that the letters can only be upper case and that the password is TEST.

   a. Write representative test cases for the code. Note the time it takes to write the tests.
   b. Write an exhaustive test case for the code and record how long it takes to write it. (That you can exhaustively generate all four-letter passwords in a short period of time shows why they are woefully insufficient.)
   c. Write an implementation of the code to pass the tests you wrote for Exercise 4a. Will it also pass the exhaustive test?
   d. Write an implementation that passes the representative test but does not pass the exhaustive test.

5. The context for this question is a children's word game:

> Someone writes a relatively long word on a piece of paper or a chalkboard. Each child then writes as many other words using the letters from the original word as he or she can. Each letter of the original word may only be used once. The person with the longest list of acceptable words is declared the winner.

It is your pair's task to write code that will determine whether the words in the word list can be formed from the letters of the original word. Write representative test cases for this code. Try to keep the number of tests small, but cover many different cases. (Note that the issue here is availability of characters, not cross-checking the entries against a dictionary.)

6. The object of the game MasterMind is to correctly guess a secret pattern of four colored pegs. For each guess, a player proposes a four-peg pattern, which is then evaluated by the opponent who originally made the code. For each correct color in the correct position, the guess is given a black marker; for each correct color in the wrong position, the guess is given a white marker. At most, each guess can only get four markers. For example, suppose the secret pattern is

GREEN, BLUE, RED, BLUE

and the current guess is

YELLOW, GREEN, ORANGE, BLUE

the guess is given one black marker for the BLUE peg in the fourth position and one white marker for the GREEN peg in the second position. If the current guess was

BLUE, BLUE, GREEN, RED

then it would be given one black marker for the BLUE peg in the *second* position and two white markers, one for the BLUE peg in the first position and one for the GREEN peg in the third position.

You and your partner write the portion of the code to correctly generate the number of black and white markers given the current guess and the secret pattern. Note that both the secret pattern and the guesses can have repeated colors; therefore, be sure that your representative test cases cover all possible combinations.

Part II

The Iteration—

Shaping the Development Process

During the spike, you figured out how to pair program, test first, and refactor. You also began to develop a self-awareness that will benefit you during the remainder of this course. These are the XP practices concerned with the development of code. Now you are ready to meet with your client and begin the actual project. You'll be estimating how long a story will take to develop and how much work your group can accomplish in a week. You will be negotiating with the customer. You will be taking user stories that contain user written descriptions of product features and breaking them into tasks that the programmers can accomplish.

In Chapter 5, *The Client*, you will begin to explore the relationship you and your team of developers will have with the client. In XP the client is considered to be a member of the team. The customer makes business decisions and the developers make technical decisions. The customer is the one who pays for software that doesn't come in on time or has less functionality. The developers can advise the customer why a decision may not be in the best interest of the project, but the customer makes the final decision. In a short project such as this, your instructor may step in to help with the process to make sure that you are able to deliver something of value.

In XP there are short cycles called iterations. In this course you will release the software to the client at the end of each iteration. The recommended time for an iteration in this class is two weeks. Exceptions are the first iteration, the last iteration, and iterations that may surround a holiday. Releases should be scheduled before the project begins and you must never miss a release. The process of planning for an iteration is described in Chapter 6, *The Plans*. At the end of the iteration you will look back at what you've accomplished and gather data that you will use to prepare for the next one. The end of the iteration is described in Chapter 9, *Evaluation and Regrouping.* Wrapping up an iteration leads right into beginning the next one so you'll notice some overlap in these chapters. Although during the spike you experienced much of what goes on during an iteration, this is more clearly described in the context of an ongoing project in Chapter 7, *The Values, Principles, and Practices.* Potential hazards are described in each of these three chapters as well.

You don't want to work hard for two weeks on a user story, present it to the customer, and hear, "That's not what I wanted." In XP the user stories are supposed to represent a common understanding of what the customer is requesting. This is not a requirements document, it is a quick and easy to understand sentence or two on an index card. It is possible that the developers and client each have a different understanding of a user story. There are plenty of opportunities to identify this misunderstanding during the process, but a good fail-safe method is to use acceptance tests. A client creates an acceptance test for a user story that basically says, "If the application can do this, then you have satisfied the user story." There is no ambiguity in this. You'll learn more about helping the customer write and run these in Chapter 8, *Acceptance Tests*.

Chapter 5

The Client—

Meeting Another Team Member

In eXtreme Programming (XP), your relationship with the client helps determine the success of the project. This is not true in other methodologies. Commonly the client just comes in for milestone meetings and is presented with PowerPoint demonstrations and carefully constructed demos of the parts of the code that happen to work.

In an XP project, the client needs to be available as much as possible. The programmers have to feel comfortable asking the client questions when they arise. As an analogy, the customer has to feel comfortable about watching the sausage being made while looking forward to eating the final product. Remember that one of the core principles of XP is that news (bad or good) should be delivered early. Imagine that you are working on a GUI for the client and you're not sure whether they want to use text entry, checkboxes, or a modal dialog box. You might have a preference but customers get to make these decisions. You save a lot of time if you can call the customer and explain the decision confronting you. Suppose the client requests the dialog box. You and your partner code it up quickly and check back with the client asking, "Is this what you were talking about?" The client says yes or no and then you understand what to create. The alternative is to guess what the client wants and to create a whole infrastructure that depends on this choice. On demo day the client lets you know they don't really like the interface and now you're left digging through code you haven't touched in weeks.

Of course, in this simple example it probably wouldn't be hard for you to change this piece of the user interface. The point is that many decisions like this happen every day. The cumulative savings are even more dramatic and the psychological effect on the programming team is also striking. The standard XP analogy is washing pots as you dirty them and not letting them sit around until you run out of pots and have to wash them all at once. This example isn't intended to imply that XP clients are any less fickle than traditional clients. Any client can tell you they want one thing one day and change their mind a week later. As you will see in this chapter, the difference is that the XP client knows the cost of change.

Much of XP requires the use of social skills. In pair programming you need to get along with another programmer who is sharing a keyboard, mouse, and responsibility for the code that is being created. An XP team enjoys collective code ownership. The potential for conflicts and hurt feelings exists as any programming pair can change the code created by any other members of the team. You may have noticed by now that the same issues arise in XP that arise in the more traditional programming model. The difference is that the XP methodology forces you to confront the issues and deal with them. There's no way to hide in your cubicle and e-mail the people sitting ten feet away from you. You actually need to talk to people.

In this chapter you'll consider the relationship that you, your team, and the client are developing from both sides. Finally, you'll follow the cycle that starts with the client creating user stories, continues through your coding those stories, and ends with the partially completed application back in the client's hands.

THE CLIENT'S JOB

If you are a student in a college software-engineering course, then your customer is not the same as a customer for a commercial project. Your client knows that at the end of the course your work on the project ends. To some extent, this is a mismatch for an XP project. This brings you back to the situation where the first thing you know about a project is the delivery date. You know that date even before you meet the client and hear about the project. The nature of the academic calendar makes this a rigorous requirement.

As Kent Beck describes in *XP Explained*, the four variables in software development are cost, time, quality, and scope. In an academic setting, time is taken out of the customer's hands. Cost is also irrelevant. In an academic setting it may help to occasionally provide the team with pizzas or a case of a caffeinated beverage, but traditional costs don't apply.

The remaining variables are quality and scope. On a shipping product you would hate to make decisions based on quality, but in this short-term, intense experience with a fixed-end date at some point the customer is going to have to decide that something is acceptable. If the client only has three more weeks of developer time, then correcting an awkward format of the output data or reducing the five-minute application start-up time might not be as important as adding two additional features that will make the application more usable. The client is the person who makes the "good enough" decision.

At all times the customer gets to decide on what will be done next. This means that, ever cognizant of time constraints, the client is making the decisions about scope. As a developer, there are parts of the system that you'd really like to include. You may feel that this feature is essential to the product or you've just always wanted to write something like this. In either case, the client is the person who gets to decide what will and won't be included in the product and at what point in the development it will be completed.

As an XP programmer, you get to decide how the tasks will be accomplished. Imagine that the customer needs you to store values in a file that your application will later read and display on the screen. The customer shouldn't decide whether you store this information using comma-separated values, XML, or by serializing objects and saving them. The customer could require that the files be human readable or that some other application also be able to share the files. These requirements could force you to make one decision or another but they are based on real customer requirements. The client gets to decide the scope of the project, the developer gets to decide how each task is accomplished. The client does not, by and large, make technical decisions.

The television documentary *Project Greenlight* showed the process of a movie being made by a first-time director chosen as the result of a competition. The HBO series is as much a lesson in project management as it is in actually making a movie. In one episode the director of photography didn't think a particular scene was artistic enough. The actors did a great job, the director liked the scene, but the director of photography wasn't satisfied, so he intentionally shook the camera near the end of the scene. Therefore, the director couldn't choose that take because the camera had been shaken. The director of photography had taken one of the director's decisions away from him. As developers you will do this, perhaps without realizing it. You will couch choices to the client in such a way that they feel forced to make the decision you're leading them to make. Be careful of this practice. If the customer feels manipulated you will have lost a level of trust that can't be regained. Let the client make client decisions. Don't shake the camera.

Outside of the academic setting, some customers won't be comfortable with the idea of using this unfamiliar methodology. You can't actually do XP unless the customer knows and agrees. On the other hand, you can learn many of the XP practices and decide whether XP is for you without initially involving a potential customer. Also, XP requires a lot from a client. If the client hasn't signed up for an XP project they may be unwilling to change just to accommodate your newly found "religion." A reasonable compromise is to find a proxy for the client. Find someone in your company who is willing to play the role of the customer. Actual XP projects will sometimes find themselves using some sort of proxy for the customer when customers can't agree to the level of on-site contact that the development team needs.

HOW IS THIS CLIENT DIFFERENT FROM "REAL" CLIENTS?

One of the key ways in which this client differs from a real world client is that either the instructor or the students solicited the client's involvement. Your client wasn't shopping around for the best development team to realize a vision. In fact, your client is performing a service for you. Without a real customer with a real software request, you wouldn't be able to learn software engineering in this lab type of course. There are also differences in the investment made by the customer as well as in the commitment to this project. The customer's expectations are different and the relationship between you and the customer is different because you are seen as a student.

Just as your client isn't shopping around for developers, you may not have too much choice of who your client is. Depending on your class structure, you may be able to request one project over another but for the most part you can't refuse a client the way you can in a commercial environment. The main issue here is whether the client is committed to really trying the XP approach. You'll need to trust that whoever agreed to take on the client actually spent time explaining what would be involved.

The worst (but sometimes necessary) situation is when your instructor is forced to take on the role of the client. When you approach this multitasking individual, you need to make sure that you are speaking to the appropriate persona. Some instructors describe making this clear by setting times when they are the customer, coach, or instructor. Joe Bergin of Pace University described a successful course in which the instructor literally puts on a different hat to indicate the role he is playing. The advantage is that your instructor truly understands what is required of an XP customer and can play that role as well as anyone. The disadvantages include the muddying of whom you are talking to as well as the project not feeling like a real project because your instructor is specifying the assignment at the same time your introductory class is programming it.

Investment

The customer is not paying for your work. This can affect the value your customer places on this project and can lead to some attitude problems on your part. Let's start with you. At some point in the semester the project will not be progressing well. When this happens a lot of the good will goes out the window. Someone in your group is likely to make the observation that not only isn't the customer paying for your time but you're actually paying tuition to do all this work. Maybe you'll feel better after you vent like this for a while. When you calm down you'll realize that having a real customer available to you is adding a lot of value to the class. The person playing the role of the customer isn't compensated for their time spent helping you. The least you can provide is working software.

Now look at how not paying for the software affects the customer. When companies are test marketing new products, they will often advertise the same item at different prices and note how well it sells. New companies are often surprised that more people will buy their software for $59.99 than for $29.99. If the product is offered at a lower price, some potential customers assume that it must be inferior. On this project, your customer is paying no money for the software. Understand that this will affect how your efforts and the entire project are viewed. Suppose you pay $60 a month to belong to a gym. Are you going to go? What if you are given a lifetime pass and never have to pay?

Commitment

What has a client signed up for? First they have to meet with someone to turn their ideas into usable user stories. These stories are descriptive enough that you have an idea of what you are producing for them. The customer then has to figure out how to test each of these user stories to see if your program correctly implements each story. Then the customer has to meet with your group to negotiate how much will be done during the first iteration. Throughout the rest of the semester the customer has to be available to answer your questions and to reprioritize user stories based on the velocity of the developer team. Every couple of weeks an iteration ends and the customer will get a chance to run acceptance tests on the current version. Meanwhile the customer also has a full-time job that isn't providing any release time in return for the time being spent with you. In other words, the client is expected to do a lot. The payoff, of course, is better software more quickly. This is an easier sell for a commercial endeavor.

The level of commitment varies from client to client. Some clients are very excited about this software project, have thought a great deal about what they are looking for, and are willing to spend a great deal of time communicating with you. Other clients will start out strong at the beginning of the semester but their available time will diminish as the demands of the semester increase. This can be a bit frustrating. You may get used to having quick access to your client. Early in the term, you could walk in during office hours and ask the questions you need answered. Midway through the semester there's a line of students between you and your client and they have the audacity to be asking your client (their instructor) to help them during the time your client has set aside to help them.

There are also clients who didn't quite understand all that XP requires. You've probably clicked "Agree" on a software agreement you didn't read carefully. You've probably also nodded your head to an instructor who asked you if you understood the lecture you'd just zoned out during. Some clients will hear that they are getting a software project built for them for free by students and not listen carefully to their obligations.

In a commercial application, the client has a strong interest in the project being high quality and completed on time. The customer may not initially view spending time with developers as productive but the return on this time investment will quickly become clear. The client may be evaluated by the success of this particular project. In the software engineering class the academic client doesn't have this incentive. In fact, the software engineering class is one more obligation on top of a semester's worth of obligations. While many clients will be caught up in the spirit of the developing project, others would prefer you to get the specs, go away, and show them a finished project at the end of the semester.

Relationship

One of the hard things about being your age is that people don't take you seriously enough. In ten years you may not know any more, but people will listen to your opinions differently. In many cases the customer for your project will be faculty or staff at your school. As good as your relationship with your customer is, it won't be a peer relationship. You may have to refer to your customer as Dr. So and So while you're referred to by your first name. In an XP project this is less of a problem because you should be deferring to customer decisions.

There is a positive side to this imbalance. Generally the people who agree to be customers for a software-engineering course understand the educational value to the student. Many will actually place learning above actual software delivery. Sure, they'd like to be able to use the software that they are helping create, but they understand that the main point is for the student to learn the process of developing software for a real customer. In a traditional class whether the final product really works is often hit or miss. In an XP project the application should be working at all times, it just may not end up doing much.

Problems can arise if your customer is knowledgeable about Computer Science (or has that impression). They may be tempted to make comments or suggestions about the code. This is not their role. The customer is not there to correct or improve your code. In a way the customer is a black box tester. The customer can and should take the software through its paces at the end of each iteration. At this point, comments about what is and isn't working are appropriate. Generally, questions about how you are accomplishing a specific task are not appropriate. An exception occurs in a case where there are different algorithms for calculating a desired result and one may be recognized as more reliable. Keep in mind that the customer means well and use the professor to run interference if the customer appears to step over the line.

Pace and Decisions

The difference between the pace in academia and the pace in a commercial setting is striking. When a real product is brought to market, time is important. Academia lacks this sense of immediacy. It's not that entrepreneurs don't consider the implications of their decisions, they just do so differently. Academics tend to take a long time to make decisions. It's important that they consider alternatives and possible scenarios even if the likelihood of these situations occurring is near zero.

One example is the vintage of computer sitting on the instructor's desk compared to the age of the machine sitting on a project lead's desk at a company that produces software. When your instructor's machine is three years old and clearly out of date, it is often difficult to convince those in charge of purchasing new machines that it needs replacing. To be fair, replacing computers regularly is a tremendous expense that is relatively new to university budgets.

On the other hand, a company that produces software needs to make sure that their employees have the tools needed to run the latest software (theirs and other company's). The machines on their employees' desks must support their employees' efforts not hinder them. For companies the calculation is based on different needs. Employees are being paid a lot of money. The better companies understand the cost of not technologically supporting their employees.

Don't educational institutions have the same concerns? Yes, but the institution doesn't see an increase in their bottom line by providing your instructor with the latest computer. Also, the people responsible for making the decision are often removed from the effects of the decision. They often have never been teachers and don't see the need to update equipment so often. Finally, there's a socialist aspect to equipment on college campuses. The Computer department might need to replace their machines every year or two years. The English department would like faster machines. Why should the Computer department always get the newest machines? No one complains about the Chemistry department being allowed to order chemicals more frequently than the History department, but computers are different. Because educational institutions consider all sides, computer departments often end up with aging machines.

This affects you in two ways. First, the lab machines that you'll be using may not be very powerful, and you may not be allowed to load the software you need onto them. You'll need to check with your instructor to make sure the JUnit, or whichever testing framework you need is loaded. Second, your client is an academic. You will need your client to make quick decisions. You need to be able to check and say, "We're looking at this set of alternatives, which one do you like," and get a quick answer. If you get the answer, "Hmmm, I need to think about this," you need to impress the client that during the waiting time you can't be working on the feature that they identified as being the most important. If you consistently get this answer you need to ask your instructor to chat with the client.

THE PLANNING GAME

If you're the kind of programmer who believes coding is an isolated activity best done when the rest of the world is asleep, this next stage of the XP process may unnerve you. You will have to spend long hours talking to members of your team and to the client. In this section, you'll walk through the various steps of creating, revising, estimating, ranking, coding, and accepting user stories. Although you may not be personally involved in every step, you'll find it helpful to understand the sequence of events.

Meeting to Determine User Stories

You meet with the client to get the user stories. Who are "you?" In this section, "you" refers to whoever is helping the client write the stories. It is the client's job to write the stories, but the client may not have enough understanding of what this means to do an adequate job. Perhaps one or more members of the team can meet with the client. It is probably best if the instructor, a grader, or a student who has taken the class in the past meets with the client. That person is "you."

There is a tutorial in Part 3, *Core Practices—Working Examples of Core Practices*, devoted to writing user stories but here's a summary of the process. The client has some ideas of what the application will do. There will be parts of the vision that are clearer and more detailed than others. Your job is to translate these ideas into user stories that are the right granularity. These user stories need to consist of a meaningful title and a description that is clear enough to the client and developers. The client needs to be able to determine whether or not the user story has been successfully completed.

In traditional methodologies the requirements document was phrased in terms of well-defined deliverables. It may make you a bit uncomfortable that the user stories are a little fuzzier than this. One goal is to keep the user stories in language that the client understands. You don't want the client to later tell you that you haven't produced what was required even though it conforms to the document. Some clients are not technical and don't understand what they're agreeing to if the items are phrased in your language not theirs.

For example, you ask the client, "Is there a persistence requirement?" They look confused but confidently say, "I don't think there's a need for that." You realize that you've backed the client into a corner where such bluffing is a preferred alternative to admitting ignorance and so you try again. "Would you like your work to be saved automatically or do you want to have to remember to save your own work." The client thinks a minute and asks, "Why would I want to save anything?" You follow-up by asking, "Do you work on the same document in different sessions?" "Sure." Now you are nearing an understanding. You now ask, "Do you want to have to re-enter information for the same document each time you start a new session?" The client agrees that this wouldn't be a good arrangement and suggests that users can save as often as they want using a keyboard shortcut or a menu item. When users quit the application, they will be prompted to save their existing work.

You now have a couple of usable user stories. Try to get the client to actually write them down. If necessary, you can write them on index cards and read them back to the client for approval. One technique is to interview the client about the application and every once in a while summarize the client's last statement as a user story. Stop every once in a while and get approval for the user stories you're paraphrasing. After a while the client may want to take over the writing process.

When you have enough user stories to get going on the project, stop. Have the client place the stories roughly in order of importance. You may have come up with nice features that the client wants to classify in the "only if there's time" category. Other stories may be listed as "essential, to be done first." After the rough ordering it's time for the developers to take a look at what you've come up with.

Note, for the rest of the chapter, "you" refers to a member of the development team.

Analysis and Estimation

You and your team now have a stack of index cards containing user stories. Look them over. You already know the general idea of what you're being asked to create, but these cards contain the client's description of the most immediate features. As you read the stories, remember that they don't need to communicate everything down to the last detail. You will be able to ask the client questions along the way. You aren't reading the stories with a red pen ready to mark them with petty little points. You don't want to encourage the client to write overly detailed descriptions that, paradoxically, convey less information.

Identify the stories that require clarification. Consider what it is you need your client to clarify. Estimate the coding times for the rest of the stories. You'll get a better idea of the coding time required when you read the User stories in Chapter 11; however, don't use specific units like hours or days for your estimates. At the beginning they may correspond to actual units but soon they will diverge. Ron Jeffries uses Gummi Bears as his unit of estimation. Joshua Kerievsky uses NUTs: Nebulous Units of Time. The purpose of having generic units is that you are using them to convey the *relative* sizes of stories. Since you are estimating stories and the amount of work you can do with the same units the customer can make informed choices. It's like translating the cost of items and the amount of money you have into a different currency. You and your team should have an idea of what the units represent so that you can debate your estimates in a meaningful way. You won't really know what the units represent until a couple of iterations into the project. The key is to get a feel for how long each story will take based on these units.

For each card you will ask a sequence of questions that include the following.

- Do you understand what is being described? The story should contain just enough information that you and the client have a common understanding of what is being described. Your level of self-awareness needs to be high here. If you don't understand the story then the client needs to rewrite it. Maybe you need to help with the rewriting process.
- Can you estimate the story? Later you will break it down into tasks and estimate those separately. For now, you are looking at a story such as "Need to be able to save the current document as a .txt file" and estimating how long that might take. This step is a nice failsafe for the previous step. You may think you understand

the story being described. Then when you go to estimate it you find that what's holding you up is a lack of clarity on one or another issue.

- Is there a way that the client can test that you've finished the story? For example, the client might choose to save the current document and then open it using some standard text editor to make sure everything looks right. Ideally, there should be an automated test for each task, but during this semester all you really care is that the user can specify a test for determining a story is complete, which the development team can also run.
- Is the story too large? You may understand the story and be able to estimate it and the client can test it—but the story may be too large. There are two possibilities here. The first possibility is that the story is really describing more than one feature. Don't confuse features with tasks. There may be several tasks involved in saving a document as a .txt file. A story such as "Need to be able to save (as a .txt file) and later read in the current document" can be split into a story about saving and a story about retrieving. The second possibility is that the story is just too long. You estimate the story as taking two weeks to complete. You may want to return to the client and ask whether the story can be broken down into substories, which each can be estimated and prioritized.

The cards are just promises for future conversations. They will not contain the answers to these questions. You'll have to talk with the client and with your team members to arrive at your answers.

Determining Your Workload

You can't just go to the customer and say, "We've decided these three stories will take four units each and those two will take five units each." This doesn't mean anything to the client. The obvious question, "What's a unit?" gets the response, "We don't know yet." The follow-up question, "How many units can you do this week?" can't get the same response.

You and your team need to carefully consider how much time each of you is willing to work in the coming two weeks. If you performed your XP spike before beginning the "real" project you will have a much better idea of what you're doing before you meet with a client. You'll have a better idea of how much you can do in an hour and how many hours you will really be able to commit to working. As you estimate, remember that your coding can not be done individually. This means that you have to base your estimates on time when two or more of you can gather. Allow for time when you're not working. Suppose that you plan to get together Tuesday afternoon for three hours. Someone in your group is going to be late. You're going to talk a while about stuff that has nothing to do with coding. You'll spend some time getting your development environment up and running. You'll need a break sometime in the middle to check your e-mail or to get a snack. Maybe you'll get in two or two-and-a-half hours of work. Make an estimate. Next week you'll have a better idea of how much work you'll actually accomplish in a week.

Once you've estimated the first two weeks, you'll be able to come up with a total number of person-hours that the group can collectively commit to the project each week. It may seem to you that pair-hours are a better unit for estimation but stay with person-hours. Suppose that in this case the total for your group is forty hours each week and that you've decided that a unit is an hour. Now you can go to your client and announce that you will accomplish forty units this week and forty the next.

Reevaluating and Prioritizing the User Stories

When you meet with your client, ask your client to clarify the stories you didn't understand and request that the client split the stories you thought were too long. Huddle quickly with your group and estimate these stories in terms of your agreed upon units. Now it is the client's turn to make the next round of decisions.

Hand the client a stack of cards, with an estimate on each card. The client is told, "In the first iteration we can accomplish eighty units worth of work for you. Choose the eighty units' worth of stories that you want us to work on first." The client smiles and riffles through the deck. "I want this one, this one, and . . . ." Soon the client has chosen eighty units' worth of stories. And then the client says, "Oh, and I want this one."

This is an important moment. If you let it pass you are through for the semester and may as well drop the class. You must politely but firmly say, "That's great, which stories do you want to eliminate." When you are greeted with a puzzled look, remind the client that you can only commit to eighty units in the first two-week iteration. You are just asking for the most important eighty units' worth.

The client is allowed to pick the most important tasks up to the workload that your team specifies. The client can not ask you to do more than you estimate can be done. It's like being given $20 to spend in a produce store. The store employees will allow you to buy up to $20 worth of vegetables. You get to choose which ones but they set the price. If you have $20 worth of vegetables in your cart and decide you want $3 worth of broccoli, then you need to take $3 worth of vegetables out of your cart to make room for the broccoli. In XP the developers give the client so many units to spend on development tasks. The developers have also priced each task. This one costs two units and that one costs three. The client is free to choose any tasks in any order as long as the total cost does not exceed the allotment.

Choosing and Estimating Tasks

You now have the stories that client would most like to see finished in the first iteration. Your next job is to have the team collectively break the user stories into tasks. You can think of these as the discrete steps that need to be accomplished in order to complete a user story. For the story about saving a document as a .txt document you may have a task for creating the GUI (a menu item, button, keyboard shortcut, modal dialog or some combination of these) that initiates the task and another task for the actual disk operation.

Once you've broken the stories down into tasks, the various members of your team can start signing up for them. When you sign up for a task you should estimate it. You have a number of units that you've agreed to put in this week. You need to sign up for that amount's worth of tasks. If you've committed to eight units this week then you need to end up with eight units worth of tasks.

At the end of this exercise you may notice that the total of the task estimates doesn't sum to the estimate for the story. Usually the sum of the task estimates is greater than the estimate for the story. Don't assume there will be synergistic benefits. When you estimated the whole story you weren't concentrating on all there was to do. Revise your story estimate. If the total for the first iteration is now greater than the total units you can work (in this case eighty), you need to go back and ask the client to reduce the total to the top eighty units' worth by using the revised estimates.

You're not going to want to do this. You just made the client choose and now you're going back and saying, "Some more have to go." The alternative is to ignore reality and just go ahead and pretend you can do more than you can. Remember that this isn't the last bit of bad news the client's going to get before the end of this iteration.

There's another issue that may be bothering you. You have to do all your work in pairs. You have eight hours this week that you can work and you've signed up for eight hours' worth of tasks. The problem is that some of your eight hours you need to be working on tasks belonging to someone else. Will you really work twice as fast when you're working with someone else? No, you are in the process of learning your velocity. Each week you will know exactly how many units you completed in the past week and that's how many you can sign up for in the next week. This is why stories can't be too long and why tasks should be even shorter. You might sign up for two three-unit tasks and one two-unit task. At the end of the week you've completed one of the three-unit tasks, the two-unit task, and you're almost done with the other three-unit task. Officially you've completed five units this week and that's what you can sign up for next week. The point is that it's easier to estimate what you can do and let the issues of pairing work themselves out during the life of the project.

Dealing with Disappointment

You start working on the stories that the client selected. If you've performed the XP spike then you won't have to lose time getting your environment set up. You just look for a pair to help you with one of your tasks and you start working. In a commercial setting, you would be programming throughout the day in a room where the pairs can communicate. You would start the day with a status report, share a little information, and get working. While you are taking a class, your days are also filled with other activities. You take other classes, have an on-campus job, play a sport, or engage in some other activity. Perhaps you can devote twelve hours outside of class to working on XP. It is good to have at least one time per week when the entire team can meet together. Begin this time with a look at where you are. You may also want to plan to meet for fifteen minutes before or after class to compare notes collectively.

About a week into the iteration you can see that your estimates weren't accurate. You have consistently underestimated the time it takes to complete the tasks. Meet with the group and reassess where you are. Go to the client immediately. You are there to say, "Here's what we thought we could do. Now we are predicting we will only get this much done. Please choose how you want us to spend the remaining time." Once you realize you can't do all that you promised, you are giving the client the option to choose what you spend your time doing.

The other thing that you've learned is that your estimate of your own time has been inaccurate. You thought the group would perform a total of forty people-hours the first week and it was more like thirty people-hours. Not only can't you do as much in each hour, but you weren't able to work as many hours as you thought. This is good news. To be clear, it isn't good news that you are accomplishing less, it's good news that you can measure what you are actually able to accomplish and that you can and do provide your client with this data.

This is a difficult moment. During your first meeting with the client after you've started coding you have to announce that you can't do as much as you said you would. As you'll see in all aspects of client interaction, this level of honesty will help you in the end. The client receives an accurate picture of reality at all times. The alternative is a client that doesn't see the project until the end. The team is struggling but the client doesn't know. The client sees you in the hall and asks, "How's it going?" Like any developer, you answer, "Fine." Fourteen weeks of "fine" later and the client gets a surprise. In XP there are no surprises.

You can use the latest weather techniques to try to predict tomorrow's weather. Over time you'll be fairly accurate if you just predict that tomorrow will be a lot like today. This XP technique of using "yesterday's weather" means that the client is getting a fairly accurate snapshot. You're getting better at estimating and the client gets a consistent view of what is being accomplished. Because there is so much overhead in starting up a project, the first week's numbers are unnaturally low. You may be tempted to attribute your lack of productivity to this factor. This amounts to telling your client that things are "fine." Always give your client an accurate accounting. Often in the second week you are able to go back to your client and say, "It looks as if we can actually accomplish more this week, would you like to choose four more units."

The End of the First Iteration

The first iteration ends and you have finished a few user stories. You eagerly take the first release down to the client. The client starts up your application and sees a window with a menu bar and some text on the screen accompanied by buttons. The client clicks on a few buttons. Nothing happens. The client selects a few menu items. Nothing happens. You look on proudly. The application does just what it's supposed to at this point and looks exactly as the client specified.

The client says, "That's great," but clearly looks worried. You need to step back a minute and consider this event from the client's point of view. You've brought in an application with an interface that is mostly finished. The client sees this and sees an application that is mostly finished but in which nothing works. You are pleased because this week's user stories were to produce the main window, add in the buttons that would navigate to the other windows, and to provide a menu bar.

You need to help the client at this point. You need to take out the user stories that you've accomplished and demonstrate that you've accomplished the ones that you eventually said you would. Let the client play with the application in that context. Point out that this was the first iteration of seven. Encourage the client to run acceptance tests against the stories you are delivering.

Tell the client how much work you were able to do during this iteration. Again, in XP you don't hide this information. Ask the client to pick the user stories that you'll work on in the next iteration. The client can pick any stories that add up to the number of units that you were able to accomplish in the last iteration.

Before you met with the client, your team reassessed the stories to make sure that your estimates were correct relative to the ones you completed. You don't say, "We estimated that story at two and it took us four hours so we need to double all of our estimates." You say, "We estimated the story we accomplished at two hours and this other one at four hours; do we really think this other one will take twice as long as the first one?" You are looking for relative estimates. You don't want to go back and change your notion of absolute time after each iteration. You are getting a feel for what the numbers on the cards mean. Maybe, as in this example, one unit is an hour, maybe it's half a day. As you progress through the semester, that will work itself out and the numbers will have more meaning for you and your client.

The client picks the stories for you to work on. You leave the client with precise knowledge of the state of the project. This little twinge of disappointment has realigned your client's view of reality. When it's time for you to deliver your final release there will be no surprises. Your client will know how to operate the application and also know what it can and can not do. In the traditional case, the client doesn't see the working software until the very end. That's a lot of realignment at once. Sometimes the clients are overwhelmed by the features that the team has been able to achieve over the semester. But the final product probably won't be what the client was picturing so there's a lot of adjustment.

Rinse and Repeat

Maybe your client wasn't that impressed with your first delivery. On the other hand, you delivered working software on time as promised. You demonstrated to the client roughly one iteration's worth of work. Following the delivery of your software, the client chooses the next stories for you. The client may not have liked getting all of the bad news during the first iteration, but you've earned a reputation for honesty.

As the process repeats throughout the semester the client takes more control over the direction of the software. Some of the client's initial frustration in the first iteration is that you said, "Choose the stories you want," and then a week later you said, "We can't do all of those—get rid of some." Although you always went back and allowed the client to make the decisions, much of the perception is that those initial decisions didn't matter much. As the project progresses and you get better at knowing what you can actually do in an iteration, the client's requests turn into deliverables. This means that as the project progresses, the client becomes more and more satisfied with the experience.

There will be iterations when you don't accomplish what you hoped you would. Continue to keep the client informed and to carefully track where you are at all times and this shouldn't become a problem. A client can be unhappy that the product isn't developing as quickly as they hoped, but it's hard to argue with the data you are gathering and sharing.

Chapter 6

The Plans—

Beginning an Iteration

Over the course of this project, you will cycle through several iterations. In this chapter, we'll look at the best way to prepare to get the most out of the current iteration. The first iteration is treated separately because there is a little more involved in starting the project. The first meeting with the client takes place before the first iteration and was covered in the previous chapter.

In one sense the software-engineering project you're engaged in is more realistic than past assignments in programming classes. It is a long-term project with a real customer making requests for features in a software product that will actually be used. You aren't off on your own trying to figure out what the professor is looking for on this assignment. You can't second-guess the assignment by figuring, "We just learned sorting algorithms and now we're being asked to apply them in a one-week assignment." You can't ask last year's class how they did the state pattern assignment.

There are, however, differences between working on this project and working in a commercial environment. In the real world, you'd be expected to devote forty hours or more each week to your job. In the context of this project, you are taking other classes and have other constraints. You will, most likely, spend less than fifteen hours a week on this project. When you look at your actual productive time, it can be as little as six hours a week. Don't feel bad, many people who clock forty hours or more each week aren't chained to a desk producing code that whole time. Your group of four or five developers devoting (let's overestimate) fifteen hours a week will have considerably fewer programmer hours available compared to a comparably sized team working forty hours a week.

Having less than half the time available to you for each iteration is both an advantage and a disadvantage. You can't possibly get as much work done in a week as a team working full time on the same project. This means that your customer has picked fewer stories for you to work on and that you can focus on estimating and completing these stories. You will spend less of your time with the overhead of estimating and be able to get right to coding. On the other hand, it is important that you have small testable stories from your customer. A task that you think should take about four hours could correspond to a morning for a real-world team but could be half of the time you and your partner actually spend programming during a week. If you slightly underestimated this story, you could come to the end of the week without completing a single task. An iteration can go by without its stories being completed.

A real-world team is often co-located. They don't have to worry about the details of where they will meet. They don't have to worry as much about differences in schedules. For the most part, they are all engaged in the project for most of their day. They can easily schedule a fifteen-minute stand-up meeting to share the details of what they are working on and compare notes on upcoming challenges. In addition, they spend their day overhearing snippets of conversation from other pairs. Information is constantly being shared both consciously and unconsciously. If one pair is stuck, others sense it and can offer assistance. If one pair is working on a task similar to a task handled by someone else on a past project they can immediately ask for help.

In your project, you will have to make sure you are sharing information. You will need a way to communicate where and when you are meeting. Often one pair will meet at one place and other members of the team will meet somewhere else at a different time. You'll have to be able to inform members of your team who weren't at your session what you accomplished. The more you can work in a setting where more than one pair can work at the same time, the more benefits you'll realize.

A real-world team often has an agreed upon common work environment. They will have chosen a single different IDE or it may have been chosen for them. Similarly, there will be a coding style that they know and use and a versioning system in use for evolving code. On your project, your team will have to make all of these decisions within the constraints of working on possibly different machines with different IDEs or even operating systems. The more that can be agreed upon ahead of time, the easier the process will be. As was pointed out in the pair-programming chapter, it is hard to come to agreement when working in groups without a hierarchy. It is much more important that the group agree than what it is they agree on. The start-up costs for your group are fairly high because you often install unfamiliar software and struggle to get it to work.

KICKING OFF EVERY ITERATION

The first iteration is different from all others because it includes the added burden of getting the project moving. In addition to setting up the infrastructure, there is no data yet on productivity or the quality of the user story estimates. Once the first iteration is completed, you will have a better idea of how much work you can do in a week. You also are better able to estimate the tasks that are ahead. You don't have to install your IDE again and figure out how to check in code. Further up the learning curve, you can now fall into a pattern: identify your current status, look at the next batch of user stories the client has selected, break them down into tasks, estimate and sign up for tasks, confer with the client, and get to work on the tasks.

In *Extreme Programming Applied*, Ken Auer and Roy Miller explain that "Iteration Planning makes the truth obvious. Developers and customers share what they've learned to be true since their last guess at what would be true. There's no room for fantasy." They go on to point out that in XP the two phases are *planning* and *doing* and explain the activities as follows. "In *doing*, first we write out what we want to be true (the test), then we try to make it true (the code), then we make sure we clearly understand what we have (refactor) so we can move on comfortably to the next task. In *planning*, customers state what they want to be true (the stories), then the developers try to make them true (the iteration), then both make sure of where they are (review of previous iteration) so they can move on comfortably to the next iteration."

Taking Stock of Where You Are

When wrapping up an iteration, take a careful look at what you accomplished. In Chapter 9 you'll look at the details of this process a little differently. For now it will help you to get a sense of how a careful assessment during the end of an iteration helps you start out fresh in the next one. Except during the first iteration, you know how many units you finished during the last iteration. Perhaps you finished six units in the last iteration. It doesn't matter if you bid on eight units and only accomplished six or you bid on four units and overachieved by finishing six. Your last bid was a guess. Now you know more. You know you were able to achieve six. If you have close to the same amount of time available for this iteration as you had for the last one, then you can commit to six units for the current iteration. Even if this is the first iteration of your big project, you can use what you learned about your productivity during the XP spike (this was the mini-project suggested in Chapter 2 to help you learn some of the core practices of XP before beginning on your actual project).

There may be good reasons why members of your team didn't accomplish more. You may be tempted to consider these when estimating. The rule of thumb is don't do it. Sure, the fire in the computer lab last week that caused it to be vacated during one of your sessions probably won't happen again this week. You could change your estimates based on it. If this is the sixth iteration and you've been averaging eight units each iteration but this time because of the fire you only completed six then go ahead and commit to eight units of story points.

Your goal should be to stay rooted in reality. The bottom line is that, for whatever reason, you accomplished six units of story points and that's what you should bid on this week. Maybe you're thinking, "We were so close. We didn't finish that story but we only have a little work left." Perhaps that's true but bid six. You can always go back to the client this iteration and ask for additional stories if you finish early and then help your pairs finish their tasks.

Some weeks your estimates will be over and some weeks they will be under. The number you give the client is based on the cumulative estimate of the group. One of the most valuable skills you will take away from this course is an awareness of your abilities as a programmer. Being able to estimate what you can produce in a week is something only you can develop for yourself. Despite the inaccuracies of each team member's estimate, the hope is that the aggregate of estimates will become a better approximation of the truth as the semester continues. The customer takes your cumulative estimate and chooses that many units' worth of stories.

As you begin your iteration each member of your team has a bank of so many units they can commit each week and the team as a whole has user stories that add up to no more than that much work. That is your reality.

BREAKING DOWN TASKS

At the start of each iteration you have to translate the amount of work to be done from customer-centered descriptions (user stories) to developer-centered descriptions (tasks). The goal is to complete all of the tasks for user stories during this iteration. From a customer's point of view, it is preferable to have three completed stories than five partially completed but unusable stories. This implies coordination and communication among the team and with the customer.

In a real-world project, there might be enough user stories on the table for the current iteration that this process could be sped up by holding the tasks discussion in subgroups. Such a company might also employ a large development team in which splitting up to discuss user stories is more natural. In your project, your group will be small enough and there will be fewer user stories so that it remains beneficial to have such a discussion when all group members are present. Someone may be able to point out the similarities between the current story and completed stories. Someone else may be able to point out that now that the system has a certain architecture, which may make adding this functionality either easy or hard. Look at the user stories in the order that the client has set and discuss how they might logically be broken down into tasks. You may want to consult with the customer after breaking your stories down into tasks. You're not asking for approval; you're asking whether the way you understand the requirements of the story agrees with what the customer intended.

Once the tasks have been set for this week's stories, you and your fellow developers start to bid on them. You may say, "I can do that task in two units." Someone else in your group may think they can do it in one unit. If the group feels that the low bidder understands what the task will take then that person wins. The low bidder has committed to doing the task with a partner in one unit. Keep bidding until everyone has used up his or her units. If there are people with spare units then the customer can add more stories. If you run out of people with units before you run out of stories, then you need to have the customer set further priorities. Your group may need to shuffle tasks to accommodate these priorities.

At this point, each team member should know which tasks they have committed to complete in the following weeks. The team may then want to strategize a bit about the order of tasks.

Working Plans

As you've been reminded several times already, in XP all code is written in pairs. Once your team members know the tasks that each is responsible for, you need to figure out who will pair together this week. In a real-world XP team, pairing can be decided in a more ad hoc manner because all members of the team work in the same space. In addition, they gather at least once a day for a stand-up meeting. In such a setting it's very easy to casually ask the person next to you if they can pair with you on your task.

Perhaps a good way of translating this to your situation is to estimate that about a day or day and a half in a professional XP shop is like a week in your setting. This means that each week you need to have solid plans about what you're going to work on and with whom. You may have additional constraints in choosing your partner. You might prefer to work on your database task with the member of your team who has the most experience with this sort of thing, but neither of you has any time in common this week. You may have already agreed to pair with someone on their task and find it natural to ask them to pair with you on yours.

After a few iterations, you will tend to follow a set pattern. Your team's schedule may have you regularly pairing with one person on Tuesday and a different person on Thursday. The more time your team can find when all of you can work in the same space at the same time, the more flexibility you will have.

In addition to deciding who will be working on what with whom, you need to be very concrete about where and when. Losing an hour or two of work here and there will add up in the course of a long project. You may think that advising you to be on time or to agree on a meeting place is outside the scope of a software-engineering text, but these are issues that have significant impact on the initial success of a project. Later in the project these issues are all worked out. Early on, one member will e-mail the group and say, "Hey, I thought we were meeting today at noon. Where were you guys?" Or two members of a group will meet after hours at the lab and one will say, "No, I thought you had the key" or "I thought you had our code" or "I thought you knew how to run the unit tests in this environment." At this point in the process each member of the group should be clear on (1) the tasks they've agreed to work on for this iteration, (2) the people they will be pairing with in the coming week, (3) when and where they will be meeting, and (4) who is responsible for bringing any items or knowledge needed to these meetings.

Communication Plans

You need to consider how information will be disseminated in your group. This is a critical consideration. XP depends on timely communication. The ideal setting is a single room in which the team can efficiently work with the client, who is there and accessible at all times. Already the constraints of real life force you to make compromises. You can't expect the client to arrange their schedule around yours and move their office to where the team codes. It's not always possible to find a time for the whole team to meet together. Instead, you meet in pairs whenever you and another team member have a common available time. Even if you could remember all that happened in a session, you'd never be able to adequately share it with others.

You need to have a way to leave messages for other members of the group that they can easily access from home or from campus. You may need to use different media for various communications needs.

Your solution does not need to be high tech. If your group has a dedicated lab, then a whiteboard can serve many of your needs. Simply having sheets of paper taped to the wall can work as well. More traditional solutions in the setting of a software-engineering project are e-mail, a newsgroup, or some sort of electronic bulletin board. You can write e-mail and copy all of the members of your group. This tends to be effective. It helps if members of your group can access their e-mail from various locations. Newsgroups serve the same purpose as e-mail but they include archiving of old messages and usually include a web interface as well as sending the messages as e-mail to group members. Newsgroups also ensure that no one is left off the distribution list. You may want to add your coach (if you have one), instructor, or client (if they want to be included and its appropriate) to a separate list that is set up just to cover the broader details. They don't need to know that you can't meet tomorrow as planned, but they may want to know the current status of the project. You may decide that everyone can see everything and just keep a single list. A bulletin board or a wiki (see http://c2.com/cgi/wiki? for more information on wikis) can also serve as a convenient way to distribute information. Similar to a white-board or note taped to the wall, these solutions require that you check for new messages regularly, although some include the feature of allowing members to sign up to be notified if there are any changes.

Nothing's better than a face-to-face meeting. You must schedule regular meetings with the group where issues can be resolved quickly. One of the drawbacks of e-mail is that the tone of the sender often isn't adequately communicated. In a face-to-face meeting, you hear the words as they are delivered and not filtered through your assumptions of their meaning. Also, simple issues can drag on in an e-mail conversation as each party refines the discussion in small but important ways. In a face-to-face meeting, the differences can be easily reconciled and the discussion can move on. If all but one member of the group can make a meeting, you may have to go ahead and have it, but this should not be a regular occurrence or you will isolate the missing group member. Often groups can meet for ten minutes before or after class. When you schedule programming time you need blocks of time that are two hours or longer to be effective, but when scheduling common time you should consider times of less than a half hour in which you can have brief but necessary meetings.

At this point, you should know how to contact the other people in your group, where to check for messages from them, and when to agree to hold in-person meetings.

Integration Plans

You meet with your group weekly to figure out who is working where, on what, and when. Then you go your separate ways. Suppose the stand-up meeting takes place Monday at 9:30 A.M. The first pair gets together at mid-morning on Monday and completes a task. Their code is compiling and passing all tests. Now what? Another group is working Monday afternoon. Their task doesn't really have anything to do with the first group's work. One option is that they just work on their task and then the group working Tuesday night works on their task and so on. Soon we have many versions of the code that will need to be integrated in one big ugly session that could go late into the night. This can't happen in your project because continuous integration is one of the XP practices.

Once you've made changes to the code, checked that the code changes compile, and checked that all tests pass, you need to update the common code base that is shared by everyone, and then everyone needs to be notified that the code has been updated. Before starting a session, if you receive notice that the code has been updated, you need to download the latest version of the code. It's a good idea to make sure it compiles and all the tests are passed. It's good to know where you stand before you start.

Code sharing does not need to be high tech. If your group has a single machine that's designated as the integration machine, just upload your code to it using an identifying naming convention, save the existing code, and then test your code. If it passes, notify the others in your group. You can also post an archive of the current code on a web page that the group members can access. Some newsgroups and bulletin boards allow you to post files. You can also look into setting up a versioning system such as Concurrent Versions System (CVS). You need to avoid situations in which two teams download the code, each team changes part of it, and the first team to save finds their work is gone after the second team updates. You are now part of an interdependent group and must find a mechanism for dealing with these situations.

At this point, your group must know where new code will be saved, how to recognize the latest code, how to notify others, and how to save and retrieve it from this site.

THE FIRST ITERATION

The previous section outlined what should be done before each iteration. You will need to set up some of the infrastructure during or before the first iteration. If you are using a newsgroup to communicate, that can be set up during the first week of classes before starting on the project. You should also think about how to integrate new code at this point. However, there are obstacles during the first iteration that won't be found until later in the project. Unfortunately, in an XP project all of your stumbling is public. Your client knows how much you accomplished during those first couple of weeks.

Installing Software

Your group needs to agree on some basics before getting started. Are you going to use an IDE or just a text editor and the command line? If you are using an IDE, you'll need to find one that will run on all of the systems you are using for development and you will need to make sure that you are licensed to run it on these machines. The instructor or school may choose the development environment for you. In any case, make sure you are familiar with it fairly quickly.

Take time when you begin your project to investigate the machines on which your application will have to run. You don't want to have your application work on your development machines and just sit there or spew exceptions on the deployment machines.

One of the places where students get into trouble is in setting the `CLASSPATH` and `PATH` variables on their development machines only to find that the deployment machines may or may not have these same settings. Often in the case of a stand-alone application that runs on a single machine, the better choice is to set these variables using batch files or shell scripts or to distribute an executable file or double clickable application.

You should also check to make sure that your application doesn't depend on special software or versions of software installed on your machine. You don't want to write an application that takes advantage of the latest release of Java and then find that your client's machine doesn't support it. At some time during the first iteration, you should check that your application can be installed on the client's machine, or if it needs to run from an external drive. The software releases aren't real unless you actually release the software to the client and let them use it.

You also need to think about how you are going to release your software to the client machine. You may want to designate some member of your group as the installation person for this iteration. That person needs to know what you're installing and what the software requirements are. The installer needs to know where the client is allowing you to install the software and the restrictions on installation. It is a good idea to rotate the installation person so that by the final week of the project everyone has installed the software at least once.

First Estimates

The good news is that you will get better at everything you are asked to do as the project progresses. The bad news is that you won't start out being very good at most of the methodological things. You've never written unit tests—you'll have to learn how. You've never pair programmed—you'll have to learn to drive and to copilot. You haven't had to estimate user stories, tasks, or your own level of productivity. How do you possibly begin?

The first thing you're asked to do, even before you get your user stories from the customer, is to estimate how much work you can get done in the next two weeks. For each week, seriously consider how much time you will be able to meet with someone else from the group. This will involve discussion with your team members to determine their availability. Once you get your estimate you'll need to reduce it by some amount. You have to understand that you won't be working on this project every minute you are in a room with a coding pair. During the first week it is a good idea to estimate that you will spend half the meeting time working on the project. That may or may not be a good estimate. But any number you come up with at this point will be a guess. Make your guess and move on.

Next, you receive a stack of stories from the customer and are asked to estimate how long each story will take you to complete. Resist the temptation to answer, "I don't know," and think back to programs you have written that can be compared in any way to the stories you're being asked to code. As a warning, you'll tend to underestimate stories. It takes a lot longer to complete stories than you may initially think. Come up with estimates for the stories. Any story that seems too long or that you can't figure out how to estimate should be sent back to the customer with questions. Better yet, if it's your question, you should ask it.

You have now completed estimating how much time you can give to the project during this iteration and you've estimated a stack of user stories. When you began estimating stories, it may have felt somewhat arbitrary. After a while, you should be able to look and say, "Well, this one looks a bit harder than that one and we estimated that at a three so this should be a four."

The customer then uses your estimates as if they are real. According to the customer, your team said it could do twenty units of stories so they'll pick twenty units. You get a smaller stack of stories from the customer. These are the stories the customer thinks will get done this iteration. You next follow the section above that described estimating tasks. The difference is that at this time you don't really know what you're doing. Do it anyway. Make your estimates and proudly announce them. You have no data points at this time and do nothing but guess. Be up front with the customers and they will value your word.

Coding Conventions

It's often the small things that sidetrack a project. This is because we often don't notice the small things and so we don't fix them. The big things call out for attention and we fix them instead. Coding conventions is an area that doesn't seem so important but falls under the "communication is good" category. Coding conventions are important enough that they are another core XP practice.

Code communicates meaning to those who read it. If your group can agree on coding conventions then it makes it easier to read the code written by others in your group. These conventions can include such trivial issues as whether you place the opening bracket to a method like this:

```
public void something(){
  //body of method
}
```

on the same line, or like this:

```
public void something()
{
  //body of the method
}
```

on the next line. No doubt you already know the answer to the question of which convention you should follow. It doesn't matter. Pick one and follow it.

You will also want to establish conventions for naming methods and variables. You may want to talk about how you will package files in this project. Some people like a lot of small packages, some like big, some don't care about size but want the packages to represent a logical division of responsibility in the application. Once again the answer is that for each issue you should pick a convention and follow it. If there are conventions that are particular to your language (as there are in Java), find and follow them.

Chapter 7

The Values, Principles, and Practices—

Living the Iteration

In the last chapter, you covered the steps for preparing for the iteration. At this point you should know what you're working on, when, with whom, and where. In this chapter, you'll review the core practices used in each iteration. Other issues that come up during an iteration are also addressed in this chapter. What do you do when you're on a roll and your session is coming to an end or if you have a great idea and no one's around? In this chapter, we'll also look at the values and principles that underlie the XP practices.

THE CORE OF THE ITERATION

You and a pairing partner sit at a keyboard and look at your task. Quickly you discuss what you think might be involved and share thoughts on a possible solution. Maybe you take the time to sketch a quick diagram. Now you think of a test that the code needs to pass for you to be satisfied that the task is accomplished. This won't be the only test required. There will be others, but start with just one for now. Create a class for the test method or find an appropriate existing class. Write the test. It won't compile. Write enough code to make it compile. Once the code compiles rewrite the code to get the test to pass. Look for refactoring. Repeat this process until you are confident that you have a test suite that covers enough of the task. When all tasks pass, you can feel pretty good about marking the task completed. You'll find more details on these practices in the tutorials in Part III, *Core Practices—Working Examples of Core Practices*, on refactoring, testing first, and pair programming. These activities form the core of what you, as a developer, do every time you sit down at a computer to work on this project.

As you participate in these core activities, there's a lot going on behind the scenes. You are using other XP practices to support your progress. You are adhering to the coding standards your team agreed to even if you don't agree with them. Code should have a unified, easy to read look about it. No one owns any part of the code, so feel free to refactor the code that you or others created and don't mind or hardly notice when someone else refactors your code. Everyone is responsible for all the code. If you see a horribly coded method, you can't say "not my mess" and move on. Whether you wrote the code in the first place or not, it is now your mess. Fix it and then move on.

You don't have to consult large design documents that were created before the problems in this project were well understood. You don't need to check that your ideas fit within the architecture that was worked out by someone else. The fact that you are allowed to have ideas about design and implement them on the fly is a bit novel. What makes it work is that everyone has bought into the notion of simple and just in time design.

You are working at a reasonably sustainable pace so as not to burn yourself out. In this way, when you are copiloting your partner can drive fearlessly because you are alert enough to provide support, insight, and a critical eye. You need to be rested enough that you are able to drive without making too many of the small mistakes so that your copilot can concentrate on the larger issues.

As you complete a task, you run the acceptance tests that the client has designed for this user story. If you have time, you run the entire set of acceptance tests. You check that the code on the integration machine is the same as the code on which your work is based. If it is then go ahead, integrate your code, and notify your group. If it isn't then reconcile the differences before checking your code in. Check your code in early and often.

Whenever you have a question of how to proceed that could affect the customer, take a moment to contact them and ask them. Because of the scheduling constraints of your group members, much of your coding time may be after hours when the customer isn't available, but write the client an e-mail and you should have a reply by the next time you get together to code. This is why you want to split your development time throughout the week. That way, you're not more than a couple hours of development away from getting the client's answer. That's very fast. You aren't asking the client whether you should implement a feature using Java servlets or JavaServer pages (JSPs), you're asking them whether they would prefer the user experience to be one way or another.

Every two weeks you'll provide the customer with a new release. As you get close to the scheduled release time, you'll figure that you could complete more stories if you had just a little more time. In XP, release dates don't slip. You will release on that date barring a catastrophe or something less dramatic but nevertheless important. You can slip features but you can't miss deadlines. This is a commitment you have made that you must keep.

The one core XP practice that you haven't paid much conscious attention to thus far is "Metaphor." In a way, this is the fuzziest of all XP practices. The idea is that you and your team will have a way of thinking about your project that will give rise to useful terminology that will help your team understand each other as you discuss directions you are taking.

PROBLEMS THAT ARISE

There's a lot to take in as you begin to program using XP. You can't possibly understand all of the subtleties of XP during your first couple of iterations. Initially, you'll learn the basics of how to do the individual practices. Soon the synergies will become apparent. You'll need to watch yourself and refine the way you pair, refactor, test first, and so on. It's like learning a new sport. At first, you're just happy when you can hit the ball or skate without falling down. Once you can repeatedly meet these minimal standards, you begin to actually enjoy the activity and can start working on the finer points. You can work on developing a consistent stroke or learn to move equally well to your right and left. In this section, you'll look at issues that come up as you are first learning to program using XP.

Do We Really Have to Pair Program?

The XP rule is that all code is produced by a pair of programmers working together at the same machine. There will be times when you're in your room late at night, get a great idea, and write some code that implements your idea. This is great. You are encouraged to think about the software in these magically productive moments. Now that you've written the code, throw it away.

"Oh, come on," the little voice in your head might say, "What's the big deal? It's just a little bit of code and it works. Check it in and move on." Throwing away working code is difficult. If you are up against a deadline where you have a lot of work to do, throwing away working code actually feels like the wrong thing to do. It's not. You can cut corners in almost every XP practice. The practices aren't what make XP extreme. The rules of XP are, by and large, based on programming's best practices. In other words, these are individually recognized as beneficial behaviors while programming. What makes XP extreme is that you are doing all of them all of the time. You will find that (1) you don't have to do them *all* all the time and (2) when you don't do all of them all the time you will pay for it in some way.

The first reason to throw your code away is to avoid encouraging such behavior. Particularly when you are beginning, there seem to be obstructions to pair programming. It takes effort to find a common time to code with someone else. You often have to find a location that's less convenient than just working in your room. Roughly half the time that you're pairing you'll be working on a task that your partner signed up for instead of the work you committed to finishing. As soon as you allow yourself not to pair sometimes, you'll have a hard time committing to pairing again. This is the proverbial slippery slope that it is best not to start down.

A second reason to throw it away is that this code has not benefited from having a second pair of eyes on it as it was written. Maybe if you had suggested this approach your pair would have been able to suggest a simpler alternative. Even if your way of addressing the problem is the one chosen, it is because two of you agreed on this approach. In addition, the programmer pairing with you would understand and be aware of this code. This larger knowledge base is a benefit as each of you later pair with other developers.

Another consideration while working on your own is that you've probably had to change some of the existing code in the project to introduce your idea. Perhaps if you downloaded the latest build before you worked, wrote test first code, and ran the tests every time you compiled, you would have a great deal of confidence. You are, however, concentrating on your specific task and don't have the copilot reminding you not to cheat the process. This isn't so much a case of having another pair of eyes on your code as having a witness in the room. It's often hard to come up with all the tests you need on your own or decide that you have enough tests just so you can get on with the task you want to address. You sometimes miss a refactoring or decide to ignore it for now and lose track of it.

If you aren't going to be able to use the code you write, then you may wonder why you should bother writing it in the first place. The easy answer is that you don't need to write it. Just jot down a note on an index card about your idea and try it the next time you meet with a partner. Many programmers aren't wired that way—when they have a cool idea, they just have to try it out. Something draws you to the program to tinker with it. In the best of all possible worlds, you'll write the unit tests first. However, there in your room no one is looking and you know you'll be throwing the code out anyway so you just go ahead and start coding your solution. You quickly find out whether your solution should work or not. The code may not be pretty but you have confidence in the technique.

The next time you pair you can suggest the approach that you tried on your own. You can provide the added endorsement that you've actually tried it and it works. But now, in addition to better understanding the code, you have the help of a second programmer. So, if you are alone and the programming muse calls to you, go ahead and answer. Code your solution, throw it away, and bring what you learned from the exercise to the next pair programming session.

No All Nighters

The XP practice of "forty-hour weeks" has been renamed "sustainable pace." This practice was put into place to point out the problems with using overtime as a solution to being behind on a project. Sure, overtime may work this week. You're behind and need just a little more time to squeeze out the extra tasks you're working on. Even XP recognizes that this may be required once in a while—it just can't become the rule.

Think of this rule in terms of dieting. You can lose weight on almost any fad diet that comes out. There's probably a diet that tells you to eat a hot dog for breakfast, drink a banana daiquiri for lunch, and enjoy a bag of chips for dinner with a cheap cigar. Each of these diets backs their advice up with some sort of scientific sounding reasons that it should work and claims of how much weight you can lose up to in the first two weeks. As anyone who's been on a fad diet knows, the difficulty isn't taking off those pounds, the difficulty is in keeping them off. The more scientifically sound diets advise you not to lose weight eating any differently than you would be able to eat for the rest of your life. Add more vegetables, reduce your fat intake, and so on. Lose weight by eating a regime you can sustain as long as you want. If some day you go to an all-you-can-eat buffet, that's okay. If you want an ice cream for dessert once in a while, that's okay too. You can't do these things all the time or even with any degree of frequency, but sometimes you just have to have good ice cream.

Overtime is the same. Once in a while, it can be just what your team needs but as a rule, it isn't good for you. What your team needs is time to recharge. You need to be fresh when you come to your code. You need to be able to truly relax when you aren't working or you won't be any better the next time you come in to do your work.

In an academic setting, you don't have forty hours each week that you can ordinarily devote to a single course. Some schools have multipliers that can be used as guidelines. For every hour spent in class, it is expected that students will spend so many hours outside of class. A software-engineering course is an upper level course in which the class time is the tip of the iceberg. There is a lot of hidden time spent with your group doing the real learning. Your group, perhaps with the help of your instructor, will determine how much time you might be reasonably expected to devote to this class. Once you have figured out how much time you spend programming each week, you'll need to divide this time up according to slots that at least two group members have available. These times should be somewhat distributed through the week and should ideally include at least one large block during which everyone can work in one place.

There is a long-standing badge of courage in the life of undergraduates: the all nighter. Spending all night cramming for an exam, writing a paper, or finishing up a programming assignment may fill you with pride at what you were able to accomplish when your back was against the wall. Maybe this effort was required. Maybe the fact that you had to work until the early hours of the morning is an indication of a lack of planning. This isn't a lecture. Go back and look at that paper you finished at 3 A.M. Would it have been better if you'd written it when you were awake?

On an XP project, you've agreed to meet with your group at eight o'clock some night for a three-hour session. The end of the session comes and you are so close to getting the next feature working. Maybe it's the end of the iteration and you want to make sure the user story can be completed for this release. Stop and stand back from the process a minute. Make a decision to go forward or not but make this decision consciously. If members of the group are tired and want to leave, let them. If some of you want to stay (at least a pair's worth), then go ahead and stay. Set a deadline. Agree to work another hour but no more. Make sure at the end of the iteration when you look back at how things went, you discuss this "overtime" experience and specifically prohibit it in the next iteration. Look at the code that was produced and see if, over time, it needs more refactoring than other bits of code. If so, you've learned something about putting in all nighters. If not, then you've learned that occasionally when you need to, you can devote the extra time in this manner.

In talking about sustainable pace, you don't just need to worry about scheduling sessions that are too long—too many short sessions can cause their own problems. There is overhead involved in sitting down to code. It takes a while to get the environment up and running, to load the current version of the code, and to get your head back into the project. Although you may have to use them, blocks shorter than ninety minutes aren't long enough to push the project forward enough. It seems that you're just beginning when you're time is up. Pair programming is an intense activity during which time passes quickly. The advantage of shorter blocks is that you're aware of how little time you have and tend to use the time more efficiently; the disadvantage is that there's less time to use.

The Simplest Thing Isn't Obvious

Many times in XP you are told to do the simplest thing that could possibly work. There are many reasons for this advice. One reason is to stay focused on the task at hand and not think about needs that aren't here yet. Another is that your code must communicate its meaning. In XP you will spend a lot of time in someone else's code or in code you wrote long enough ago that you don't remember quite what you were thinking at the time. You need to be able to quickly understand what each piece of code does. Finally, XP is all about taking small, testable, reversible steps. Keep it simple, keep it small, and you will go faster.

You don't overdesign the system because of some anticipated need that hasn't arisen yet. You are asked to create a method that returns the number of elements in a `Vector`. The simplest design might be this one.

```
public int getSize( Vector vector) {
  return vector.size();
}
```

But you think that maybe you'll want to be able to accommodate other types of collections. Maybe you should take in an object of type `Collection`, obtain the corresponding `Iterator` and iterate through the list until you get to the end. Without too much effort, you've designed a more flexible solution. This will still work for `Vector` but it will work for so much more.

```
public int getSize( Collection collection) {
  Iterator iterator = collection.iterator();
  int size = 0;
  while (iterator.hasNext()){
    size++;
    iterator.next();
  }
  return size;
}
```

Yuck. All you want for now is the size of a vector; you don't need that extra stuff. Maybe later you will. It didn't take more than a minute to write the more flexible version. What's the problem? You don't need it yet. If it only took you a minute then it can be written when you need it—if you need it. Often you find that you design for needs that never arise. By the time that these needs do arise your code may have been refactored in such a way that this solution is not the best one for that time anyway. You'll hear XP practitioners talk about YAGNI. This is the acronym for "you aren't going to need it." Whenever you find yourself making a system more complex for an anticipated need, remind yourself, YAGNI.

The second reason for simplicity is communication. Look at the two code snippets. What you want to communicate is that the method returns the size of a Vector that is passed in as a parameter. The first version of the method communicates this intent much more clearly than the second method. In *eXtreme Programming*

eXplained, Kent Beck explains that the simplest design has:
"four constraints, in priority order.

1. The system (code and tests together) must communicate everything you want to communicate.
2. The system must contain no duplicate code. (1 and 2 together constitute the Once and Only Once rule).
3. The system should have the fewest possible classes.
4. The system should have the fewest possible methods."

Notice that the order matters a lot. While refactoring you split up long methods by taking lines of code that belong together and creating a new method that names the action taken collectively by those lines of code. In other words, you've created a method and the code does no more than it did before. This seems to violate rule 4. However, the code communicates its meaning much more clearly and rule 1 has precedence over rule 4. These four rules can be used very effectively for simplifying your code.

Even with these guidelines, however, deciding on the simplest thing can be difficult. The simplest thing is in the eye of the beholder and is very dependent on the knowledge and experience of the programmers. Initially, a switch statement may seem like the simplest solution. At some point, a State pattern may become obvious to a developer who's experienced with design patterns, while another developer may feel that the switch statement is still the easiest solution. If you and your partner disagree about the simplest thing, it may indicate that you or your partner needs to educate the other about a technique. Once you explain what a State pattern could do in this case, your partner may see it as a simpler solution. Alternatively, once your partner understands a State pattern they might be able to better explain to you why their solution is simpler. In any case, discussing the simplest thing will lead to more understanding on both sides. As with everything else in XP, discuss, decide, and move on quickly. Nothing is undoable.

Hey, That's My Code

You and a partner write code to pass a test and moved on to another task. You were driving at the time so you think of the code as yours even though you're careful to refer to it as "the code we wrote." Weeks later you're working on another task that causes you to revisit your code and you can't believe it. Somebody has changed your code. Not only that, but the replacement code is much worse than the code you wrote. You stop what you're doing and change it back. You run the tests and all tests pass. You move on.

In such a case, take a hard look at why you changed the code back. Were you personally affronted that somebody had changed your code or were you genuinely trying to make the code better? It's difficult to answer objectively. If your pride was interfering, then it will also help provide the rationalization to mask its motives.

Look at a simpler and not atypical case. You prefer a certain convention for the opening bracket for a method or loop. Maybe you like it on the same line as the method name or maybe you like it on the next line. The details aren't important. This time when you come back to your code, you notice that the code is the same but the bracket convention has been changed. You get annoyed. Why would someone make such a stupid, inconsequential change to your code? And then you change it back. There's a bigger issue here. You probably need to have coding standards for your group. But in the event that your standards don't include bracket placement, leave the brackets where they are. Your group couldn't agree on where the bracket should be so you don't have a right to continue the argument by changing them to your way.

It should be as cut and dried if you had returned to your code and found it better than you left it. You'd leave the improvements in, wouldn't you? What if the code was different but you didn't think it was any better or worse? Unless there is now an obvious refactoring that is better than your original solution or the one you now see, leave it alone.

Separate yourself from the code you wrote. It's not yours. You don't need to defend it against enemy attack. You won't be held accountable for the lines you originally wrote. Ideally, you won't even recognize the code that's yours and the code that's someone else's. With coding standards and pairs moving in and out of everyone's code with an eye for refactoring, you need to let go of the notion that certain code belongs to you. In retrospect, code you particularly liked doesn't tend to be as great as you remember it and code you thought was just awful often isn't as horrible as you remember. Most of the time, you will write code that is just okay.

THE LARGER VIEW OF XP

When no one is looking, what is it that keeps you from taking shortcuts? Maybe you can get your whole team to agree that you can include code that you wrote on your own. Everybody agreed. What keeps you honest isn't a set of rules. What keeps you honest are your values and principles. For example, the person in front of you drops their wallet and doesn't notice. You call after them and let them know. You could have just let them walk away and taken their money. It wasn't some rule that made you react that way; it's in your makeup. You aren't the sort of person who could do that. You have values and principles that tell you how to behave even in cases where no rules apply.

There are occasions when you must ignore a rule to do the right thing. This is not to be confused with the times that you ignore a rule because you don't feel like following it. Here you directly disobey a rule because of a greater good and are willing to suffer the consequences. It is the same with XP. Doing XP is more than just following the practices.

In *eXtreme Programming eXplained*, Kent offers values and principles for eXtreme Programming. You will find that after a few iterations you will find yourself modifying some of the practices. Unlike the cases in the previous section, you won't make modifications for expedience. You will be making decisions in the light of your understanding of the values and principles of XP together with your experience of following the practices as they are written.

Values

The values of XP don't look like much when they're written down. These values are communication, simplicity, feedback, and courage. The first three pervade all that is written in this book. One of the book's reviewers also pointed out that, although he doesn't highlight it in his book, Beck also emphasizes the importance of respect. In some ways this is the most important of all of the values.

At every step so far, the description of what you should be doing has involved communication in a deep way. You communicate with the customer, with the rest of your team, with the person that you are pairing with, with your coach, and with your instructor. You look for simplicity everywhere. Your design, your code, and your processes should all be simple. One of the rewards of XP is feedback. At each stage, everyone knows what is and isn't working. The unit tests for the current version of the code will always be working. A quick glance at the current state of the acceptance test tells every one which of the customer's concerns were met.

The importance of simplicity and the problems with realizing it were discussed earlier in this chapter. Let's look more closely at the pervasive values of communication and feedback and then briefly discuss courage.

Start with a small example of communication. You could write a method like this.

```
public boolean a(){if(b()&&c())return true;else return false}
```

Alternatively, you could write the same method like this.

```
public boolean checkIfMoveIsAllowed() {
  if (movedPieceRemainsOnPlayingBoard() &&
       targetSquaresAreAllUnoccupied()) {
    return true;
  } else {
    return false;
  }
}
```

There is a clear correspondence between the two methods. The second method doesn't do anything that the first one doesn't. The compiler and the Virtual Machine could care less which version you submit. If you are new to the project and could inherit either version of the code, which would you choose?

The second version communicates its meaning better. The whole reason that you take the time to write clear, well-constructed code is to communicate better with another person or possibly with yourself at another time.

When it comes to interpersonal communication, the XP practices are a little more prescriptive. You don't want the interaction with the customer to be the typical conversation.

Customer:	How's it going?
Developer:	Fine.
Customer:	Think you'll make the deadline?
Developer:	*<fill in whatever you'd like here, the Customer isn't listening>*
Customer:	That's good.

In XP there are checks built in to make sure you are actually communicating. Customers communicate what they want by creating user stories. Developers indicate that they understand what is being asked for by estimating the stories or asking for clarification on those they don't understand. All the while there is a running conversation going on so that potential misunderstandings can be identified and addressed. The developers tell the client how long they think a story will take to complete. The customers have to really hear this estimate and understand it because they are using this estimate to determine what they want the developers to work on during this iteration. Iterations don't last very long. It won't be long before the developers and the customers meet to discuss exactly what's been done and what needs to be done next.

Developers are required to communicate with each other all the time as well. You can't write code without sitting down with someone else. Each of you has a specific but dynamic role that involves constant conversation. The group meets as a whole to plan the iteration, discuss progress, and bid on tasks. As pointed out previously, even the code you write is intended to communicate with the other developers.

There are other instances of mandatory communication, but the key is that it pervades an XP project. As you adapt XP to your local situation, communication must remain a feature of the enterprise. An early indication of trouble is that someone on the project is not communicating. You can't let this go unresolved. As soon as you notice someone not attending meetings or actively participating in the process, try to draw them out. This doesn't need to be done publicly and the XP coach may be the best person to address this issue. A problem with communication, even a small one, can have disastrous effects.

Feedback is also evident everywhere in an XP project. Feedback is immediate, specific, and comprehensive. You don't have to guess how far along you are on any aspect of the program. If you are working on a task, you can see that your unit tests are all passing. Your team knows when you have updated the current build because you notify them. There is a mechanism for tracking progress on stories and tasks for use by the development team. You meet frequently to discuss your plans, but these discussions always begin with an honest assessment of where you are.

The customer also is continually updated as to the status of the project. The customer knows which user stories have been completed and has the ability to run acceptance tests that verify this fact. The customer knows the stories currently being worked on because the customer has decided what they will be. There is no way you'll get to the end of the project and surprise the customer. The feedback is continuous and covers areas that give the customer and the developers the real data they need.

Much project development is based on guesses. eXtreme Programming is no different. The developers estimate how long stories and tasks will take as well as how much they will accomplish each week. When the project begins, these guesses have a low a degree of accuracy as the ones your group made. The first difference between XP and other methods is that the guesses only apply to the next couple of weeks. If you take a guess with a high margin of error and try to extrapolate from this guess, then being off a day or two during a two-week iteration corresponds to being off by as much as three months in a one-year project. The second difference is that you continue to evaluate your early guesses and use your actual productivity to create the next round of guesses. As you gather more data, your guesses are more rooted in reality and your margin of error decreases. In addition, because of the information you communicate, the customer can constantly make decisions about what is most important to include in the project next. The customer can react to the velocity of the developers and bring the project in on time with the functionality most needed for release.

In his article, "When Is it Not XP" (www.xprogramming.com/xpmag/NotXP.htm), Chet Hendrickson writes, "Courage is the trademark of Extreme Programming. It is our goal. It is the yardstick we should use to judge a project." Courage allows you to move quickly and confidently to do the right thing because you are well grounded in reality and have open communication. While Beck presents courage as a core value, Hendrickson's article discusses how courage is made possible by the other three values of communication, simplicity, and feedback. In this setting, courage is almost like an acceptance test for the other three. If courage is missing, then one or more of the other three are missing. In a more concrete way, Hendrickson points out that the lack of courage can indicate a failure to correctly following all of the XP practices.

Principles

In between the high-level values that give us the broad guidelines to make our choices and the low-level practices that provide the rules that govern our day-to-day behavior, there are basic principles. As you try to learn and follow the practices of XP, you will come to areas that don't seem to be covered by the rules. You may need more guidance in making your choices than you feel is presented by the practices. Therefore, you ask your coach. The coach looks wise, nods, and tells you that you need "Courage." You roll your eyes. Coaches can use the values to help you better understand the difficulties you are having, but in *eXtreme Programming eXplained*, Beck provides basic principles that provide more concrete benchmarks.

For example, a core value is "feedback," while a principle is "rapid feedback." It's not enough to provide data on what's going on, you must do so quickly. "Simplicity" is a value that you strive for but the corresponding principle is "assume simplicity." These may not seem to be different. Assuming simplicity means that you don't just nod to the goal of having a simple solution but that you assume it actually exists most of the time. You are more likely to chase a goal that you assume is attainable.

Much of XP evolved to meet the demands of software projects with changing requirements. In XP, two principles address this fact of software life. "Incremental change" encourages you to make very small changes that collectively make a difference. You've seen this stressed throughout the discussion of the XP practices. Take small steps and run fast. The other principle is "embracing change." This is the principle that tells you not to stress. Things will change; enjoy the ride.

The final fundamental principle is "quality work." You've seen this throughout the XP practices as well. Unit tests tell you that what you're producing works. Refactoring helps you improve the code. Collective code ownership allows you to clean up a mess when you find it. You are obligated to do the best job you possibly can.

Beck also suggests principles that aren't fundamental but help support the development process. Some are generic such as "teach learning," "accept responsibility," "play to win," "open, honest, communication," and "work with people's instincts, not against them." Although you wouldn't think that someone could stand up and sensibly advocate against any of these principles, you will see projects that don't support them. Many projects are run by people concerned with not being blamed for failure. They aren't playing to win; they are playing to avoid personal loss.

"Small initial investment" encourages developers to try the simplest thing. If you're not sure what to try, conduct "concrete experiments." You've already seen the value of such experiments during your XP spike. They provide you with the data you need before you make larger decisions. The way you measure what you've done to help with predictions on what's to come is with "honest measurement." Measure what you can and don't imply that you know more than you do.

The final principle is "local adaptation." One of the many misunderstandings of the XP community is that this methodology is rigid and prescriptive. In his book introducing the methodology, Beck recommends that you adapt the practices to your local conditions. He cautions you to carefully consider what you are doing differently, but recommends that XP will have to be tailored to your own needs.

Chapter 8

Acceptance Tests—

Determining That a Story Is Completed

It is important to know when you are finished with a story. It is even more important to be able to demonstrate this to the client. As mentioned in Chapter 5, it is unfortunately too common to see a flashy PowerPoint demonstration accompanied by a demo that is rigged to work in some limited setting. In XP the software is regularly released to your client who then gets to play with it as much as they wish.

In this course, you may meet clients who really exercise your application and can tell you what does and doesn't work. You may have to remind them that some of the features that don't work aren't supposed to work yet. On the other hand, they may be pointing out gaps in your implementation that need to be addressed. If the client shows you how to replicate a situation where something goes wrong, they are providing you with very valuable information.

At the other end of the spectrum are clients who will welcome you every two weeks when you come to install your latest release. They will watch you demonstrate the new features that you've installed since their last release and will complement you on your progress. They won't touch the application until your next visit. There may be good reasons for this. They are certainly busy with other obligations and they can't commit time to testing software that is incomplete. Another reason is a lack of technical savvy. They saw you demonstrate the application and it worked. There's no need for them to test it further. It's nice to have their confidence, but the feedback you get from them isn't helpful.

Acceptance tests provide a way for a client to tell you, "When I do this and get that result then this story will be completed to my satisfaction." When a client can be that specific about the criteria for a story being completed, they have the client equivalent of a unit test. They get to track the progress of the project by observing the total number of acceptance tests growing and the percentage of passing tests generally increasing.

Having definite criteria for completing a story gives the developers more confidence that they are done. The customer tells you a story is done when it passes a certain test. If you can replicate that test and get the code to pass, then you cross that story off your list for now.

AREN'T WE TESTING ALREADY?

Before you write a line of production code, you and your current pair are supposed to write a unit test. The progression is that first the test may not even compile, then you add enough code to get it to compile even though it may fail, then you add enough code to get it to pass. Finally, you look to see if you can refactor the code now that the unit test is in place. You continue to write tests and the code that makes them pass until you have completed the requirements of your task. When all of the tasks for a story have been completed, you have completed your story.

The problem with this scenario is that all of the steps taken after receiving the user story are based on decisions made by the development team. The team decides how to split the story into programming tasks. In order to accomplish the programming tasks, the pair decides what is required for each task. The development team writes the unit tests in support of these divisions. The customer can't make the decision of how to split the stories and the customer can't write unit tests. The result is that the unit tests validate that the program is correct according to the developer's point of view.

The customer must be able to describe how they will know that a story is complete. In other words, the customer has asked for a feature or functionality that is described in a story. The customer needs to have a way of determining that the code satisfies the requirements of the story. If a story can not be tested, it should be eliminated or replaced. You don't want to keep going to the customer and showing them that you've completed their story only to have them repeat, "No, that's not it." In frustration you would ask them what is it they really want. Acceptance tests capture this. Where a user story is an understanding between the client and developer, an acceptance test is a requirement to be fulfilled by the development team.

A unit test is a white box test (meaning the tester can look at the code being tested) to execute and verify correctness of a small portion of code. In a unit test you may do a little setting up and then call a method you want to test and check its result against the expected result. A unit test knows the signatures of the methods it is calling. In fact, the unit test is often the time when these signatures are first designed. A unit test can be written by a developer working on a specific task because everything the developer needs to write the test is locally visible.

An acceptance is a black box test. The client says, "Here's the setup, here's the input, here's my expected output." At first this may sound like a unit test. In a unit test you have a setup, then input information to the system, and test the results against expected outputs. But the client's acceptance test can be as simple as the following:

Test Panic Button

On the startup window when I press the button marked "panic" the background color of the window should turn red.

As a developer you might be tempted to raise an eyebrow and say, "They don't even know it's a JFrame not a window." Maybe the customer actually has a JOptionPane in mind. The issue here is that the customer has completely specified a behavior that you can test against. You can startup the application and see a button with the label "panic" somewhere on the startup window. Go ahead and press it, the background of the startup window should turn red. You now have confidence that it will do so when the customer tests it on delivery day.

In one sense, acceptance tests are very much like unit tests. You want to build a suite of them and know which ones are running and which ones aren't. If someone introduces code that breaks a test that used to run, you want to know about it right away. As with unit tests, your acceptance test suite will not test absolutely everything. You may show the release to the customer and announce that you have completed a story only to have the customer show you a feature they expected to be part of this user story. Help the customer write a test for that feature and correct your code to pass this test. Remember that you have access to your customer in between releases. You can ask questions and run tests during an iteration.

The granularity of an acceptance test is different from that of a unit test. A unit test might test a single case of a single piece of functionality from a single task in a user story. A single acceptance test, in validating some facet of a user story, may exercise the functionality of many unit tests. Acceptance tests work the application the way a user would. The unit tests work the application the way a developer would.

Acceptance tests exercise everything that unit tests do and much more; this may seem to imply that unit tests are unnecessary. Unit tests are still critical to developers to know that their code is correct. There is a hierarchy of correctness. The code won't compile if it is not syntactically correct. If it doesn't compile then it can't be tested further. If it does compile then the unit tests can be run. These tell us that the application does what we think it should and that no subsequent code has broken its functionality. If the code doesn't pass the unit tests, there's no point in testing it further. If it passes the unit tests, then all of the little pieces of the code work individually and we can run acceptance tests to make sure that all the pieces combine to do what the customer wants. Although developers benefit from acceptance tests, they are really for customers. Unit tests tell developers their current status and level of correctness. By viewing the number of passing acceptance tests the customers can view progress in the project and better make decisions. These tests give the customer a clear picture of the current status and level of completeness.

RUNNING ACCEPTANCE TESTS

Acceptance tests are a fuzzy area in eXtreme Programming. Unit tests are written to exercise code in the development language. We know how to parse unit tests. For the most part we just use the compilers that support the language of the code being tested. Acceptance tests are written by nontechnical people speaking in the language of their application. The Fit framework has recently been released on http://fit.c2.com. Fit allows you to easily automate acceptance tests.

You may be tempted to run acceptance tests by hand. Running acceptance tests by hand makes it easier for your customer to define the tests by themselves. The downside, of course, is that they will be run less frequently. With a little effort you can use Ant to enable you to push a button that will compile your code, run the unit tests, and then run the acceptance tests. You would benefit most from having this ability when you integrate your changes to the current release. At that point you compile your code and run the unit tests. If any unit tests are broken you need to back out of your changes. You'd also like to be able to run the suite of acceptance tests to see if you have passed more of them or broken any existing ones. If this process is automated you will be in a better position to identify the cause of any problems.

In the setting of this course, students are often integrating code at the end of a two- or three-hour session. Often only one pair is working at a time so that only the pair currently working is changing the code. After they are done coding for the session and all of the unit tests pass, they can run through the existing suite of acceptance tests. More likely, they will tend to only run through the acceptance tests they are currently working towards.

You actually don't save any time by not running acceptance tests early and often. You only need to run acceptance tests for stories you're actually working. It's also a good idea to rerun acceptance tests that have already passed, just to ensure that recent changes haven't broken them. Unit tests don't allow you to play with the application. After you've been coding for a while, you're going to want to run the application and play around with it. Acceptance tests just tell you how to play around with it so that you know it's doing what you want.

UNDERSTANDING THE TESTS

As an example application, suppose you are writing software for the cash registers in a grocery store chain. You have already completed user stories for taking input from the optical scanners and from the keypad. You are now working on this user story.

User Story: Generate a Receipt

As items are entered by the clerk, their name and price are added to a receipt and the price is added to the subtotal.

Perhaps you can anticipate some of the issues the developers may face, but for now assume they split this user story into tasks as follows.

Task 1: Record items on Receipt

Display a Name—Price pair on a receipt.

Task 2: Calculate Subtotal

As items are entered, update the subtotal to reflect the current subtotal

---

The setUp() method for the test class might look like this.

```
protected void setUp(){
  receipt.addItem("Seedless Grapes", 1.75);
  receipt.addItem("2% Milk",2.29);
  receipt.addItem("Coffee", 6.47);
}
```

One unit test for the first task might look like this.

```
public void testDisplayItemsOnReceipt(){
  assertEquals(receipt.getItem(2).getName(),"Coffee");
  assertEquals(receipt.getItem(1).getPrice(),2.29);
}
```

One unit test for the second task might look like this.

```
public void testSubtotalCalculation(){
  assertEquals(receipt.getSubtotal(), 10.51);
  receipt.addItem("Cough Drops", 2.27);
  assertEquals(receipt.getSubtotal(),12.78);
}
```

All of the unit tests pass and the development team is ready to mark this user story as completed. The customer then arrives with the following pseudocode acceptance test.

Acceptance Test: Shopping cart for *Generate a Receipt*

Set up: Coffee at $6.47 per pound, seedless grapes at $1.75 per pound, 2% Milk at $2.29 per gallon, cough drops at $2.27 per bag.
Scan items: 1 lb Coffee, 1 lb seedless grapes, 1 gallon 2% Milk, 1 bag cough drops
Verify: subtotal is $12.78

Writing acceptance tests and unit tests are separate activities with different purposes, so it is unlikely that the client would come up with that exact acceptance test. The client, under normal circumstances wouldn't have any idea what the unit tests look like, so they would certainly choose different items, amounts, and prices. The point will be made more clearly that in this example the acceptance test uses the exact same data that were used in the passing unit tests, the acceptance tests can turn up problems that were missed.

The customer is indicating in this acceptance test how the system will work. Before this story is even tested, the system will need to know the prices of the individual items. Getting those prices into the system is the focus of a different user story. Once they are entered, a normal transaction consists of entering an item name together with an amount that is given either in weight, volume, or some other unit. The unit tests for the "Generate Receipt" user story as well as the "Enter Item Prices" user story could all be passing, yet this acceptance test could fail.

Think about ways in which the unit tests could pass while an acceptance test could fail. Maybe the developers didn't split up the tasks for "Generate Receipt" correctly. Or maybe Enter Item Prices hasn't been implemented yet. In both cases, the unit tests for Generate Receipt work, and the acceptance test does not. This might also occur if an incompatibility exists between the implementations of the user stories Generate Receipt and Enter Item Prices. There's an off-by-one error in retrieving the stored prices that doesn't show up in the unit tests, because both implementations are self-consistent. Therefore, only in the acceptance test is the price for seedless grapes charged for coffee, and the milk prices register the cost for bananas, which yields an incorrect subtotal.

User Story: Setting Prices

A manager will be allowed to enter and modify prices for any existing item.

User Story: Retrieving Prices

When an item is entered, the corresponding price will be displayed. If no price is found, the clerk will be allowed to enter a price for the item for the current transaction.

Because prices can be stored and retrieved for each item, the client will assume that an item can be entered as described in the acceptance test. Remember that a user story is a general agreement between the client and developer. The acceptance test is a much more formal requirement. The acceptance test can also open up a dialog. In this case, if you were the developer you might say to the client, "You realize that your acceptance tests assume that the prices are entered at another time, and that the items are entered with some identifying name or number along with a quantity."

The client responds, "That's right. I just want to scan in the items or enter their code and weigh them. The system should have the price stored somewhere."

Now that you look back at the user story you can see that the acceptance test is completely consistent with it. They asked that you make sure that, "As items are entered by the clerk, their name and price are added to a receipt and the price is added to the subtotal." The acceptance test has just clarified how the process should work. As you've seen each time, XP both requires and depends on communication. Acceptance tests are one fail-safe method to test information that might not be understood from a user's story. Another safeguard is the constant communication between developers and clients.

As a final point on this acceptance test, the client never considered how the code might be written. The client isn't at all constrained by the access level of methods or classes. The client just tells you what they want to happen when they push this button and expect you to make it happen. They know you've finished when they push the button and see the results they asked for.

WRITING THE TESTS

As you saw in the last section, there are benefits to having the acceptance tests sooner rather than later. On the other hand, as you begin to work on a story, your understanding, and possibly the customer's understanding, of the story may change. The continuing conversation between you and the customer may help them refine their acceptance test. Although XP facilitates working with change, you don't want to waste time on meeting a requirement that will definitely change in the next day or so.

When a customer writes a user story it must be testable. This does not mean that there must be one or more acceptance tests written at the time the story is written. It means that in the judgment of the customer and the development team, it is possible to test this story. Having a story that is not testable can be grounds for asking that the customer recast the user story. Consider the following stories about the cash register program.

Friendly interface

The user interface should be friendly and easy for the clerk to use.

Responsiveness

The price should be retrieved quickly once the item has been scanned in or entered.

Visibility

The customer should be able to see the current state of the purchase.

Each of the stories needs clarification and isn't obviously testable as it currently appears. Perhaps the activity of trying to write acceptance tests might clarify what is meant by a story, but just asking how you would test it would be enough to suggest a rewrite. In the Friendly Interface story no direction is given. The client could have one idea of a friendly interface, while the development team might assume that a DOS prompt is friendly enough. In any case, how would the client write an acceptance test for friendliness? Further discussion might lead to what aspects the client wants provided in the system. The Responsiveness story just needs a clarification of what is meant by quickly. What is an acceptable response time? For Visibility, the client probably has a clear and specific idea of what is requested. The story needs to be rewritten to indicate that the running subtotal is displayed along with the last five items purchased or some equivalent level of detail. The client's stories must be clearly testable.

A client can sketch out the acceptance test at the time the user story is written, but it is probably premature. As the customer prioritizes stories, you get an idea which stories will be chosen before others. At the beginning of an iteration, the customer decides on the stories that the team will work on for that iteration. As the team goes off to divide the stories into tasks and estimate those tasks, the customer should begin to think about how those stories will be tested.

Usually this only requires that the customer think about testing three or four stories or less. This is a manageable number. In the user story practicum in Part 3, *Core Practices—Working Examples of Core Practices,* you are taken through a blow by blow example of helping the customer write user stories. Initially someone on the development team may have to also help the customer write acceptance tests. You can help the customer by asking questions such as, "What will you need to see to know that this story is complete?"

A single user story may require more than one acceptance test. Once the simple acceptance test described above passes, you may want to add tests in which items are purchased in amounts other than one unit. Instead of buying a pound of grapes, another test might buy one pound two ounces. This would ensure that the application isn't just returning the price of a single unit but is actually computing the value based on the amount purchased. Another story may buy two pounds of coffee to see if the system accepts this larger purchase or if it assumes that there was an error in entering the order.

You've seen that a single acceptance test may span more than one user story. The purpose of the acceptance test is to determine that this user story has been acceptably completed. In so doing, the test may need to call upon other parts of the system. This is another argument for not writing acceptance tests until they are needed. At the time you write an acceptance test you need to rely on the currently working parts of the system. In the example, since price entry and lookup are complete the current acceptance test could use that functionality.

Suppose price entry and lookup hadn't been completed. You would have to talk to your customer to find out whether the scope of the story had expanded. Perhaps you would want to discuss whether they needed to change their priorities to allow the other stories to be completed first. Another approach would be to request that they change their acceptance test or that they allow you to interpret it differently to accommodate the current limitations of the system.

Even though an acceptance test might span the code written for more than one user story, it is still targeting a single user story. If you are writing an acceptance test, name it and indicate the user story it is intended to test. Describe the set up that is required before running the test. In the example, the prices for the various items had to be entered into the system before the items were scanned. Next, describe the action that is performed to run this test. In this case it was to scan in several items; it could be to read a file, access some data, or press a sequence of buttons. Finally, specify the correct result of running the test. You could be expecting a value in return or for the state of the system to change in some way. The change must be demonstrable and measurable. Make sure the developers understand the test and know how to run it if it is to be run by hand. Finally be available for and receptive to questions about the test you've written and the corresponding user story.

AUTOMATING THE TESTS

The customer writes the acceptance tests. To be more precise, the customer specifies the acceptance test. The customer may need help in actually writing the test from the development team, particularly in situations where the tests will be automated. Until recently each project seemed to have its own custom solution. One goal of these solutions was to allow the customer to write the acceptance test without doing much in the way of programming. Then it was up to the development team to parse the tests and make the appropriate calls into the code base.

Some teams are using JUnit to run acceptance tests. The advantage is that the tests can be automated and easily run while results are displayed. One disadvantage is that JUnit doesn't display the proportion of unit tests being run successfully in an easily read way. It displays a red bar for a single failure in the entire test suite. For acceptance tests you'd also like a graphical representation of what percent of tests are passing. Even better is to see a histogram that lets you track the increase in total acceptance tests as well as the percent passing. A more significant disadvantage is that the client can not generally write the tests and often can't easily read the tests to make sure they are testing what is desired. A nontechnical client can read and often write extensible markup language (XML); but a nontechnical client can't be expected to read Java code and certainly can't be expected to or even allowed to write test code. As the developer, you don't want to spend time debugging code written by the client.

We'll look briefly at two solutions in this section. One uses XML to specify the acceptance tests. The developers then can use such programming languages as Python, Ruby, or Java to parse the XML. Nathaniel Talbott has had success with getting clients to write acceptance tests using a subset of Ruby. This makes it easier for Talbott, as a developer, to use the acceptance tests as real code. Other developers agree on a vocabulary and syntax with their clients and parse the client tests that conform to these rules. Ward Cunningham has recently released the Fit framework that allows the customers to write their acceptance tests as HTML tables. Although Fit has not been available for very long, it is quickly being adopted. You'll find a tutorial on Fit in Part III, *Core Practices—Working Examples of Core Practices*, and a brief description of the framework in this section.

Using a Custom Framework

The acceptance test from the last example may be written in XML so that it can automatically be parsed and run. In that case, it might contain information that looks more like this.

```
<priceCheck>
  <setup>
    <item>
      <name> Coffee </name>
      <unit> pound </unit>
      <pricePerUnit> 6.47 </pricePerUnit>
    </item>
    <item>
```

```
        <name> seedless grapes </name>
        <unit> pound </unit>
        <pricePerUnit> 1.75 </pricePerUnit>
      </item>
      <item>
        <name> 2% Milk </name>
        <unit> gallon </unit>
        <pricePerUnit> 2.29 </pricePerUnit>
      </item>
      <item>
        <name> cough drops </name>
        <unit> bag </unit>
        <pricePerUnit> 2.27 </pricePerUnit>
      </item>
    </setup>

    <scan>
      <item>
        <name> Coffee </name>
        <unit> pound </unit>
        <amount> 1 </amount>
      </item>
      <item>
        <name> seedless grapes </name>
        <unit> pound </unit>
        <amount> 1 </amount>
      </item>
      <item>
        <name> 2% Milk </name>
        <unit> gallon </unit>
        <amount> 1 </amount>
      </item>
      <item>
        <name> cough drops </name>
        <unit> bag </unit>
        <amount> 1 </amount>
      </item>
    </scan>
    <verifyEquals>
      <calculatedValue> <subtotal /> </calculatedvalue>
      <actualValue> <12.78> </actualValue>
    </verifyEquals>
  </priceCheck>
```

You would not expect your customer to transform their acceptance test into this format without your help or the help of a tool with a friendly interface. Once an acceptance test is in this form, extracting and converting the needed information is easy using an XML parser. The development team will still need to do custom work to enable each application to pass this data to the application they are working on and to extract the results.

You could create a document type definition (DTD) or schema for your acceptance tests and have your client use an XML editor to build their acceptance tests. Usually this works by their specifying a root element. Each type of test may have a different root element. In this example, the root element is priceCheck. Whether your client could create the XML or not, they can certainly read and understand it. Once they do, they can mimic the existing tests to create more tests.

The final step in using these tests automatically is to build an application that parses the test and transforms it into calls to your application. The parsing program need not be written in the same language as your application. Some proprietary versions use Python to parse the acceptance tests and run applications against them. Others use Ruby to help the customer generate tests in near natural language. These in-house products often have a web-based reporting tool so that the client can easily access the results of running these tests. If you don't have access to such a tool, the client does need to choose this activity as being worth the time of the team as it takes you away from coding story points. As mentioned earlier, setting up a custom automated way of running acceptance tests is currently costly.

The Fit Framework

The Fit framework provides a nice solution for automated acceptance tests. The customers produce HTML tables and the developers write the glue to tie the tests into the code. The parsers are provided with the framework, which is available from http://fit.c2.com.

As an example, the previous acceptance tests might appear in a table such as this.

fit.ActionFixture		
start	GroceryCheckout	
press	scan	
enter	item	coffee
enter	amount	1 pound
press	scan	
enter	item	seedless grapes
enter	amount	1 pound
press	scan	
enter	item	2% Milk
enter	amount	1 gallon
press	scan	
enter	item	cough drops
enter	amount	1 bag
check	subtotal	12.78

If you write out the HTML for this table, you would see the mappings you made from the XML version to this version. The advantage of using this framework is that many of the tasks you'll be performing each time are done for you.

In this case, the top line of the table indicates that the class ActionFixture in the Fit package will be used to process this table. Other fixtures will be discussed in the acceptance test tutorial in Part III. Somehow the prices would need to be entered for reference. That could be done with another table, they could be stored in the GroceryCheckout Java class referenced in this table following the start keyword, or they could be read in from a text file or other source. The words press, enter, and check are also keywords, which are understood by the action fixture.

The HTML files that contain tables like this are processed into other HTML tables that contain the results of running the acceptance tests. This allows the developers and the customers to view the results of these easily run tests using a web browser. Again, it is early in Fit's life, but it addresses many of the requirements of developers and customers in writing and running acceptance tests.

EXERCISE

1. Chapter 11, the Core Practices chapter on user stories, provides a complete set of user stories from an actual XP project. Write acceptance tests for these stories. Consider whether acceptance tests alter the priority order of the stories.

Chapter 9

Evaluation and Regrouping—

Wrapping Up an Iteration

An iteration does not need to end with a release. A release may come at the end of two or more iterations. In this project, the release is the culmination of each two-week iteration. In the context of this course, you want to get the product in the hands of the client as quickly as possible. Because of additional start-up problems, you may want to have two iterations before the initial release or you may want to schedule a special three-week iteration for the first release.

Actually, where one iteration ends and another begins is a bit fuzzy. In some projects as the release date nears there is so much scrambling to get the code finished that the introspection suggested below won't happen. In this chapter, you'll see that performing the assessment before delivering the release makes better use of your client's time to help plan the next iteration. These could be divided into two meetings with the client, but in the academic setting it's better to take advantage of the time you have with the client while delivering the software. If you decide that some of these items belong at the beginning of an iteration, that's fine. Just make sure your team shares an understanding of what must be done before and after each release.

FINISHING UP EACH ITERATION

At the end of an iteration, you should take stock of where you are. The first thing that the client will want to know about the project is, "What have you done this iteration?" You need to know what's working now that wasn't before. You also need to know if something that was working is now broken. Examine what worked well during the past two weeks and what didn't. Figure out if you can address the problems that arose. Estimate how many units each of you can accomplish during the next iteration and check your estimates for user stories. All of these activities help prepare you for your meeting with your client. Show the client the current state of the application and discuss what needs to be done in the next iteration together.

RUN ACCEPTANCE TESTS

There's an old joke about a little boy who's asked to spell banana. He proudly says "b a n a n a n a n a n a n a n a n a" and then clarifies, "I know how to spell it, I just don't know when to stop." As you saw in Chapter 8, the tests tell you when you have completed a story. There is a small danger that you will continue to code after the client's requirements for a story are met. There is a much larger danger that you will think you are finished before you are. The acceptance tests measure whether the individual pieces of the tasks that you have verified using unit tests combine to provide the functionality the client thought they were describing in the user story.

Ideally, acceptance tests should be run all the time. If they are automated, they can be. After you complete a task, run the acceptance tests that include that task. After you complete a user story, you must run the acceptance tests for the story. If the acceptance tests don't all pass, you haven't completed the story. Chances are, you need to examine the acceptance tests carefully to see what you're missing. You may need to go back to the client to figure out the differences between the way your team is reading the user story and the way the client intended it. You only get credit from the client for completing user stories. Passing the acceptance test tells you that the user stories are complete.

Remember that your time scale is different from one in a commercial environment. There, if the acceptance tests aren't run all the time, they should at least be run once a day. This converts to just under once a week in your setting. Therefore, once a week all of the acceptance tests for your iteration should be run. This takes time. Someone needs to be responsible for this task, which need not be done in pairs. If you have an odd number of people available during a work session, while two people are pairing the third can be running the acceptance tests. Nothing prepares you for your release better than being able to confidently say to the client, "Here's what we've done this iteration and here are the tests we're currently passing."

There are many ways to chart and track the acceptance tests that are currently passing. One chart can just indicate numbers. You can draw a bar chart on which the entire bar represents the number of acceptance tests currently in the suite and the highlighted portion of the bar represents the number of acceptance tests currently passing. If the highlighted portion drops, something is wrong and needs immediate attention. Another chart can indicate user stories that are complete. For each user story, list the tasks and keep a Gantt chart (if that is a tool you like to use) or some other time-based indicator to indicate the amount of time spent on each task. Such charts indicate the date and time the task was begun and the date and time it was completed. On the same chart you can list the acceptance tests and mark their status as passing or failing during these different time periods. This helps you see when a story is complete. However you decide to track progress, make it easy, visible, and informative.

In short, you will run your acceptance tests at least once a week. Your group will have a member responsible for running all of the acceptance tests on the code before it is released. Progress toward passing the acceptance tests will be charted.

ASSESS WHAT WAS COMPLETED

What makes your team agile in an XP project is knowing where you are at all times. If the client suddenly asks you to change directions, you have solid footing and can discuss what the implications of the change will be. For the most part, your assessment will be couched in terms of tasks. You and your team have signed up for tasks and are busy making them work.

The client, however, is only interested in completed stories. You may have had what you consider to be a fairly productive week. Of the twenty units your team signed up to do eighteen were completed. Suppose your team worked on four stories that were each worth five units and that the incomplete tasks were one unit's worth on the third story and one unit's worth on the fourth story. From your client's point of view you have completed ten units worth of work. The client doesn't care that your unit tests are passing for the eight units of stories you've completed on the last two stories. Sure, the good news is that you only have a little work to do on those two stories, but look at the discrepancy in assessment. Counting by tasks, you completed 90% of the work you set out to do. Counting by stories you completed 50% of the work you set out to do.

Which method of assessment is the correct one? Both are valuable. You need to understand your achievements to improve your estimates for the next iteration; therefore, it is important to know that you have been able to produce eighteen units worth of work. You also need to understand your achievements in terms of the deliverables. A story is either complete or it's not. Suppose you go to a restaurant and order a meal. After an hour, you ask where your meal is. The waiter says, "The cook tried really hard to make your meal and almost finished. It's the end of his shift so could you come back tomorrow?" This is what you are telling your customer.

Perhaps you could have gone to the client and asked them to choose which story they would like you to complete and put both teams on the same story. You still would have completed eighteen units but the two teams would have completed three stories, an increase in virtual productivity of 50%. More likely, both teams were "almost finished" and thought they would complete their work in time to get all four stories finished this week. You will get better at knowing what is almost finished as you gain experience.

Before you meet with your client, make a careful assessment of what you've done during this iteration. Understand what you've done from the customer's point of view. Present completed stories as achievements. Discuss completed tasks in incomplete stories in the context of the work to be done in the next iteration.

DISCUSS PROBLEMS THAT CAME UP

There are always issues that need discussing. Most problems should be dealt with as they arise so they don't fester, but some problems won't become apparent until your group consciously examines the just completed iteration with the advantage of distance. Keep the discussions nonpersonal. Discuss the action and not the person. Saying "you're rude and irresponsible" to a group member may be true but it won't be as effective as saying, "Forgetting to show up last night caused a lot of problems." Once an issue has been discussed and resolved, let it go. Here are some examples of possible problems.

Be aware of a group member (even yourself) who is trying to lead the group by making decisions. It is natural that some members will be better organized than others and that they will help the group understand what decisions need to be made. Often these people will poll the group to find common meeting times and announce that "Sunday afternoon from three to six everyone is available, let's meet then." These aren't the kind of decisions to be wary of. You do need to watch to make sure that no one has decided that it is their responsibility to assign tasks for the week or to evaluate the progress of other members. You make your own commitments for work for the week. Others may have valuable insight into your abilities that you don't. Listen to them and use them. If you feel you are being told what to do, raise this issue early. This area can lead to bitter discussion later if it isn't dealt with as soon as it arises.

Deal with an undependable group member (even yourself) early in the project. Being late to a session holds up everyone's work because XP code is produced in pairs. Even worse, deciding just to skip a session, even with a last minute warning, can have dramatic effects. Emergencies will come up and you will have to deal with them, but having to cancel a session because you forgot you had something else due is not an excuse that carries much weight.

Problems might include machines, software, or areas of XP or the project that are causing you difficulty. Ask for help. For example, you might say, "I've noticed that when I pair I almost never drive. Does anyone have any suggestions?" People you pair with may have been waiting for you to drive and may welcome the opening to make suggestions. You might notice that "we've been having trouble writing tests for the GUI" only to have another group let you know what's worked for them. Anything is fair game here. Remember that XP is about communication, so help each other to resolve the problems that are coming up in the course of an iteration.

BUDGET FOR THE NEXT ITERATION

Before you decide how many units you plan to budget for the next iteration, you need to examine all of the facts about the last iteration. You won't necessarily just bid the number of units you completed. There may be reasons to adjust this number up or down. After the last two steps, you have a clear idea of what you accomplished in the last iteration and you also have an understanding of the problems that arose. Some of the problems were unusual and won't come up again. You may therefore be tempted to estimate for the next iteration as if you accomplished more. As mentioned in Chapter 6, when preparing for the iteration, generally, you shouldn't do this. This iteration will probably go smoother than the last, but other unexpected issues will arise. It may pay off to consider your experience with unanticipated problems to be the norm. Then you will have a buffer for the next iteration.

Rather than dealing in straight units, you'll find it helpful to keep track of how much time you allotted to work this iteration as well. For example, if you planned to work twelve hours in two weeks and accomplished four units then you are taking about three hours per unit. If instead you spent twenty-four hours in two weeks to complete four units then you are taking six hours per unit. Knowing this figure will help you make a more accurate bid if the amount of time you have available changes in each iteration.

Your commitment to this project must be serious, but there are weeks when you will be able to put more or less time into this assignment. When there are midterms in other classes you may have to put more time into that work and will have less time available to devote to this project. You may have a couple of days off from your job, which will allow you to put more time into this project. But remember that you aren't just scheduling for one. You can't code on your own. This means that you are affected when other members of your team aren't as available. It also means that if you have extra time you need to find another member of your team available to meet at that time.

Combine all of this information into an accurate bid for this iteration. If you are going to put in roughly the same amount of time, the safest bid is to bid the number of units you accomplished last iteration. If you are going to put in a different amount of time, then adjust your bid based on the number of units you can produce per hour.

Again, make sure that others are available for pairing at these times. For example, if you worked for twelve hours on the last iteration and completed four units, and this iteration you can work fifteen hours, then bid five units. Notice that a unit means different amounts of time for different people in your group. You are predicting that your efficiency will be about the same and basing your productivity on this estimate.

Once the entire team has made their estimates, you can comment on each other's numbers. If someone appears to have made an overly optimistic estimation then perhaps a kind word can point this out. If someone appears to have decided to contribute too little this week, then again a group member can quietly indicate this. There are real-world constraints that some members of your group will not want to go into in depth. This project is a large part of your life right now, but there are other areas. A family problem or other issue may command a group member's attention so that they can't devote as much time to the project this iteration but it may not be something they want to share with the group.

ESTIMATE USER STORIES

Each iteration provides you with more data that you can use to better understand where you are and where you are going. Your first estimates of user stories were incomplete in two respects. First, you didn't estimate all of the stories. Second, the stories you did estimate were done before you really knew much about estimating or about the project.

At the end of an iteration the group should look back on the stories that were estimated but haven't been completed yet. These might be stories that are partially completed or they might be stories that haven't yet started. You are not going to go back and reestimate these stories in terms of your new understanding of what a unit is worth. You are going back to compare your estimates for how long the completed stories actually took. Ask yourself whether you still think one story will require about the same amount of work as another. Is that story still about twice as long as this one? You are reevaluating your judgments of relative length. You may have estimated one story as two units and another story as four units. If the first story took five units worth of work once the individual task estimates were added up and you still judge the second story to be twice as long, then the second story needs to be reassessed at ten units. This story is now too big and needs to be split by the client.

Part of this process of reestimating stories is revisiting dependencies. When you first estimate a story, you ask how long it will take to complete just this one story. You may have the feeling that if another story is completed first, this story will take much less time. At the end of an interaction, you are able to account for this information. You know what stories have been completed and so as you revisit your already estimated stories you may say, "Oh, this will take much less time now. All we have to do is add a field to the existing record." This look around helps give you a more global view of the software. You've had your head down working on specific tasks for two weeks. This exercise reminds you of interdependencies you may have forgotten.

In addition to revisiting stories you've already estimated, you also need to estimate further down in the stack of user stories. If the client hasn't dramatically reordered the stories to be done, then you need to stay just a little bit ahead in case they decide to reach further ahead for the stories for the next iteration. You can prepare for the client meeting by providing estimates for the stories the user might choose.

DELIVER TO THE CLIENT

Depending on how much you accomplished in this iteration and how prepared you are, the client meeting can be the high point of the iteration. In reality there should be no surprises for the client. They should know what they're going to get and they should know how it will look and feel and work before the meeting happens. You don't need to prepare a flashy presentation and not all of your group members need to be there.

At least one person should arrive early enough to install the software and test it before the meeting. It is best to have at least two people involved in this process in case anything goes wrong. Once the software is installed, show your client what you've been able to do this week. It actually works better to have the client operate the software, play with it, and run it through the acceptance tests for the stories you've completed. This allows you to observe the client using the software. Observing the client gives you clues as to what the client is looking for. Second, using the software allows the client to get a feel for it and better express to you early on what isn't right.

If the client doesn't like something about the software and suggests a change, consider the change and suggest what it will take to make the change. Do not talk the client into or out of the change. If they decide to go ahead, have them write a user story that captures the change or have them amend an existing user story. They need to write an acceptance test that verifies the change has been made and you need to estimate the additional work. Unlike a traditional software project, the requirements are not frozen in an XP project. Just as you've learned more about XP by doing it, the client learns more about the application they want by playing with it.

On some projects, the client comes to the developer area and tests the application on the integration machine or one of the developers brings a laptop to the client and demonstrates the application on it. If you have access to the client's machine, you should install the software and let them use it. You will be alerted to configuration problems and difficulties with installation early in the project and the client will have ownership of the application.

PLAN WITH THE CLIENT

Once the clients have played with the application and understand the current state of the project, they may have different ideas of what needs to come next. Hand them the stack of user story cards ordered as they were at the beginning of this iteration. Then hand the client some blank cards in case new stories need to be written. You are handing the client the keys to the car and hopping in the passenger seat to see where they take you. Tell the customer how many units can be chosen in this iteration and, if needed, help guide them through this planning phase.

After a couple of iterations, the client should be able to reorder the stories, determine if any additional stories are needed, and select the stories to be worked on during this iteration.

You may need to explain a bit about your estimates. The client may want to know why you accomplished so much or so little in the previous iteration. There's no reason not to be forthcoming with your client. Your client is a member of the team with whom you interact regularly. Your client understands, for example, that the academic calendar might mean slow downs around midterm time. The client may want to know why you've changed the estimates on some of the stories. Tell them. You don't have to discuss technical details, but you should be able to explain your reasoning to a nontechnical person or you should reconsider the validity of your reasoning.

The more the client knows, the better positioned they are to help you. Now that the client understands your bids for the next iteration and your revised story estimates, they will choose the stories that are candidates for this iteration. As before, it is up to your team to then break down the stories into tasks and estimate these tasks. If the client is willing to look at the task breakdown, let them comment on any issues they anticipate arising. If the task total changes the estimate of what can be done this week, allow the client to reorder the stories.

Now that you know what you are going to work on during the next iteration, it's time to start. This is a good time to head to another room with your team and have the standup meeting that starts the next iteration.

COMPLETING THE LAST ITERATION

There is a tendency in an XP project to assume that, because the client has been getting releases all along, you don't need to devote much time to the final installation. This is, however, the end of an extended project where the client has given a lot of time to help you build their software. You want to leave them with working software that includes the documentation they may need for its use. You also gave them a little bit of the software at a time throughout the life of the project. This final release is a time when you can prepare a presentation that summarizes all of the software's abilities. The requirements of each step are summarized below.

Just as there was added overhead in starting the project, finishing up the last iteration includes extra tasks you may not have anticipated. Therefore, you may want to have an extra week between your last iteration and the final presentation. You need to figure out what portions of the project you were able to deliver to the client. You will probably need to prepare a presentation for your instructor, and you will have to prepare a final installation for your client. Finally, you have had an unusual relationship with the client. You need to bring it to an appropriate close. Don't just hand over the software and say, "See you later." Take time to express your appreciation and find out how the project went from the customer's point of view.

INCLUDE THE WRAP UP IN YOUR ESTIMATES

Some instructors build in a buffer week for you to prepare the final software, the documentation, and your presentation. If not, figure this into your estimates for the last iteration. Some of the time you will be devoting to the class will not be devoted to the project. As always, let your client know this up front. You may not need an entire week, but remember that you've never done this part of a project, so you may not be very good at estimating your needs.

ASSESS WHERE YOU ARE

Run the acceptance tests and figure out which stories you actually completed. As you get close to the end of the last iteration you may want to devote a little extra time to completing those tasks you're really close to finishing. Overtime is not recommended, but an extra push here at the end is going to be sustained in any case. At each point, you are keeping the client up to date on what is going to make it into the final release. Even at the end of the project, they are setting priorities and telling you what they would prefer you work on.

PREPARE THE FINAL PRESENTATION

Your final presentation for the class will show others what you've done during the course of this project. It may be hard for you to prepare this presentation because you've been thinking in terms of little pieces each week or so. Now you are taking a big look back and talking about what the client wanted in the beginning. You can discuss the process of getting the project to where it is now. You need to highlight those features included in the final product. You should address changes that the client made to the initial description of the product. This should be a professional presentation made to both the class and the client.

PREPARE THE FINAL INSTALLATION

Although you should have been cleaning up your code along the way, make sure that the code distributed at the end is clean. You don't have to include your classes that were used to support test cases and you should make sure that no stale class files remain.

You may have removed the source files but forgot to remove the corresponding class files. Your actual installation does not need to include the source code; although, you should provide the source code (including the tests) so that the software can be maintained and improved. Deliver the presentation to your instructor and the client in a form that you would like to receive it in if you were later called in to work on this software.

In addition to the binary files and source material, you need to prepare documentation for your software. The documentation does not have to be overly involved, but at a minimum it should cover installation of the software and include system requirements, needed software, and configuration requirements. The documentation should also remind the user how to operate the application. You don't have to cover every case in a long tutorial, but you do need to provide documentation so that if the user puts the application away for six months or more they can still reconstruct how to use it. Your instructor will provide more details on the documentation requirements for this course.

Although it is not required, nice packaging is appreciated by the client. Whether you are burning a CD or just providing a disk, take the time to create an easy install in an attractive package. Just as presentation counts with food, presentation implies something about your software before it is ever run. As before, arrange your meeting with the client, but this time allow them to install the software without assistance. You're probably not going to be around the next time it needs to be done.

Part III

Core Practices—

Working Examples of Core Practices

Ideally, you will learn eXtreme Programming (XP) from someone with experience. In addition to your instructor, it is quite helpful to have a coach. The coach can pair with you and model desired behavior. The coach can just sit nearby and listen as you pair and as your team meets with the client, bids on tasks, and wrestles with the other activities that are part of XP. Your coach can remind you of the underlying principles and values that give XP its soul.

Sometimes, however, a coach is not available and there are specific points you need to understand. In Part III you'll find tutorials that take you through the details of creating user stories, testing first, refactoring, playing the planning game, and managing and building your code. In XP, all of these topics address practices that are intertwined. Each practice supports others and each benefits from others. However, for the most part, these practices are presented in isolation.

For example, it would be dangerous and difficult to refactor without a comprehensive suite of unit tests. The details of refactoring are presented in Chapter 13, *Refactoring—Sharpening Your Knife,* without providing the supporting unit tests. Similarly, you don't just start writing tests and then code when you practice test-first programming. You need to have user stories that have been broken down into tasks. You are engaged in some subtask with your pairing partner when you write your tests and then the code that makes them pass. Even so, in Chapter 10, *Test First—Learning a New Way of Life*, you will make several passes through the testing cycle without really considering the tasks and user stories that led to the code you're writing. Chapter 10 includes passing references to tasks and to refactoring, but focuses on presenting testing first in isolation.

By separating the activities, you will have a better guide to what you should be doing at each point. Certainly, you need to have user stories before you can plan your iteration. In Chapter 12, *The Planning Game—Negotiating the Future,* you will learn how an existing set of user stories changes during the course of estimating the stories and breaking them down into tasks. Chapter 11, *User Stories—Exploring with the Customer,* concentrates on the process of developing the user stories in the first place. Chapter 14, *Customer Written Tests—Automating the Acceptance Process,* details using the Fit framework to create and run acceptance tests. Acceptance tests are used to help you break down and understand user stories. You won't know that you have completed tasks and stories until the tests are passing. Certainly, these three chapters are interdependent.

Many students have never managed a large, long-term project. In Chapter 15, *Development Mechanics—Organizing Your Project,* you'll look at details that aren't necessarily required for an XP project, but may help you manage any project. In Chapter 15 you will look at creating and using packages. You will create different directories for holding your source code, test code, documentation, and compiled classes. You will be led through the process of integrating code and preparing for deployment. Fortunately, in XP you engage in these activities early and often so you will get quite good at them.

Chapter 10

Test First—

Learning a New Way of Life

In this chapter, you'll follow an example of writing test-first code to create a version of Conway's *Game of Life*. This program is a classic and you may have a favorite way of coding it that is much simpler or more flexible than the one presented here. You could, of course, refactor this code to improve it but refactoring is a topic for another chapter. Here the goal is to take you through the cycle of writing a test, writing the code that makes the test code compile, and then run. As you'll see in the section on testing GUIs, you don't test everything; you just test what can break.

In this and the other chapters in Part III, each practice we focus on will be viewed somewhat in isolation. Ordinarily, user stories are broken into tasks. You would be working on a particular task when you decide to write your first test for it. In this chapter we will look at test-first development in a way that allows us to focus on both writing and running tests and then seeing the effect of this technique on your code.

OVERVIEW OF TESTING FIRST

Like most of what we do in XP, the testing cycles are short. You should be able to code a little and see the results quickly, although how quickly will depend on the task at hand. The key idea is that you cycle through tiny steps and end up coding more quickly and more robustly than if you try to take on a big task all at once. As you code, you will develop a suite of unit tests that you will run as often as possible. Save, compile, run the tests.

As an analogy, think of this suite of tests as if it were a spelling and grammar checker in a word processor. These tools make sure that the words you use are spelled correctly and that the sentences you put together obey basic rules of usage. The tools don't tell you that what you are writing will interest your reader nor will the tools make the argument you are trying to make. In the same way, the unit tests you write will tell you that local pieces of code behave the way they are intended to. Unit tests do not offer information about global behavior. For that, the client (perhaps with your help) will write acceptance tests. This is like having someone else read what you've written and tell you whether it convinces or moves them

When using a spell checker you'll come across words that the spell checker doesn't recognize. (In this document the word "refactoring" was consistently flagged.) A good spell checker will allow you to add words to its dictionary. Similarly, as you program, you may find a section of code that passes all the tests but still has a bug in it. Add that test to your suite of tests and then fix the code. A spell checker won't catch a mistake such as, "Can you *here* the music?" The word "here" is spelled correctly; it's just the wrong word. The question should read, "Can you *hear* the music?" This mistake can be picked up only by a tool that understands the context in which "here" and "hear" appear. Perhaps a second pair of eyes will pick up this mistake, perhaps not. There are errors in your code that can't be picked up by unit tests. Again, a full set of acceptance tests does address these problems.

Here's a look at the testing cycle:

1. Think of the next small step that you want to accomplish. You'll get a feel for the size of the step as you work through the example in this chapter. You may be tempted to take larger steps. But, by taking small steps that you can validate, you'll end up moving very quickly.
2. Think of how you will test what you've accomplished this step. This is white box testing. You have complete access to the code you're testing. Suppose you are testing that two `int`s are summed correctly. You might check that the sum of four and five is nine. This example is intentionally over simplified.
3. Write the code for one of your tests. Although you can choose another testing framework, JUnit is the one described in this book. Details of the JUnit framework appear later in this chapter. You will need to check out the JUnit javadocs to see the test methods that you can use. In the case where you're summing two `int`s, make up a name for the method you'll be testing. Let's call it `add()`. You'll need a class containing this method. Let's call it `Calculator`. Then, if `calculator` is an instance of `Calculator`, `calculator.add(4,5)` should return `9`. Once you save your test and try to compile it, you'll discover that there's a problem. Your code won't compile. Your next step is now clear.
4. Write just enough code so that your test compiles. You need to make sure there is a `Calculator` class and that it contains an `add()` method that takes two `int`s and returns an `int`. What may be difficult at this point is that you aren't trying to write the code that does everything it needs to do. At this point `add()` could just return the integer `-3`. This doesn't happen to be the correct answer, but it will help your code compile. Once it compiles you move on.
5. Your test should be failing at this point. There are simple cases in which just adding a constructor will enable your test to pass. In most cases, there will be a middle ground where your code compiles but the test fails.
6. Now write just enough code to make your test pass. In this example with `add()`, it should just return the sum of the two `int`s passed in. You may be tempted to

take care of other issues, but you need to stay focused on your current goal, which is to pass the test.

7. Look for the next test you have to write. Go back to step 2 and consider whether there are more tests that have to be written to make sure that you have achieved your small step. You don't need to test every case. You don't need to add two positive `ints`, a positive and a negative, and so on.
8. Now return to step (1) and continue with the next small step. Now you see that you've been in a nested loop all along. You can refactor code at any point of the process if you need to. The best time to refactor code is after it passes all of the tests.

You'll work through actual code examples in the rest of the chapter to see how this process comes together. The key is not to do more at any step then you need.

THE RULES OF LIFE

John Conway's *Game of Life* takes place on an infinite grid with square cells. Each cell has as neighbors the eight cells that touch it. At time zero, you can set up the board in any state you wish and start the game. The state of the board at each discrete point in time is determined by the state of the board at the previous time by the following rules:

- A live cell stays alive only if it has two or three live neighbors, otherwise it dies.
- A dead cell comes to life only if it has three live neighbors, otherwise it remains dead.

These are also sometimes listed as three rules.

- A cell with two live neighbors remains in the same state.
- A cell with three live neighbors will be alive in the next period of time.
- A cell with fewer than two live neighbors dies of loneliness and with more than three dies of overcrowding.

There are many variations on this game. Some are played on a finite board with different rules for dealing with the edges. Some are played on a board with different shaped cells and different rules for life or death. In this example, assume that the board is a 30 by 40 cell rectangle and that you identify the left and right edges and the top and bottom edges. In other words if you are traveling across the third row from right to left and fall off the end of the board, you will reenter on the right side of the board still in the third row. (Some may recognize this as the torus identification.)

In each time period, you will visit each cell in the board twice. There are other ways to implement this game, but this will do for the example. The first time you visit a cell you will check to see if it will change in the next time period. The second time you visit a cell you will change it if it needs changing. You can implement this in a single pass but then you have to be careful that cells that change don't change the information of neighboring cells before the neighboring cells decide whether or not they need to change. You can also implement this so that not all cells must be visited in each pass. Again, this nicety is beyond the needs of this example.

SETTING UP JUNIT

The tool you'll use for running the unit tests that you'll be writing throughout this course is JUnit. JUnit is an open source-testing framework for Java programmers originally created by Kent Beck and Erich Gamma. You can find out more about the project, download the latest version of the software, and investigate extensions and alternatives to JUnit at www.junit.org.

Using JUnit is as simple as downloading the zip file and unzipping it. There really is nothing to install. Commercial Integrated Development Environments (IDEs) such as Borland's JBuilder and IntelliJ's IDEA, as well as open-source IDEs such as Eclipse and Netbeans have integrated JUnit into their environment. When you use one of these tools, after setting application-specific project properties, you can usually run your test suite automatically. Even without such tools, JUnit has been designed to facilitate the automatic running of a suite of tests. Read the examples and articles that are included in the download of www.junit.org and you will be well on your way. The JavaDocs for JUnit are also included in the download.

As you begin a new project you need to provide some basic structure for running your suite of tests. The basic structure is generally the same on each project. Once it is in place, you can concentrate on adding tests and writing the code that passes them. In the following section you'll look at the specifics of setting up the basic structure you'll need.

Setting Up the Infrastructure

You will create a suite of tests that in turn call other suites of tests or classes that extend the JUnit class `junit.framework.TestCase`. The classes that extend `TestCase` will contain a number of tests that will be described in the section titled *Extending TestCase*.

For now, create a class named `AllTests` in the top level of your package hierarchy. In this example, you'll create a package called `life` and inside of it a class called `AllTests`. For those who are not familiar with working with packages, this means that you will create a directory named `life`. Inside this directory, you will create a file named `AllTests.java` with the following code.

```
package life;

import junit.framework.Test;
import junit.framework.TestSuite;

public class AllTests {
  public static void main (String[] args) {
    junit.textui.TestRunner.run (suite());
  }
  public static Test suite ( ) {
    TestSuite suite= new TestSuite("All JUnit Tests");
    return suite;
  }
}
```

The method `suite()` will be where you link to your other suites or test classes. For now, `suite()` doesn't call anything. You just call the `TestSuite` constructor. Later you will add `TestCase` classes or other suites to the `TestSuite` that you are calling `suite`. This does requires that you add the two import statements at this point to import the `Test` interface and `TestSuite` class that implements this interface.

The method `main()` can be used to run your test suite using the text-based TestRunner. In the next section, *Running a Suite*, you'll see how you might run `AllTests`. First, you'll need to compile `AllTests.java`. You'll need to include the `junit.jar` file in the classpath when you compile and when you run `AllTests`. From just outside of the `life` directory compile `AllTests` using the following command.

```
javac -classpath <junit.jar's classpath> life/AllTests.java
```

The code should compile at this point. If it doesn't you may have to add `:.` to the end of the classpath to point to your current directory on a UNIX-based machine or `;.` to the end of the classpath to point to your current directory on a machine using Windows.

Running a Suite

It may seem premature to run the suite. It doesn't do anything yet. The key in test-first design is to compile and run the tests very frequently. The more often you run the tests, the easier it will be for you to track down mistakes. The difference between the code that passed all of the tests the last time you ran them and the code that is currently failing tests must be the code you've written since the last time you ran the tests. The more frequently you run the tests, the more certain you can be of where the problem lies.

You could easily say that there are no tests to run and you'd be right. However, if you wait you won't know if it's the initial setup that's wrong or if it's the test code you'll be adding. Run the tests.

There is a variety of ways to run the tests. As `AllTests` contains a main() you can just run AllTests from the command line.

```
java -classpath <junit.jar's classpath> life/AllTests
```

As was the case when you were compiling, if this doesn't run you may have to add `:.` to the end of the classpath on a UNIX-based machine or `;.` to the end of the classpath on a Windows-based machine. If it runs successfully you should see an indication of how much time it took and a message that reads something like `O.K. (0 tests)`.

You can also run the tests using one of JUnit's GUI test runners. From the command line, from just outside of the life directory, you would enter the following command.

```
java -classpath <junit.jar's classpath> junit.swingui.TestRunner
life/AllTests.java
```

This time you are running the application with `main()` method in the class `junit.swingui.TestRunner` and passing it the argument `life/AllTests.java`. If this is your preference, then you can eliminate the `main()` method from `AllTests.java`.

You've heard about the green bar that you get when your tests pass. You may feel a bit cheated at this point because there is no bar at all. Then again, there are no test cases to pass or fail either. As you add test cases, you will either get a green or red bar.

As mentioned before, many IDEs have integrated support for JUnit. Most that do allow you to choose whether you want to use the GUI or text-based test runners. Many IDEs also offer their own test runner, which presents the results of running JUnit differently from the standard offerings.

CREATING YOUR FIRST TEST

The following is our plan for setting up the first test. Begin by creating a class called `TestCell` that extends `junit.framework.TestCase`. You'll add a pointer from AllTests and your test suite fails. Things will seem to get worse before they get better. If you try to add a method that specifies an actual test, your code won't even compile. Your test refers to a class that doesn't exist yet. Even if the class existed, the methods your test is calling in the class haven't been written yet. Next, stub out the class and get your code to compile. Again, your test will fail. Write just enough code to get the test to pass. Once the test passes you can take another look at your code and decide if you need to do any refactoring.

Extending TestCase

Create a subdirectory of the life directory called model. Inside model, create a new file called `TestCell.java` containing the following code.

```
package life.model;

import junit.framework.TestCase;

public class TestCell extends TestCase{
}
```

You will use this basic template for all of your classes that will contain the actual tests. They will all extend `junit.framework.TestCase`. If you are using a version of JUnit prior to the 3.8 release, your class will also require a constructor like this.

```
public TestCell(String name){
    super(name);
  }
```

In any case, you will then create methods for running various tests. These methods will have the following signature:

```
public void test <name of test here>();
```

JUnit uses reflection to run any method that begins with the name test. For each testxxx method JUnit calls the method setUp() followed by testxxx() followed by tearDown(). This allows you to put code in the body of setUp() that initializes variables and sets up the fixture the way you want. If you need different set-ups for your tests, create a new class that extends TestCase. The tearDown() method is similarly used to clean up changes you've made to the environment so that test results don't interfere with each other. You can explicitly call the test methods and not use reflection if that is a requirement.

Add the line highlighted below to the suite() method in AllTests.

```
public static Test suite ( ) {
    TestSuite suite= new TestSuite("All JUnit Tests");
    suite.addTest( new TestSuite( life.model.TestCell.class ) );
    return suite;
}
```

This addition adds the contents of the class TestCell to this TestSuite so that the tests you add to TestCell will be run as part of this suite. Save and compile AllTests.java and TestCell.java. Run AllTests whichever way appeals to you. Perhaps to your surprise, you get the message that there is one failure. If you're using the GUI test runner you'll encounter your first red bar. You are given the helpful message that the cause of the failure is that there are no tests in the class TestCell. This is a relief. You knew there weren't any tests yet. You'll actually come to appreciate seeing the test suite fail before it passes—this let's you know that the mechanism is working. In this case, you know that running AllTests actually does cause TestCell to be called.

Where Do Tests Come From?

Test first is a great practice whether or not you are doing XP. If you are doing XP then you are writing tests to accomplish the next step in a task. A task is a developer-defined component of completing a user story. Perhaps you have a user story like this.

Initialize Board

The board will consist of a rectangular grid of square cells. Each cell has as its neighbors the eight cells that border it in any way. A cell is initially dead.

Then maybe one of your tasks is:

Initialize Cell (Task for Initialize Board)

Create a cell that is initially dead and has links to its eight neighbors.

Your first step may be to create a `Cell` object that is initially dead. You'll write the test for this and then write the code in a minute. In order to concentrate on different issues in test-first programming, the sequence in this chapter does not follow a set of tasks to be completed. For each step, however, you can imagine the task that underlies the example being presented.

Writing Your Test

Start by writing a simple test. Create a new `Cell` object and then check to make sure that the newly created `Cell` isn't alive. Give your test method a descriptive name because if it fails the error message containing the method name will help you locate what's going wrong. You could write the first test method in `TestCell` like this.

```
public void testNewCellIsDead(){
  Cell cell = new Cell();
  assertTrue(!cell.isAlive());
}
```

When you try to compile this code you will get compiler errors that indicate that `Cell` is an unknown type and that `isAlive()` is an unknown method. Of course, they're unknown; you haven't created them yet. You have correctly written code that tries to create a new `Cell` object even though you know that the class used to construct such an object doesn't exist yet. In writing this test you've made some decisions about what the `Cell` object looks like. You know that it has a no argument constructor and contains a method named `isAlive()` that returns a `boolean`.

The `assertTrue()` method that you used in `testNewCellIsDead()` is provided in the junit.framework.Assert class. Check the JUnit JavaDocs for the full list of assert-like methods that are available to you. Most are named `assertTrue()`, `assertEquals()`, `assertNull()`, `assertNotNull()`, or `assertSame()`. `Assert` is the parent class to `TestCase`.

Getting It to Compile

What's the least that you can do to get the code to compile? You need to create a class named `Cell`. Inside of the model directory create `Cell.java` containing the following code:

```
package life.model;
public class Cell {
}
```

Save your work and recompile the project. You may notice that the test code still can't compile. You're right, but take small steps.

The compile fails because `Cell` doesn't contain an `isAlive()` method yet. Add this code to `Cell` now.

```
protected boolean isAlive(){
    return true;
}
```

The code compiles. As soon as code compiles, run your tests. This process has to become habitual. Save, compile, run the tests. The test fails. You get an `AssertionFailedError`. Your test expected `cell.isAlive()` to be false in this case. Your next task is to get the test to pass.

Getting It to Pass

If the goal is to get the test to pass, the easiest way would be to just return `false` instead of `true` from `isAlive()`. Try that. Save, compile, and run the test suite. The test passes. This hardly feels satisfying.

Maybe what's needed is another test that forces a better solution. Add this test to the `TestCell` class.

```
public void testLiveCellIsAlive(){
  Cell cell = new Cell();
  cell.setAlive(true);
  assertTrue(cell.isAlive());
}
```

Here you create a new `Cell` and set it to be alive and then check that it is alive. Save and compile and you see that it won't compile. Add the `setAlive()` method to the `Cell` class. The simplest version does nothing for now.

```
protected void setAlive(boolean alive){
}
```

The code compiles but the new test fails. The methods `setAlive()` and `getAlive()` are obviously accessors, so introduce the `boolean alive` and rewrite the body of the methods. Cell.java now looks like this.

```
package life.model;

public class Cell {
  private boolean alive;

  protected void setAlive(boolean alive){
    this.alive = alive;
  }

  protected boolean isAlive(){
    return alive;
  }
}
```

Save, compile, and run the tests. Both tests pass. Look around to see if any code needs to be cleaned up.

Look Around for Refactoring

There isn't much code so there isn't much to clean up. The `Cell` class looks pretty good. Refactoring can be as simple as changing the name of a method or variable. If you feel the need, go ahead and change one of the names. If you change the variable alive, you will also have to change references to it. Similarly, if you change the names of the accessor methods you will have to change the references to them.

You can, however, benefit from refactoring the `TestCell` class. In each of your test methods you have declared and initialized a `Cell` object. Instead, create an instance variable and initialize it in the `setUp()` method as follows:

```
package life.model;

import junit.framework.TestCase;

public class TestCell extends TestCase{
```

```
    Cell cell;

    protected void setUp() {
      cell = new Cell();
    }

    public void testNewCellIsDead(){
      assertTrue(!cell.isAlive());
    }

    public void testLiveCellIsAlive(){
      cell.setAlive(true);
      assertTrue(cell.isAlive());
    }
  }
```

This removes duplicated code and makes sure that we've initialized the `cell` variable before running each test. Refactoring does not have to be grand and dramatic. You've made a small change that will make future tests easier to add. Your test code may end up being twice as long as your production code. You'll need to keep your test code clean so that it can be easily understood.

Take a quick look back at what you've done. You started with a simple test: when a cell is created verify that it is dead. By writing this test you helped shape the code being tested. A second test kept you honest. Now that those two tests were passing you looked to see if you could clean up your code. This clean up applied to both the production code and to the test code. You worked in small steps and began to feel the rhythm of save, compile, and run the tests.

WRITING MORE TESTS

Be wary of times when you choose not to test first. You will think of a new really easy feature to implement and just want to write the code without the tests. You should resist this impulse for three reasons. First, your accuracy in judging what is easy may not be consistently reliable. Second, having the test code will allow you to refactor with confidence. Third, long after you've forgotten about what you were thinking when you wrote this code, someone will come along and break what you've done. If you have a test in place then, assuming that they run the tests before they check their code in, they will know immediately that they've broken your code and will know where to look. It is easier to write the tests as you go and you will write better code if you write the tests first.

Checking for Changes in Live Cells

So far, you've written code that allows `Cell` objects to be initialized and set to be alive or dead. Now you can write the algorithm for getting from this time period to the next. Start with a test. You know that a live cell with two or three live neighbors will stay alive in the next time period, otherwise it will die. Here is a sequence of tests you could write for this case.

```
public void testLiveCellWithTwoLiveNeighborsStaysAlive(){
    cell.setAlive(true);
    for (int i = 0; i <2; i++){
      cell.incrementNumberOfLiveNeighbors();
    }
    assertTrue(!cell.needsToChange());
  }

  public void testLiveCellWithThreeLiveNeighborsStaysAlive(){
    cell.setAlive(true);
    for (int i = 0; i <3; i++){
      cell.incrementNumberOfLiveNeighbors();
    }
    assertTrue(!cell.needsToChange());
  }

  public void testLiveCellWithFourLiveNeighborsDies(){
    cell.setAlive(true);
    for (int i = 0; i <4; i++){
      cell.incrementNumberOfLiveNeighbors();
    }
    assertTrue(cell.needsToChange());
  }

  public void testLiveCellWithOneLiveNeighborsDies(){
    cell.setAlive(true);
    cell.incrementNumberOfLiveNeighbors();
    assertTrue(cell.needsToChange());
  }
```

Of course, you would write these tests one at a time and get them to compile and pass. You could write more tests but this is a representative bunch that you hope will cover enough of your cases. Add these four tests to `TestCell` and you'll find that it doesn't compile. You need to define the methods `incrementNumberOfLiveNeighbors()` and `needsToChange()` in `Cell`. The intent of `incrementNumberOfLiveNeighbors()` is to increase this particular cell object's count of its live neighbors. Introduce an instance variable of type `int` called `numberOfLiveNeighbors` and let the body of `incrementNumberOfLiveNeighbors()` increase the value of `numberOfLiveNeighbors` by one. The method `needsToChange()` needs to return false for a live cell with two or three neighbors and true otherwise.

Here's the code for `Cell` including an accessor method for `numberOfLiveNeighbors`.

```
package life.model;

public class Cell {
  private boolean alive;
  private int numberOfLiveNeighbors;

  protected void setAlive(boolean alive){
    this.alive = alive;
  }
```

```
  protected boolean isAlive(){
    return alive;
  }

  protected void incrementNumberOfLiveNeighbors(){
    numberOfLiveNeighbors++;
  }

  protected int getNumberOfLiveNeighbors(){
    return numberOfLiveNeighbors;
  }

  protected boolean needsToChange(){
    if (isAlive() &&
       (getNumberOfLiveNeighbors()==3 ||
        getNumberOfLiveNeighbors()==2) ) return false;
    else return true;
  }
}
```

Save, compile, and run the tests and you'll see that all six of the tests pass. Look at the `needsToChange()` method. It only works for live cells. It can't possibly work for dead cells because it always returns true for them. This is a recurring theme. Don't write the logic for the more complicated case because you don't yet have an official need for the harder case. When you have that need, you will have tests to help you keep on track.

Check for Changes in Dead Cells

You can come up with analogous test cases for dead cells. Add these four tests to

```
TestCell.
public void testDeadCellWithTwoLiveNeighborsStaysDead(){
    for (int i = 0; i <2; i++){
      cell.incrementNumberOfLiveNeighbors();
    }
    assertTrue(!cell.needsToChange());
  }

  public void testDeadCellWithThreeLiveNeighborsLives(){
    for (int i = 0; i <3; i++){
      cell.incrementNumberOfLiveNeighbors();
    }
    assertTrue(cell.needsToChange());
  }

  public void testDeadCellWithFourLiveNeighborsStaysDead(){
    for (int i = 0; i <4; i++){
      cell.incrementNumberOfLiveNeighbors();
    }
    assertTrue(!cell.needsToChange());
  }

  public void testDeadCellWithOneLiveNeighborsStaysDead(){
```

```
        cell.incrementNumberOfLiveNeighbors();
        assertTrue(!cell.needsToChange());
    }
```

The code compiles with these additions, but three of the four tests fail. Change `Cell` accordingly. Here's the new version of `needsToChange()`.

```
protected boolean needsToChange(){
    if (getNumberOfLiveNeighbors()==2) return false;
    else if (isAlive()) {
      if (getNumberOfLiveNeighbors()==3  ) return false;
      else return true;
    } else if (getNumberOfLiveNeighbors()==3) return true;
    else return false;
}
```

Run the tests and you'll see that all ten of them are now passing.

What You Don't Have

You don't have an exhaustive set of tests and you probably won't need them. A comprehensive test suite would require eighteen tests to check the behavior of live and dead cells with zero to eight neighbors. What you have instead, is a representative collection of tests. You have tests that check what happens when live cells have one, two, three, or four neighbors. Testing both one and four may be excessive but it allows you to check that live cells can die from loneliness and from overcrowding even though the resulting `needsToChange()` method lumps these cases together. You may be tempted to check for zero, five, six, seven, and eight neighbors. At this point that would be overkill and wouldn't add anything. If later you notice errant behavior you may come back to add more tests. You weren't forced to alter the logic of `needsToChange()` until you also tested what happens to dead cells with one, two, three, or four neighbors. In checking for changes, you have a representative set of tests.

You also don't have a running application. You can't start up your Game of Life and see some shell running. This may seem contrary to your experience. Usually you get some part of your application working and then you run it to make sure that it is correct. In this case, what would you look at? You haven't even thought about the GUI yet. Even so, you have a lot of confidence that this corner of your application works as needed. You've produced one class containing thirty-two lines of production code and two classes containing ninety-eight lines of test code. Although the division does not need to be this dramatic, you should be concerned if you have more classes than test methods.

ALLOWING CELLS TO CHANGE

At this point, you may be tempted to add a GUI. Try to delay creating your GUI until the model is a little more complete. Sure, you can go ahead, create your GUI, and later refactor it; but the fear is that you'll put too much functionality in your GUI. Your goal is to make the user interface as thin as possible. The client prioritization of user stories will drive the order in which you add functionality. For the purposes of this example, let's next add the ability for a live cell to die and for a dead cell to come alive.

The Test Cases

You want to choose a representative set of test cases. You know that `needsToChange()` is working properly. You only need to check that a live cell that needs to change does and a live cell that doesn't need to change doesn't. Similarly, check for proper behavior in a dead cell that needs to change and one that doesn't. You can add this check to your existing tests. Change `testLiveCellWithTwoLiveNeighborsStaysAlive()` as highlighted below.

```
public void testLiveCellWithTwoLiveNeighborsStaysAlive(){
    cell.setAlive(true);
    for (int i = 0; i <2; i++){
      cell.incrementNumberOfLiveNeighbors();
    }
    assertTrue(!cell.needsToChange());
    cell.change();
    assertTrue(cell.isAlive());
  }
```

This won't compile because `Cell` doesn't contain a `change()` method. Add the following method to `Cell`.

```
protected void change(){
}
```

The code now compiles and the tests all pass. So, you've handled the case where nothing is supposed to happen. Now change `testLiveCellWithOneLiveNeighbor-Dies()` as highlighted below.

```
public void testLiveCellWithOneLiveNeighborsDies(){
    cell.setAlive(true);
    cell.incrementNumberOfLiveNeighbors();
    assertTrue(cell.needsToChange());
    cell.change();
    assertTrue(!cell.isAlive());
  }
```

The code compiles but the test fails. Change the `change()` method like this.

```
protected void change(){
    if (needsToChange()) setAlive(!isAlive());
}
```

The tests pass. Change two tests for dead cells to confirm that the code behaves correctly. Here are the adjusted tests.

```
public void testDeadCellWithThreeLiveNeighborsLives(){
    for (int i = 0; i <3; i++){
      cell.incrementNumberOfLiveNeighbors();
    }
    assertTrue(cell.needsToChange());
    cell.change();
    assertTrue(cell.isAlive());
  }

  public void testDeadCellWithOneLiveNeighborsStaysDead(){
    cell.incrementNumberOfLiveNeighbors();
    assertTrue(!cell.needsToChange());
    cell.change();
    assertTrue(!cell.isAlive());
  }
```

They compile and all tests pass.

Refactoring

As an illustration of how you might refactor at this point, notice that the `change()` method calls `needsToChange()`. This means that when you poll all of the cells to see if they need to change and then you come back to tell the cells that need to change to go ahead and do so, at that point you're asking them whether they need to change. Instead, refactor to store the information of whether or not a change is needed in a private boolean named `changeNeeded`. Alter the `needsToChange()` method like this.

```
private boolean changeNeeded;
protected boolean needsToChange(){
  changeNeeded = false;
  if (isAlive() ){
    if  (getNumberOfLiveNeighbors() !=2 &&
          getNumberOfLiveNeighbors() !=3){
      changeNeeded = true;
    }
  } else if (getNumberOfLiveNeighbors()==3)
    changeNeeded = true;
  return changeNeeded;
}
```

The code compiles and the tests pass. Now you can refactor the `change()` method to check the results of `needsToChange()` on the previous polling of cells.

```
protected void change(){
   if (changeNeeded) setAlive(!isAlive());
 }
```

The code compiles and the tests run. At this point, you may want to change the return type of `needsToChange()` to void and introduce an accessor method, `getChangeNeeded()`. This would require refactoring the tests. It's probably a bit cleaner because `needsToChange()` would then do what its name suggests and `getChangeNeeded()` would be used to find the status of the result.

In addition, as one reviewer noted, this particular refactoring may be viewed as dangerous because we've introduced the instance variable `changeNeeded`, whose significance is temporary. More appropriate examples of refactorings are included in the Refactoring tutorial in Chapter 13. Rather than continue with this path, let's look at the GUI for a `Cell`.

TESTING GUIs

Before discussing how you might introduce tests for the GUI for the Game of Life, consider how you might have tested this application in the past. You might have coded enough to get the game running and tested it with different configurations to see if everything seems to be behaving properly. In a small application like this one you could probably get away with that strategy. In the Game of Life, there are certain patterns that have well-known behavior. For example, suppose your initial board configuration has three live cells: one cell somewhere in the middle of the board along with the cell immediately to its right and the cell immediately to its left. In the next time period, the middle cell will remain alive while the right and left cells will die. In addition, the cells immediately above and below the center cell will come to life. In other words, the horizontal row of three live cells will be replaced by a vertical row of three live cells with the same center. This so-called "Blinker" pattern will repeat. This is a nice visual test. Start with the horizontal row and you should see this oscillating pattern. The test first idea is that you don't want to have to wait that long to see if your application is behaving properly. If you have to wait that long, you will then have to search for where the errors are. In test first, you have a pretty good idea where the problem lies and can begin working on the problem instead of spending a great deal of time locating it. You'll need to keep your GUI thin and continue to write automated tests.

A Second Extension to TestCase

Create a new subdirectory of `life` called `gui`. In it put `TestCellPanel.java` with the following code.

```
package life.gui;

import junit.framework.TestCase;

public class TestCellPanel extends TestCase {
}
```

You'll also need to add the following line to the `suite()` method in `AllTests` so that the tests in `TestCellPanel` are called.

```
suite.addTest(new TestSuite(life.gui.TestCellPanel.class));
```

Save, compile, and run the tests. You'll get a failure that lets you know that everything's okay. The test runner is complaining that `TestCellPanel` doesn't contain any tests. It doesn't, but the warning let's you know that `TestCellPanel` was successfully added to the suite of tests being run. Next, you'll add tests.

Tests for Cell's GUI

What do you want to test for the component that provides the GUI for a `Cell` object? Suppose you use a `JPanel` for this component. What do you need to test? If you set the background color using `setBackground()` you don't really need to check that it's been set. You shouldn't need to check that the properties and methods inherited from `JPanel` have been correctly implemented.

You also don't need to see the GUI to test it. You want the testing process to be as automated as possible. You don't want to have to dismiss windows or click buttons and check for the results every time you run the test suite. This means that you don't have to create some sort of `JFrame` that holds a `BoardPanel` that in turn holds a grid full of `CellPanel` objects. You just need to begin by creating a single `CellPanel` and by testing its functionality. At some point you will need to see the GUI to make sure that it looks the way you want it to. This isn't a process that you can automate with testing and you want to have the tests in place first so that you can be sure that your adjustments to the look of the GUI aren't breaking any tests.

Start, as you did for `Cell`, by testing that a newly created `CellPanel` object is off. The test might look like this.

```
public void testNewCellPanelIsOff(){
  CellPanel cellPanel = new CellPanel();
  assertTrue(!cellPanel.isOn());
}
```

This won't compile. Create a `CellPanel` class that extends `JPanel` and provide it with an `isOn()` method that returns a `boolean`.

```
package life.gui;

import javax.swing.JPanel;

public class CellPanel extends JPanel {

  protected boolean isOn() {
    return false;
  }

}
```

The code now compiles and the tests pass. For a next test, let's create a CellPanel and then turn on the associated Cell and make sure the CellPanel reflects the change. Refactor your test code by introducing a `setUp()` method along with the new `test.AnAliveCellPanelIsOn()` method. The new TestCellPanel class looks like this.

```
package life.gui;

import junit.framework.TestCase;

public class TestCellPanel extends TestCase {
```

```
  CellPanel cellPanel;

  public TestCellPanel(String name){
    super(name);
  }

  protected void setUp(){
    cellPanel = new CellPanel();
  }

  public void testNewCellPanelIsOff(){
    assertTrue(!cellPanel.isOn());
  }

  public void testAnAliveCellPanelIsOn(){
    cellPanel.getCell().setAlive(true);
    assertTrue(cellPanel.isOn());
  }

}
```

This won't compile. You have to write a `getCell()` method. To pass the tests you'll have to fix the `isOn()` method. Here's one possible solution. Note that you've had to add a constructor along with an instance variable to hold a handle to the `Cell` object. If you haven't worked much with packages, it may not have occurred to you that you need to add an import statement to import `life.model.Cell` as it isn't visible from `life.gui.CellPanel`. The changes to CellPanel.java are as follows.

```
package life.gui;

import life.model.Cell;

import javax.swing.JPanel;

public class CellPanel extends JPanel {
  private final Cell cell;

  public CellPanel(){
    cell = new Cell();
  }

  protected boolean isOn() {
    if (cell.isAlive()) return true;
    else return false;
  }

  protected Cell getCell(){
    return cell;
  }

}
```

This still won't compile. One solution is to change the access of the `isAlive()` and `setAlive()` methods in `Cell` to public because they are being called from outside of the `life.model` package.

Testing Communication from Cell to CellPanel

This still isn't setting any visible properties in the CellPanel. You can amend the tests to require that the CellPanel changes colors.

```
public void testNewCellPanelIsOff(){
  assertTrue(!cellPanel.isOn());
  assertEquals(cellPanel.getBackground(),cellPanel.DEAD_COLOR);
}

public void testAnAliveCellPanelIsOn(){
  cellPanel.getCell().setAlive(true);
  assertTrue(cellPanel.isOn());
  assertEquals(cellPanel.getBackground(),cellPanel.LIVE_COLOR);
}
```

As you may have come to expect, this code requires many changes in `CellPanel`.

```
package life.gui;

import life.model.Cell;

import javax.swing.JPanel;
import java.awt.Color;

public class CellPanel extends JPanel {

  private final Cell cell;
  private boolean on;
  public static final Color DEAD_COLOR = Color.white;
  public static final Color LIVE_COLOR = Color.black;

  public CellPanel(){
    cell = new Cell();
  }

  protected boolean isOn() {
    setOn(cell.isAlive());
    return on;
  }

  protected Cell getCell(){
    return cell;
  }

  public void setOn(boolean on){
    this.on = on;
    if (on) setBackground(LIVE_COLOR);
    else setBackground(DEAD_COLOR);
  }

}
```

The tests all pass, but once again this solution doesn't feel satisfying. The isOn() method shouldn't have to poll cell. The cell object should notify the corresponding

CellPanel of any changes. You may recognize this as the Observer design pattern. eXtreme Programming practitioners use design patterns, UML, or anything else that happens to solve the problem without introducing unnecessary overhead. When it is appropriate to introduce a design pattern that simplifies your task, go ahead and use it. You may also be coding along and just recognize that you're in the middle of refactoring toward a design pattern. Renaming classes and methods to communicate this fact may help those reading your code. You can find more information on this topic of refactoring toward design patterns on Joshua Kerievsky's web site http://industriallogic.com.Surprisingly few changes have to be made to the existing code to make this work. In the CellPanel class change the body of the constructor to this.

```
cell = new Cell( this );
```

You are giving cell a way to communicate back with this CellPanel. Second remove the line setOn (`cell.isAlive()`); from the `isOn()` method. There are also a few changes that need to be made in Cell. You need to add two constructors, a CellPanel variable, and change `setAlive()` to reflect the changes in the GUI. Here are the changes to Cell.

```
package life.model;

import life.gui.CellPanel;

public class Cell {
  private boolean alive;
  private CellPanel cellPanel;
  private int numberOfLiveNeighbors;
  private boolean changeNeeded;

  public Cell(){
    cellPanel = new CellPanel();
  }

  public Cell(CellPanel cellPanel){
    this.cellPanel = cellPanel;
  }

  public void setAlive(boolean alive){
    this.alive = alive;
    cellPanel.setOn(alive);
  } //rest of class omitted as nothing changes
}
```

The code compiles, the tests run.

Testing Communication from CellPanel to Cell

Suppose we have a story that allows the user to click on a cell in the GUI to toggle its state. `CellPanel` is also used to send messages to `Cell`. You want to make sure that when the user clicks on a `CellPanel` the change is reflected in the corresponding `Cell`. This example is used to demonstrate how you might write a unit test for validating the result of clicking on a particular `CellPanel`. Add the following tests to TestCellPanel.java:

```
public void testClickOnDeadCellTurnsItAlive(){
  assertTrue(!cellPanel.isOn());
  cellPanel.dispatchEvent (
    new MouseEvent(cellPanel,MouseEvent.MOUSE_CLICKED,
      0,MouseEvent.BUTTON1_MASK,0,0,1,false));
  assertTrue(cellPanel.isOn());
}

public void testClickOnLiveCellTurnsItDead(){
  cellPanel.getCell().setAlive(true);
  assertTrue(cellPanel.isOn());
  cellPanel.dispatchEvent (
    new MouseEvent(cellPanel,MouseEvent.MOUSE_CLICKED,
      0,MouseEvent.BUTTON1_MASK,0,0,1,false));
  assertTrue(!cellPanel.isOn());
}
```

You'll also need to add the following import statement.

```
import java.awt.event.MouseEvent;
```

In the first test you verify that the `CellPanel` object is not on. You then send a mouse clicked event to the `CellPanel` object and check that the result is that the `CellPanel` object is now on. The mouse click has to result in the `Cell` object being updated, which in turn results in the `CellPanel` object being updated. This is the sequence as described in the Gang of Four description of the Observer pattern. (Note that the *Design Patterns* book written by Gamma, Helm, Johnson, and Vlissides is commonly referred to as the "Gang of Four" book.) As you might expect, the code compiles but nothing happens. You need to add a `MouseListener` of some sort to `CellPanel`. Here are the changes to CellPanel.java.

```
package life.gui;

import java.awt.event.MouseAdapter;
import java.awt.event.MouseEvent;

// unchanged code omitted ...

public CellPanel(){
  cell = new Cell(this);
  this.addMouseListener(new ClickHandler());
}

  // more code omitted ...

public class ClickHandler extends MouseAdapter{
  public void mouseClicked(MouseEvent e){
    cell.setAlive(!cell.isAlive());
  }
```

```
}

// still more code omitted...
```

If you were familiar with this pattern, you may have been tempted to dive right in and start writing code. Write the tests first, take small steps, and your code will be more robust.

A LOOK BACK

It is difficult to test first all of the time. Even devoted XPers will try to just knock some code out once in a while. For the most part, they end up regretting it. Ron Jeffries is kind enough to own up to this publicly in *Extreme Programming Installed*, but everyone does it.

What happens when you notice yourself coding without tests is important. It's like quietly meditating while trying not to let your mind wander. At some point your mind wanders. The strategy is to notice your mind wandering and return to meditating. What often happens is that you will berate yourself for letting your mind wander and now you are on a path further from your goal. When you notice yourself not testing, return to testing. Programming as part of a vigilant pair will help keep you from wandering. A partner need not be a testing master to observe that you've started coding without tests and to suggest that you form your test before proceeding.

Do not test everything. Only test code that can break. In the running example you wrote code that ended up testing accessors. This was because the methods existed before they became accessors for a variable. If you had started with a variable `xxx` and methods `getXxx()` and `setXxx()` there would be little need to write tests to make certain the accessors were working properly.

The key to test-first programming is to take very small steps where nothing could go wrong. Fix what does go wrong. Move on. If you've followed the example in this chapter, you've already begun to feel good when the tests all pass. Maybe you've even come to see compiler messages and unit test messages as helping you fix your code.

EXERCISES

1. Just before moving on to test the GUI it was suggested that you change the return type of `needsToChange()` to void and introduce an accessor method `getChangeNeeded()`. This would require refactoring the tests. It's probably a bit cleaner because `needsToChange()` would then do what its name suggests and `getChangeNeeded()` would be used to find the status of the result. Complete that refactoring.
2. You've seen tests that verify that live or dead cell that gain between one and four live neighbors behave properly. Add a test to show that a live cell with two live neighbors dies when one of its neighbors dies. Create a method called `mournNewDepartedNeighbor()`.
3. Each cell should have eight neighbors that it can update when it changes state. Add this facility. Create the tests first.

Chapter 11

User Stories—Exploring with the Customer

You're sitting in a theatre engrossed in an off-Broadway musical that follows programmers as they pair together on an eXtreme Programming (XP) project. In the climactic moment, the actor playing the client comes in to make an important announcement. Unfortunately, you can't hear it because the cell phone belonging to the man in front of you starts to ring. The play ends and you realize you'll never know whether the client was happy with the deliverables or not. You fume because there's nothing much you can do. You know you'll end up complaining to your friends about how rude people in theatres can be. On the way home, your mind replays the scene. In your imagination, you file a complaint with the cell-phone task force.

The task force immediately dispatches a sketch artist named Stanley, who asks you to describe the man who disturbed you. You say, "He was about forty years old, he had light brown hair, and he was follicly challenged." Stanley looks puzzled until you clarify: "balding." (In your daydream, you're pretty witty.) Stanley asks you to describe the shape of the criminal's head. You remember that it was long and thin. Stanley asks, "What about the nose?" Now it's your turn to look puzzled. Stanley flips to a page in his book where a dozen basic nose styles are displayed. You point and say, "Like that one, only there was a bend in the middle." Stanley sketches a bit and asks you if that's right. You say kind of, but the nostrils were a bit bigger. This session could go on quite a while, but you are jolted awake as you find yourself back home.

This dynamic between the aggrieved theatre goer and the sketch artist is the same as that between the client and the development team when user stories are first described. The client needs the help of the development team to turn the image of what the application should look like into a realistic sketch. The developers know what many of the options are, but they can't know the option that matches what the client sees. An experienced client may be able to write user stories alone, but most will need help. The client describes the application they want to the developer, and the developer asks questions and provides options to help the client with the description.

Just as the mouth that the sketch artist draws can not possibly be correct down to the last detail, the user stories that the client ends up with aren't legally binding agreements. The sketch allows the victim to say, "Yes, that looks like the man that answered his cell phone." The user stories allow the client to say, "Yes, that is what I want the application to do." The sketch artist shouldn't say to the victim, "No, the mouth looked more like this." In the same way, the development team shouldn't say to the client, "No, you really want the application to behave like this."

In this chapter, you'll listen in on a conversation between a developer and a client trying to come up with an initial set of user stories. This conversation is based on a real project with a real client for an XP software engineering class. In this case, the client was Dwight Olson, the chair of the Mathematics and Computer Science department at John Carroll University. The user stories mentioned in this chapter were actually used by the development team as they worked on this project. Because real conversations aren't as directed as examples need to be, this fictionalized account combines two meetings held early in the semester. You've been cast in the role of the developer. To give you an in-depth view of this process, you'll see all of the initial stories that came out of these two meetings.

BEFORE THE FIRST MEETING

Your role in the first meeting is similar to that of a reporter. You are interested in the story that the customer has to tell, but you need to help the customer get it into a form that makes sense to your readers. As with the reporter, you as a developer will learn more if you do a little research first. Think back to interviews you've heard or read in which the interviewer asks a simple question that could have been easily looked up ahead of time. You don't want to hear an interviewer ask, "Where did you grow up?" or "When were you born?" when this information is readily available. It is better to ask, "As a teenager in Seattle in the late sixties, what influence did Jimi Hendrix have on your music?" There are, of course, interviewers who go too far in the other direction. They will ask questions that are intended to show their knowledge rather than to elicit information from their subject. Neither extreme is helpful. While meeting with the client, you will need to have enough knowledge to be able to ask relevant questions and to make helpful suggestions while letting the client tell the story.

There are some things you should probably know about Dwight and this project. Each semester he has to figure out what courses his department will offer and who will teach them. He'd like a software application that automates the part of the process that amounts to just copying information from past semesters and facilitates filling in the schedule with the new information. He has a vision of how this software should look. By the way, this isn't the first time he has agreed to be a client for the software engineering class. Twice before, he has worked with a group trying to build this scheduler application. Once the application was not completed and the other time the final version was too limited and too difficult to use.

Dwight is actually interested in working with an XP group. He's heard about the differences between the traditional methodology that he has experienced on past efforts and XP. He understands that more will be expected of him and he is willing to be available throughout the semester. This is an important fact to keep in mind. You don't have to get a complete and detailed picture in the first meeting. You will be able to go back to Dwight and clarify areas you don't completely understand. On the other hand, he'll be able to contact you and change his mind about features that he was sure that he needed.

WRITING YOUR FIRST USER STORY

It's a week into the semester; you're still working on your spike to try to figure out what XP is all about. You don't really start this project for another week, but you'd like to get a look at what you'll be doing for the next twelve weeks or so. The beginning of the semester is a busy time for a department chair but Dwight welcomes you into his office, clears some papers off a table, and invites you to sit down. The two of you chat a bit about how the semester is going. You may be anxious to get down to business, but you remember that XP is all about communication and relationships. You also remind yourself that he is being nice enough to give you a lot of time this semester despite his previous experience of getting nothing usable in return. You absentmindedly play with your stack of blank index cards while enjoying the conversation.

Taking Stock of Artifacts

Dwight pulls a folder from his top drawer and says, "Here's what I'm looking for." He takes a couple of sheets out of the folder and shows you schedules from past semesters. On one sheet, the courses are in order by course number and section. The course title, faculty member, and class-meeting times are included. On another sheet is a list of faculty members with course numbers and meeting times. For Dwight, there is an obvious metaphor for this software you are creating. Your computer might use folders and files so that a filing cabinet is a metaphor for how you store documents on your computer. Here Dwight is suggesting how he thinks of your project. It will help you and your team to use the language that fits with his view. The sheets of paper that he is showing you are the artifacts that he associates with the course-scheduling process.

"Each semester," he explains, "I have to look at the courses we need to offer and schedule the faculty members who'll be teaching them. Take first semester Calculus as an example. Looking at the number of incoming freshmen, we'll have to offer a certain number of sections. We'll need to spread them out during the day so that students can fit them into their schedules along with their required courses for other majors."

Perhaps it occurs to you that the course schedule is more or less the same from year to year. You ask Dwight, "Are you really creating the schedule from scratch each semester?"

He thinks a moment and answers, "Well, the fall and spring semester are different. We run more Calc 1 classes in the fall and just a few in the spring. With Calc 2, it's just the opposite; more classes run in the spring than in the fall. But from year to year the schedule is basically the same."

"So," you suggest, "couldn't you start a semester's schedule by modifying the schedule you had for the same semester the previous year?"

"That would work for the one hundred and two hundred level courses. But some of the upper level and graduate courses rotate on a two-year schedule. For those courses, it might be better if we started a new schedule document from the schedule for the same semester two years before," he replies.

Write a User Story

You've heard a clear description of a required feature for the scheduler. You write the following description on an index card.

Create Document

When creating a document for a new semester. The classes, sections, times, and Faculty members assigned to teach the classes from the same semester two years before are used as the starting point.

You could record these user stories using a word processor or spreadsheet. Index cards are less permanent. However, you can easily pass an index card to Dwight and he can make changes. If an idea comes to him while you're writing a card, he can take a blank one and write down his own user story.

You read the user story back to Dwight and ask him if that's what he'd like. He thinks a moment and says that it is mostly right. He doesn't think he wants the faculty members included in the new schedule. While you're making the change, you replace the word "classes" with "courses." It shouldn't matter to Dwight, but there will be confusion if classes could refer to both Java classes and to the classes taught by the department. Even though you are making small changes, you read him the revised user story. A recurring theme of XP is short feedback loops.

Create Document

When creating a document for a new semester. The courses, sections, and times from the same semester two years before are used as the starting point.

He nods and says, "That sounds good." You hand him the index card. It's only fair: he showed you his artifacts so you show him yours. You need to explain user stories to him.

"All I've done," you begin, "is take what I think you said and create what we call a 'user story.' It has a short title, 'Create Document,' that helps us identify it. The description on the card then serves as a common understanding of this feature. I may have to ask more questions later when we start coding it up, but for now I think I understand what you're saying. There is one other requirement for a user story—it has to be testable. There has to be a way for you to test whether or not we've actually given you what you want. In this case, it's pretty easy. You create a new document and you should see the information from two years ago."

Remember that this is as new a process for Dwight as it is for you. It might help both of you if you explain to him how these user stories will be used. "Once we have a bunch of user stories," you continue, "the team will estimate how long we expect each one to take and how much time we have available. We'll ask you to pick the ones you want first. You get to decide what's most important to you at any time. You might decide this story isn't important to you this week and next week decide it's the one you must have next. You can even decide that you no longer want the application to work the way you described. You have total control of the stories. If you'd like, you can write them."

Dwight smiles and says, "That's okay. You can keep writing them."

STORY GATHERING

Now that you have your first story, you can ask questions to help the client come up with more stories. Try to let the client lead. You may lead the client to many stories but they won't necessarily be the client's priorities. Ask open-ended questions. Don't ask, "Would you like the background to be blue?" Instead ask, "What would you like the panel to look like?"

Find a Starting Point

Dwight has told you what he wants to happen when a new document is created. In this case you can follow the process from the beginning. At other times you may want to begin at the end and work backwards. In this case, you ask, "What would you like to happen when you first start up the application?"

"I don't know."

"Do you want a screen to pop up with various choices?" you prompt.

"No," he answers, "most of the time I'll just be working on an existing schedule. I think I'd like the program to just bring up the last schedule I was working on."

You write your second user story and read it back to him.

Starting Application

The application begins by bringing up the last document the user was working with.

Dwight thinks that user story sounds pretty good. You point out that that means there has to be a way of saving the document.

Following a Path

The story you wrote for starting up the application has led to a story on saving the document. The danger in following this path is that you haven't even decided what goes in the document. The danger in not following this path is that you'll forget the features that are popping into your mind right now. Continue brainstorming. Write the story for saving the document now.

Saving Document

User saves the document when they want.

Again, Dwight is happy with this story. He adds that he wants to make sure he's given a chance to save his work if he accidentally closes the application. You change the story like this.

Saving Document

User saves the document when they want. User is prompted to save when he closes the application.

Dwight frowns and says, "No, I don't think those two belong together. Go back to the original story for Saving Document and create a new story for Closing Document." You discard the expanded Saving Document story and create the following separate story.

Closing Document

If user closes Application, they are prompted to save.

Dwight is now happy with the separate user stories. Looking back, you've actually covered a lot of ground pretty quickly. He knows what he wants to happen when the application starts and when the application quits. He also has described when he can save his work and how he can start up a new document.

Going Too Far

You're on a roll. You've suggested some solid user stories that have the right amount of granularity. At this time, it might be nice to experiment with the schedule, perhaps try a few things out and decide which looks best. You create the following user story.

Experimental Changes

If the user wants to play around with the schedule without erasing the current state, they can. At any point, they can choose to revert to the earlier version, to accept these changes as the current version, or to create another experimental version.

You proudly read it to Dwight. He politely explains that he doesn't really see the need for it. You agree that he probably doesn't need it right away but suggest that you put it in a pile of ideas to be implemented later. Dwight says, "No, I don't really think I would ever use that feature."

What went wrong? It was all going so nicely. Experimental Changes describes a very nice feature. It might be one that you would find very useful. Usually these moments happen when the development team is working and the client is nowhere in sight. Someone on the team thinks of a cool feature to add to the program and takes a few days to add it. The client doesn't want the feature and will never use it. In XP, the client is always allowed to make these decisions for himself. So really nothing went wrong. You had an idea and the client made the decision that he wouldn't use this feature. Sometimes it's hard not to take these rejections personally. Dwight didn't say the idea wasn't good; he said it wasn't for him.

GETTING BACK ON TRACK

Although there is nothing wrong in suggesting features and certainly nothing wrong with the client rejecting your suggestions, you will have more success at this point in the project if you can let the client suggest the features that are important to him. One way to get back on track is to return to the beginning. You've written the story called Starting Application. Pick up there and ask the client, "When the application starts up and loads the last schedule you worked with, what do you want to see on the screen?"

Dwight picks up the first piece of paper he showed you earlier and says, "Something formatted like this one." You write this as a story and show it to him.

Scheduling View

The scheduling view lets the user see the current state of the schedule by course number. This view shows course number and name, section number, credit hours, meeting times, and instructor's name.

Dwight likes this story. It captures what he's looking for. It also suggests other user stories.

Exploring Time Slots

You ask Dwight what he means by meeting times and how he wants to enter them.

"That's an interesting question," Dwight says. "The answer is pretty complicated. There are set time slots for classes that meet Monday, Wednesday, and Friday (classes are 50 minutes long and meet on the hour) and set times for classes that meet on Tuesday and Thursday (classes are 75 minutes long and meet at 9:30, 11:00, 12:30, etc.). Some of our classes meet four days each week so the time may be different on some days than others. For example, if a class meets four days a week (MTWF or MWThF) at nine or noon, the Tuesday and Thursday class times are automatically adjusted. The nine o'clock class moves to 8:30 and the noon classes move to 12:30. Some of the time slots are only available to three credit-hour classes. Also, I can create special time slots late in the afternoon or in the evening for graduate courses."

"As for entering them," Dwight continues, "I'd like to be able to click on a button and have all of the possible times listed so I can just select the one I want. Also, I'd like to be able to look at all of the classes scheduled at a particular time to see if I have conflicts."

"Hold on," you say, scribbling wildly, "here are the stories I think you're describing.

Time Slots

A time slot consists of the days the class meets, together with the time. The application should be aware of standard time slots and allow the addition of nonstandard slots for the current semester.

Drop Down List of Blocks

When choosing a time slot a drop down list should help with user selection.

Credits Determine Blocks

A Three-hour class can only be offered in set slots.

Four Day Class Adjustment

In a class that meets four times a week at 9 a.m. or at noon the Tuesday/Thursday times are adjusted. The 9 a.m. class moves to 8:30 a.m. and the 12:00 class moves to 12:30.

Viewing the Time Slot Schedule

The user should be able to view all classes currently scheduled for a given time slot.

Dwight looks the list over and says, "There are also slots that aren't available for certain classes. I can't schedule a freshman class at certain times because of the freshman seminar, for example." You write this.

Section Rules

The user can define rules so that courses can not be scheduled during certain times.

Dwight looks at it and says, "Put that in the pile of stories to be done later. I'd like it eventually, but it doesn't need to be one of the first things you do." You agree and look at where you are. You now have a good sense of how the time slots work in the scheduler, but you need to know more about the other entries.

Courses and Sections

Dwight points out that you haven't really dealt with courses and sections yet. The first semester course in Calculus may be offered at different times or by different instructors. These are called sections. Dwight says, "Even though this document starts with the corresponding semester from two years earlier, I'm going to need to make adjustments. I'll need to be able to change the list of courses being offered. I'll have to decide how many sections of each course we're offering. Then I'll need to be able to choose a time slot for the section."

You present him with the following cards.

Which Courses

The user should be able to add courses to or delete courses from the schedule.

Assign Number of Sections

For each course, the user can select a certain number of sections.

Schedule Section

A user should be able to schedule a section by selecting a time slot.

This last story seems close to the drop-down list of blocks story, but that one was about how a time slot is selected and this one is about being able to assign time slots for sections.

Then Dwight says, "You know what I really want? I want this program to figure out the section numbers automatically. For each course, we assign section numbers with this complicated routine. For day classes we start with the number 50 and number the courses in order early to late on Monday, Wednesday, and Friday followed by the courses early to late on Tuesday and Thursday. There's a whole system. Then we start numbering at 1 for the evening courses starting with the Monday and Wednesday classes and then the Tuesday and Thursday classes."

You sketch the following card.

Number Sections

The application should be able to generate section numbers for each course. The sections are numbered as follows. Day classes start with 50 in order MWF early to late then TTh early to late then MTWF early to late then MTWTh early to late then MWThF early to late. Night classes start with 1 in order MW early to late then TTh early to late.

"That's it," he says. "I'd also like to be able to see when a course is offered during the week. I'd also like to look over the whole week for all the courses" He accepts these stories.

View Course Distribution

A user should be able to see when in the week a given course is offered to make sure that it is well distributed.

Viewing Entire Schedule

The user should be able to view the entire week and see what classes are offered in each time slot.

Working with Faculty

Based on Dwight's description, you come up with these stories to specify how faculty will be treated in this program.

Faculty List

User can add or subtract faculty members or list them as inactive.

Teaching Preferences

User can view list of faculty appropriate for teaching a given course.

Teaching Assignments

User can assign an instructor to a given section.

View Faculty Schedule

A user should be able to select a view showing a faculty member's schedule by week and by class.

Teaching Assignment Errors

The user is notified if an instructor has a scheduling conflict when it occurs.

WRAPPING UP WITH THE CLIENT

You've gotten a lot accomplished in this meeting. You don't have the entire application specified down to the last detail. You couldn't possibly do so with any degree of accuracy. As the client sees what you're building, his understanding of what he will be getting will adjust and the requirements and, therefore, the user stories will change. You need to close the meeting by making sure the client understands where he is in the process and what's coming next.

Stopping the Client

Take the stack of user stories and pass it to Dwight. Ask him to look through them and see if anything jumps out that is missing or needs to be changed. Be careful how you phrase the question. You don't want to encourage the client to keep finding one more story. If the client interprets your question as saying that you're looking for more stories, he may try to come up with some, thinking that he's helping you. If you sense this happening, you need to explain that you're just making sure that there's no really important feature that he just hasn't thought of yet.

You look at the stack and realize that you already have plenty to work with. You can probably already see that it won't all get done this semester. After looking at the existing stack, Dwight may come up with a story that is more important than many of the existing stories. You can help take the pressure off of him by reminding him that new stories can be added at any time during the life of the project. Just as your job at the beginning of the meeting was to encourage your client to start creating stories, now your job is to help the client stop.

Ordering the Stories

Now suggest that the client put the stories roughly in order of importance. Not all stories will be equally important. If the client has difficulty you can remind him of the two stories that were already ordered: one he decided would never need doing and the other could wait. Maybe the first ordering can be in rough piles labeled "right away," "next," "later in the semester," "might not be delivered," and "not this semester." It's easier to start with this rough sort. These categories are tied to the fact that you will be abandoning this project at the end of the semester. Ordinarily a project continues until the client says "stop."

Next, ask him to go back to the "right away" and "next" stacks and put those stacks in order of importance. You need to stress that nothing is written in stone. At any point in the project Dwight can reorder the stories. There may be a cost in reordering, but he has the right to decide what is worth that cost. As he orders the two piles, he may pull stories from "next" and put them ahead of "right away." This is great. The client is handling the user stories and getting a feel for how he can control the project. He is reconsidering priorities in a way that will help your team later when you need quick answers from him. Let the client know that before you write any code you will be back to allow him to pick the stories he wants you to work on. Once the cards are in order, you can explain the planning game.

Preparing the Client for Reality

One of the keys to the relationship between an XP client and a development team is that the client's expectations are based on reality as soon into the project as possible. At this point, however, Dwight has no clear picture of the process. You realize this when he hands you the stories from the "right away" and "next" stacks and asks, "Can I have these by next month when I start working on next semester's schedule?"

"I don't know," you say with confidence.

"Well," he presses, "how much do you think you might be able to give me by then?"

"I don't know yet," you answer again, "I don't have any guesses of how much work is involved and how much work we can do."

Dwight looks a bit puzzled. After all, you've been asking him to write concrete stories and to order those stories. He's just asking you how long they might take.

You explain, "I'll take these cards back to the team and we'll estimate the cards that were in the 'right away' and 'next' piles. We might estimate more of them if that will help. Then we'll estimate how much time we can spend in the first two weeks. The estimates will be in units that probably stand for some amount of time, but we can't be sure what yet."

"Let me get this straight," Dwight responds, "You may take the Create Document story and say it takes five units but you aren't saying whether the units are hours or days or whatever. I'm not sure that I see the point of estimating if the units can mean anything."

"Okay," you say, " Let's stick with your example and let's say we also estimated Closing Document at one unit. If it actually takes us about three hours to finish Closing Document, how long should it take us to do Create Document?'"

Dwight smiles. "Then Create Document should take around five times as long or about fifteen hours."

"Right," you agree, "and as you complete more stories you'll have a better and better idea of what a unit corresponds to. Actually, you don't care."

"What do you mean, 'you don't care'?" he asks.

"Well at the same time, each member of the team estimates how many units he can accomplish this week. If I estimate that I can do twenty units this week and end up only doing Create Document then I've accomplished five units of work this week. Even if I do Create Document and most of Closing Document I've only completed five units of work this week. This makes next week easy. I sign up for five units of work again and see how I'll do."

"So that's why you don't care about units," Dwight says. "Whether a unit corresponds to an hour or a day, you don't care. You know how many units you can accomplish in an iteration and you know about how long it would take you to finish the user stories."

"Right," you continue, " and our estimates will improve during this project because we'll have more experience and much more data."

"Okay," Dwight says, "I get how you are using units. What happens after you estimate all of the stories and tell me how many units you can do this week?"

"Next, we'll bring the stories back to you. We might tell you that we think a story is too big and ask you to split it into smaller stories."

"How much smaller?"

"Well, one of the keys to XP is getting quick feedback so we don't want a story that we think will take too long to finish. These stories look pretty good, though."

"So," he says, "you tell me what the stories cost me in terms of units and how many units I get to spend."

"Right," you say, "we'll tell you how many units you can pick for the first iteration and you can decide which stories you'd like us to work on first. If you get twenty units of work from us, you pick out twenty units worth of stories."

"So," Dwight asks enthusiastically, "when I pick out these twenty units worth of stories, that's what I can expect at the end of the iteration?"

"Maybe," you reply.

"What do you mean, 'maybe'?" he asks. "You tell me to choose twenty for the first iteration, I choose twenty, and now you say that maybe I'll get them and maybe I won't?"

"Well, remember," you caution, "we aren't very good at this yet. We don't really know how much we can accomplish in a week and we really aren't very good at estimating stories yet."

"So what can you do this first iteration," Dwight asks.

"Well, our next step will help us estimate this even better. After you choose the stories for the first iteration, we then go break them down into what we call tasks. These are the programming jobs it takes for us to program your story."

"That's like me telling you I need to run out for an hour to buy office supplies but then I break it down to driving there, shopping, and driving back."

"Right, and you know it takes you about twenty-five minutes to drive there, twenty-five minutes back, and you usually spend fifteen minutes in the store. So now you have a better idea of how long it might take. You now are guessing that it will take you an hour and five minutes."

"But," says Dwight, "it's still a guess."

"That's right," you say, "but it's based on more detail. Say you get caught in traffic on the way there and it takes you forty minutes to get there. You could call me and say that you're running late. You still have the fifteen minutes of shopping and the twenty-five minute drive back so you can now give me a better estimate. You don't have to wait until you get back to realize that you're going to take longer."

He thinks a minute and then says, "so once you break down the story into tasks do you give me new estimates based on the total of the tasks."

"Maybe," you say. "If the new totals mean that we can't get everything done that we estimated, we'll come back to you and let you choose which of the reestimated stories you want us to work on during the first iteration."

"And then you go work on the twenty units of stories."

"Right, but if we get caught in traffic we'll be back."

"Why?"

"In your shopping example, what if it's more important that you get back in an hour than that you get your office supplies? After twenty minutes of driving in traffic you may realize that you're not going to make it to the store so you change your plan and turn around and come back here."

"So," says Dwight, "if you find a story took longer than you think then you'll know that you can't complete all the work we agreed on."

"Right. But we don't get to choose what's most important out of the remaining stories. This means that we have to come back to you and ask you to choose. Maybe what we now know is that we only get sixteen units done during each iteration and we've completed eight. We'll ask you to choose eight units worth of stories out of the remaining twelve."

"So," Dwight says, "it sounds like I will be making a lot of decisions."

"You will, and they won't all be eliminating stories. The second iteration often goes better than the first so we may come back to you and tell you that you can pick additional stories."

You and Dwight have covered a lot at the first meeting. You established a rapport. You listened as he described his project. You helped him turn his description into user stories that will help both the team and the client understand what is being built. You helped him prioritize the stories, and you prepared him for the future. These are your goals for this first meeting. You wrap up the meeting and take your stack of user stories back to your team.

CLIENT VARIATIONS

Although Dwight was a real client, he was almost too good to be true. Your clients may have a more difficult time with the process. They may not understand what they are agreeing to. At the very least, your client must have a realistic view of what they are asking for.

Much of your interaction with the client will involve your explaining to them what is coming next and coaching them on what you need. You have to explain what a user story is and you need to provide examples. If a client provides you with a bad or inappropriate user story you need to be able to help him or her see why it may need improvement.

Consider a user story that specifies that the application must be extremely easy to use. How would you test this story? How would you know when it is completed? What are the steps along the way? Be careful how you discuss this with your client. He or she may be very proud of this story. Ask what is meant by easy to use. Maybe you can suggest menu options or buttons that will bring up the last schedule being worked on.

Another weak user story may specify that you use a javax.swing.JTable to present the schedule information. This may be a great idea, but the client does not get to make technical decisions. You may say that you'll consider that as an option, but then ask which features of the JTable are important to the client. The client gets to make many decisions in this process, but technology is generally not one of them. An exception is that the client may want to specify that your application be able to read in information generated from a spreadsheet program that they like to use. Then this is a legitimate user story.

Generally, your client will try to cooperate with you in this setting. They have agreed to help on a project and are interested in their software and your education. The biggest requirements of the client in an academic XP project are availability and the ability to make decisions. You need to be able to contact the client when problems arise. If they are off campus for two months then this won't be possible. When you contact them you are often asking them to choose among alternatives. They need to make quick decisions so that the project can move on.

Chapter 12

The Planning Game—

Negotiating the Future

After testing first, the planning game may be the hardest practice in XP. It wouldn't be so hard if we were in the habit of telling the truth in estimating software practices. Of course, developers will say that they would be more honest in their estimates if management would treat these estimates in a reasonable way. So, developers learn to pad their estimates and management learns to demand that the estimates be cut down. Meanwhile, the sales staff is presenting their own version of the schedule and requirements to the customers. The weary customer just wants the truth. Customers need to build their own business plans around the delivery of your software. Like the Tom Cruise character in the movie *A Few Good Men,* customers repeatedly ask for the truth and tell you that they feel they are entitled to it. Often the reaction of the development team echoes the response of the Jack Nicholson character in the movie, "You can't handle the truth!"

In XP you will tell the truth. You will tell the truth early and often. Even a disbelieving customer will come to trust you quickly because you are backing the truth up with reality. Every two weeks the customer gets to see what you've produced. After a couple of iterations your estimates get better, and the customer comes to trust that you mean it when you say that your best guess is that you'll get a certain amount done. There aren't many rules in the planning game. Here's the first.

> *Rule 1:* The developers will be truthful in their estimates and the customers will believe these estimates.

This sounds like business as usual. After all, back in the Chapter 1 you were told about projects that promised a delivery date. The project team then set out to do the analysis, and then the design, and then the programming. Some time into the programming cycle, the developers realized they weren't going to make the delivery date. Usually a little bit before the deadline a quiet announcement is made that the delivery date will be missed. In his book *Slack*, Tom DeMarco argues that the fault is with the schedule and not with the workers. He writes, "A bad schedule is one that sets a date that is subsequently missed. . . . If the date is missed, the schedule was wrong. It doesn't matter why the date was missed. The purpose of the schedule was planning, not goal-setting. Work that is not performed according to a plan invalidates the plan."

This statement seems to fly in the face of how missed deadlines are dealt with. Isn't it the fault of the developers? It has to be someone's fault. DeMarco continues, "The missed schedule indicts the planners, not the workers. Even if the workers are utterly incompetent, a plan that takes careful note of their inadequacies can help to minimize the damage. A plan that takes no account of realities is not just useless but dangerous." In the planning game you will never plan too far ahead because the standard errors, in the technical statistics sense, are initially so large that these estimates are useless. You will estimate what you can get done in the next two weeks based on what you know of your abilities in the past during this length of time. Just as your estimates will be based on more data points as you progress, the customers will tend to have a better sense of what to expect in the next iteration as more and more iterations pass. This is summarized as the second rule of the planning game.

> *Rule 2:* The developers will refine their estimates and the customers will refine their expectations based on the actual achievements in each iteration.

Many popular games can serve as a metaphor for the planning game. Consider any card game in which some cards are revealed and then discarded; Bridge, Blackjack, Poker, and Gin Rummy are some obvious examples. Before the game begins, the chance of any given card being an ace is one in thirteen. At a later point, if a player has carefully watched the discards and knows that all the aces have already been played, he or she knows the probability of any future card being an ace is zero. By paying close attention to what has happened in the past, the player can better assess the current possible outcomes.

This is your strategy for success during the planning game. Carefully observe what's happened in past iterations and use this knowledge to predict the outcome of this iteration. A further analogy to the planning game can be made using the board game Monopoly. In Monopoly, players take turns rolling a pair of dice and moving around a board that has properties and special spaces. If you land on unowned property, you can purchase it from the bank with money you've accumulated. If you land on property owned by another player, you have to pay them rent. You can buy and trade property with other players in an effort to control all properties that share a given characteristic (i.e., same color, other railroads, or both utilities). You may have a strategy, but this strategy must be adjusted as others land on and buy property that you wanted. Each time that it is your turn, you must reassess and make your plans based on all that you know about the current state of the game. If you land on a property that costs $280 and you only have $220 then you can't buy the property without selling or mortgaging some of your other assets. At each point you have a fixed amount of resources and have to judge what you can do with them.

This is true in XP's planning game as well. In each iteration there are a fixed amount of resources. You will have a better idea of the true value of these resources as the game goes on. As in Blackjack, you will make better guesses as to the value of the hidden cards later in the deck.

What's interesting about the planning game is that the developers get to estimate their assets and the costs of potential activities. The client, however, decides how the developer spends these assets. It's as if the developers and client are part of this team that is taking their turn once per iteration. The developers, however, possess the information that the client needs to steer the development process. If the developers notice something during the iteration that needs to be shared with the client, then they should do so immediately. The sort of things that the developers need to share include informing the client that they are working more slowly than expected, that they are working more quickly than expected, or that a certain user story was underestimated or overestimated.

There's one last rule that also is related to game playing. The best game players are constantly updating their view of the game and reconsidering the options available to them. In some games (for example, the card game Set or the word game Boggle), as soon as you see a potential move, you are allowed to make it. Simply stated, Rule 3 says that you don't have to wait until it is your turn to take your turn.

> *Rule 3:* During the iteration the developers will update the client as to the progress of the iteration. The client will use this information to quickly refine what is required in the current iteration.

Notice that at each point the client makes decisions based on the information that the developers provide. There must be trust in both directions. That isn't to say that clients should close their eyes and fall backwards, trusting that the developers are there to catch them. The clients can start out by trusting the developers a little. The developers then show this trust is well founded and also that they trust the client just a little as the client begins to make decisions. It may not begin smoothly, but XP has built in checks so that the discussion can proceed in a practical and not a personal way. Consider the following interaction.

The client says, "Oh, you say that costs four units and that costs three and that costs three and that costs two. Hmmm. How much do I have to spend? Six units? Okay, I think I want the one that costs four and one of the ones that costs three." It's not that the client can't add. Traditional clients always ask for more because they suspect the developers will always deliver less.

There's no reason to fight. The developer smiles and says, "You can spend six units."

The client says, "Oh, that's right. I would like the two 3's please."

And that's the planning game. Except for the part where the developer comes back and says, "Oops, one of those threes is a four." Or the developer might say, "We've found some extra time, you can choose two more units."

> *Note:* This chapter, like all others in Part III, is a tutorial. Rather than just read it through, you should stop when directed and participate in the activity. It is unlikely that you will come up with the same answers as those provided in subsequent sections, but these answers will have more meaning for you if you play along at home.

THE BEGINNING USER STORIES

Check out the User Stories tutorial in Chapter 11 for a look at how user stories are discovered and developed. In this chapter, we'll use actual client user stories from a tic-tac-toe game. In this case, Steve wanted a tic-tac-toe game designed for his daughter to play on their home computer. Steve came in with the following eighteen user stories. Read them carefully and think about whether you have any questions about these stories.

You will be tempted to use spreadsheets and other software solutions for managing your stories, tasks, and other aspects of the planning game. Traditionally, these are kept on 3 × 5 index cards. It's not that the developers and pioneers of this methodology couldn't write applications to manage this process. They found that, for colocated teams, index cards work best. They can be passed around, reorganized, and torn up with ease. They are inexpensive, easy to use, and several people can create new cards at the same time.

Default Pieces **(1)**

Default representations for the pieces are a graphical "X" and a graphical "O."

Board Setup **(2)**

The board is a 3 × 3 grid. Each square on the grid is initially empty.

Winning the Game **(3)**

A player wins the game when three of their markers form a line either horizontally (row), vertically (column), or diagonally.

Tie Games **(4)**

If nine pieces have been played and there is no winner, the game ends in a tie.

Player's Pieces **(5)**

Tic-Tac-Toe is played by two players. One player is assigned the marker "X," the other is assigned the marker "O."

Standings **(6)**

A running tally of the number of wins for each player during a session will be kept and displayed.

Displaying a Move **(7)**

Once played, a visual representation of the piece will be displayed on the screen.

Highlighting the Win (8)

When a player wins, the winning three-in-a-row is highlighted by a line drawn through the three markers.

Taking Turns (9)

Players alternate placing their markers in empty squares. Once placed, a marker can neither be moved nor removed.

Making a Move (10)

Players select the square to place their marker by clicking on the square with the mouse.

Number of Games (11)

A running tally of the number of games played during a session will be kept and displayed.

Display Results and Replay (12)

At the end of a game, the result will be displayed and an offer of another game will be presented.

Alternate Markers (13)

Players can select alternate representations for their markers from a list or supply their own.

Illegal Moves (14)

Attempting to select an illegal move results in no action taken.

Computer First (15)

The player may select whether the computer plays first or second.

Computer Ability (16)

The computer played has two levels of ability: low—makes random plays; high—never loses.

Computer Opponent (17)

Player may choose to play against another human or the computer.

Quitting **(18)**

The session can be ended by selecting the quit button.

Stop: Before going on, take time to think through these user stories. If you were meeting with a client, what questions might you have about these stories? What clarifications or changes might you be looking for?

REFINING THE USER STORIES

The first step in the planning game is to make sure that the user stories are clear and testable. Here are the actual concerns that the developers had for Steve. In this case there were actually two developers, Kathy and Jason. To make it easier to follow this part of the conversation, we'll combine the developers into the single persona of Kathy.

Kathy starts by saying, "I'm not sure I understand the difference between user stories (9), Taking Turns, and (10), Making a Move. It sounds as if they're both about moving by placing markers in empty squares."

Steve responds, "I was thinking that Taking Turns was more of a description of what constitutes a move whereas Making a Move describes the physical action of making the move, but I can see where there's a lot of overlap."

"In fact," Kathy quickly adds, "I think we can throw story (7), Displaying a Move, into this combination as well. If you're placing a marker in a square then this requires a visual representation of the piece being placed in the square."

"Again," says Steve a bit defensively, "that's probably true but at the time I thought of them separately."

"Should we keep them separate?" Kathy asks.

"No, we can combine them," Steve agrees. He jots down the following user story.

Make Move **(19)**

Players, alternating turns, use a mouse to select an empty square in which to place their marker. Once placed, a marker can't be moved or removed.

"What do you think?" Steve asks.

"It works for me. Do you think you need to say something about the visual representation of the marker?" Kathy answers.

"I don't think so," says Steve. Remember, the user story is more of a record of their common understanding than it is a binding agreement. At this point, both Steve and Kathy agree that this story stood for the three stories it was replacing.

Kathy continues to look at the cards. Something seems to be missing. She says, "I don't mean to create more work for my team, but do you want to allow the players to enter their names?"

Steve agrees. He adds the following user story.

Player Names **(20)**

The players will be asked to enter their names at the beginning of the session.

Kathy nods and then asks, "What about stories (1), Default Pieces, and (5), Player's Pieces? They both talk about the players' markers being an 'X' and an 'O'."

Again Steve agrees. He thinks for a minute and then suggests replacing them with this user story.

Choose Marker **(21)**

Tic-Tac-Toe is played by two players. At the beginning of a session, one player chooses either "X" or "O" as his or her marker, the other player is assigned the remaining one.

"That's better," said Kathy. "What about number (14), Illegal Moves? Don't you think it would be better if the user was told that a move was illegal? If no action is taken, the user might be confused."

At first Steve thinks that this would just complicate the game and then he sees Kathy's point that a user could be confused without further feedback. He replaces Illegal Moves with this refinement.

Illegal Moves **(22)**

Attempting to select an illegal move results in a message indicating that the move is not allowed.

"I think we're going to need to change (8), Highlighting the Win, as well," says Kathy.

"Why?" asks Steve.

"This is a little more subtle," Kathy replies. "If you look at the story, you have us making the line through the three markers when a player wins."

"That's what I want," says Steve.

"Well yes," Kathy answers, "but really as soon as three markers of the same kind are in a row you can draw the line."

"That's true," says Steve, "but I don't really see the difference."

Kathy answers, "The problem lies in the acceptance testing. If you want to test that the user story has been fulfilled, in the second version you just need to see what happens if three of the same markers are in a row or not. The acceptance test there can avoid the issue of whether the program 'understands' that the game has been won. In the first version you have to tie the logic of your acceptance test to whichever object is in charge of determining a win. The second way is cleaner and can be more easily tested."

Steve asks, "Isn't this coding? It seems like the decision is yours."

Kathy says, "It's somewhere in between. I'm making a coding argument for why you may want to change how you've described your story. Not only that, but it will allow the acceptance tests that you write to more accurately reflect the status of the development."

"How do you figure that?" asks Steve.

"Look at it this way, if the acceptance test for user story (8), Highlighting the Win, depends on knowing when the game has been won, then it cannot possibly pass until story (3), Winning the Game, also passes. So if (8) is implemented before (3), its acceptance test cannot pass until (3) is implemented, at which point both acceptance tests will pass. It's a question of granularity, the line should bedroll when there are three consecutive markers, testing for a win is a separate issue."

Steve agrees and writes this replacement story for Highlighting the Win.

Highlighting a Three-in-a-Line **(23)**

Whenever three markers of the same type are in a line, draw a line through those markers.

Steve quickly adds, "You know, we should change story (3), Winning the Game, to point out that after someone wins, the game is all over."

Recognizing a Win **(24)**

A player wins the game when three of their markers form a line either horizontally (row), vertically (column) or diagonally, and the game ends.

At this point Steve and Kathy agreed that they had enough stories to begin. They were:

Board Setup **(2)**

The board is a 3 × 3 grid. Each square on the grid is initially empty.

Winning the Game **(3)**

A player wins the game when three of their markers form a line either horizontally (row), vertically (column), or diagonally.

Tie Games **(4)**

If nine pieces have been played and there is no winner, the game ends in a tie.

Standings **(6)**

A running tally of the number of wins for each player during a session will be kept and displayed.

Number of Games **(11)**

A running tally of the number of games played during a session will be kept and displayed.

Display Results and Replay **(12)**

At the end of a game, the result will be displayed and an offer of another game will be presented.

Alternate Markers **(13)**

Players can select alternate representations for their markers from a list or supply their own.

Computer First **(15)**

The player may select whether the computer plays first or second.

Computer Ability **(16)**

The computer played has two levels of ability: low—makes random plays; high—never loses.

Computer Opponent **(17)**

Player may choose to play against another human or the computer.

Quitting **(18)**

The session can be ended by selecting the quit button.

Make Move **(19)**

Players, alternating turns, use a mouse to select an empty square in which to place their marker. Once placed, a marker can't be moved or removed.

Player Names **(20)**

The players will be asked to enter their names at the beginning of the session.

Choose Marker **(21)**

Tic-Tac-Toe is played by two players. At the beginning of a session, one player chooses either "X" or "O" as their marker, the other player is assigned the remaining one.

Illegal Moves **(22)**

Attempting to select an illegal move results in a message indicating that the move is not allowed.

Highlighting a Three-in-a-Line **(23)**

Whenever three markers of the same type are in a line, draw a line through those markers.

Recognizing a Win **(24)**

A player wins the game when three of their markers form a line either horizontally (row), vertically (column) or diagonally, and the game ends.

> *Stop:* Before going on, pretend you are the client. Choose the stories that might be most important to you. Technically, this activity is not part of the current developer-centered tutorial. It does, however, help you understand the client's next step.

SELECTING USER STORIES FOR THE FIRST ITERATION

The client now has a set of user stories to prioritize. Just as in the game of Monopoly, the priorities can change every time it's "their turn." Using yet another game as an analogy, think about the game of Scrabble. Here you draw tiles with individual letters on them and alternate trying to form words from your tiles and those that have already been placed on the board. On your turn you have to reassess your options. You have additional letters that you didn't have to choose from on your last turn, and your opponent has both added and removed possibilities from the board by placing their last word. Throughout the planning game, the client will reorder the user stories based on what the developers have accomplished so far, on what the client's current most important need is, and on what the developer estimates to be the time available and the time required by the remaining tasks.

The Client Provides a Basic Ordering of Stories

To start the process, the client will broadly prioritize the user stories. This is to keep the developers from having to estimate every story at this point. In the current tic-tac-toe example there are few enough user stories that it would be possible to estimate them all, but let's just estimate the ones that the client rates at the top. In this case, Steve organized the user stories like this. The story numbers appear in parenthesis to make it easier for you to locate the original descriptions.

Top six stories (immediate and most important):

- Board Setup (2),
- Alternate Markers (13),

- Make Move (19),
- Choose Marker (21),
- Highlighting a Three-in-a-Line (23), and
- Recognizing a Win (24).

Next four (important but can wait):

- Tie Games (4),
- Display Results and Replay (12),
- Player Names (20), and
- Illegal Moves (22).

Next three:

- Standings (6),
- Number of Games (11), and
- Quitting (18).

Next three:

- Computer First (15),
- Computer Ability (16), and
- Computer Opponent (17).

Steve was only asked to pick out his top six. He did and then asked if he could then suggest the next four that he wanted the developers to tackle. When they said yes, he continued to organize the remaining stories in relative levels of importance. Although this wasn't necessary, it did provide possibly useful information.

> *Stop:* Take the top six stories and estimate how many units you think each one will take. Use two units for user story (2), Board Setup, and estimate the others in comparison to it.

The Developers Provide Rough Estimates of the Stories

The developers now take the top stories that the client chose and estimate how long these will take. These first estimates are going to be wrong. In a traditional software engineering approach you would base the remainder of the project on these estimates. In XP you'll refine these estimates before the end of the day and only depend on those revised estimates for, at most, a week.

The most important thing to remember while estimating is that you are approximating the relative difficulty of the tasks. In this example, the developers initially used units that correspond to a half-hour knowing that their notion of how long a unit will take will change during the course of the project. The developers are on short iteration cycles and so have committed twenty units to the first iteration. They figure that user story (2), Board Setup, will take about an hour and so the estimate is two units.

In looking at (21), Choose Marker, they figure it will take a bit longer. There's not much more to do, but they estimate it at three units. With story (13), Alternate Markers, something interesting happens. The developers initially estimated it at eleven units. Then they estimated user story (19), Make Move, at eight units.

They have more confidence in this estimate of the Make Move user story (19). They can't express why, but they both are pretty certain it will take around eight units. In this light they catch each other reconsidering the Alternate Markers story (13). Here they both agree that if Make Move (19) is estimated at eight units then Alternate Markers (13) should require more than eleven units. On the other hand, they argue that work on one of the stories may reduce the time required by the other. They then remember that they are to estimate the stories in isolation because the client gets to choose the order and may ignore their advice and choose an order different from the one preferred by developers. They go with their gut feeling and revise the estimate of the Alternate Markers user story (13) to fourteen units.

They present the following results to the client.

User story	Units
Board Setup (2)	2
Alternate Markers (13)	14
Make Move (19)	8
Choose Marker (21)	3
Highlighting a Three-in-a-Line (23)	6
Recognizing a Win (24)	6

Stop: For kicks, from this set of stories, which requires thirty-nine units of work, select twenty units' worth that you want. Again, this is a client activity so you are doing this just for fun.

The Client Chooses the Current Iteration

Now the client chooses as many units as they would like the developers to work on in the first iteration. The upper limit is the developers' allotted amount. In this case, the developers have said they can accomplish twenty units. The client isn't bound to only choose from this list. The client can ask the developers to estimate another story.

Also, take a look at the estimate for (13), Alternate Markers. It's more than half of the iteration's worth. It may be a good idea to break it down into smaller stories. For now, Steve is happy leaving it as it is. He selects the following stories for the first iteration:

Board Setup **(2)**

The board is a 3 × 3 grid. Each square on the grid is initially empty.

Make Move **(19)**

Players, alternating turns, use a mouse to select an empty square in which to place their marker. Once placed, a marker can't be moved or removed.

Choose Marker **(21)**

Tic-Tac-Toe is played by two players. At the beginning of a session, 1 player chooses either "X" or "O" as their marker, the other player is assigned the remaining one.

Recognizing a Win **(24)**

A player wins the game when three of their markers form a line either horizontally (row), vertically (column) or diagonally, and the game ends.

This is a total of nineteen units but Steve and Kathy agree that there is enough uncertainty in these estimates that this difference won't matter much.

Stop: Break each of these four stories into tasks. These tasks are development units where the user stories are client functionality units.

A CLOSER LOOK AT THE ESTIMATES

In some ways the estimates on both sides are still very rough. The client looked at a pile of stories and chose the ones they wanted first. Then the developers looked at those stories and indicated how long they think each one will take without fully considering what's involved. Then the client chose the stories for the first iteration based on client priorities together with developer estimates of the user stories and of their available time.

Now the developers are going to take a closer look at what is involved in coding each story. Once they've broken each story down into tasks, individuals will estimate and take responsibility for the tasks. The developers can then go back to the client with the revised estimates if the client needs to make further decisions. For example, if in the process of breaking the stories into tasks, the developers realize they have forty-three units of work instead of twenty, then the client will have to pick the most important twenty units worth.

The Developers Break the Stories into Tasks

The next step in the process is for the developers to meet and discuss how the four stories selected by the client can be broken down into tasks. These tasks are the developers' domain because this is how the developers will achieve the functionality specified in the user story. For example, here's the breakdown for story (2), Board Setup.

Board Setup **(2)**

The board is a 3 × 3 grid. Each square on the grid is initially empty.

Task 2-A: Board-GUI Task

Create a GUI that displays a board consisting of nine empty squares arranged in a 3 × 3 grid.

Task 2-B: Board-Model Task

Create an internal representation of a tic-tac-toe board that serves as a model of the game.

The developers don't need to share these tasks with the client. The idea is that now a pair can work on a specific task and start coding. They can decide how the task will be tested and start writing unit tests followed by the code that makes the unit tests pass. Here are the tasks for user story (19), Make Move.

Make Move **(19)**

Players, alternating turns, use a mouse to select an empty square in which to place their marker. Once placed, a marker can't be moved or removed.

Task 19-A: Determine Marker Task

Determine which is current marker based on current player.

Task 19-B: Place Marker Task

Respond to mouse click in empty square by placing current marker in square, and update internal representation.

Task 19-C: Ignore Bad Clicks Task

Ensure that mouse click in nonempty square has no effect.

Task 19-D: Determine Current Player Task

Determine current player by alternating between players starting with the specified starting player.

The first task (19-A) brought up an issue that the developers decided needed to be addressed in user story (21), Choose Marker. The developers weren't sure when the players should choose their markers. They asked Steve if he wanted to allow for the players to choose their markers before every game and he answered that no, choosing once per session would be fine. He added this information to user story (21), Choose Marker, and it was renumbered as (25) so that the changes could continue to be tracked. Here's (25), Choose Marker, along with the tasks.

Choose Marker **(25)**

Tic-Tac-Toe is played by two players. At the beginning of a session, one player chooses either "X" or "O" as their marker, the other player is assigned the remaining one.

Task 25-A: Choose Marker GUI Task

Create a GUI to allow player to choose X or O as their marker.

Task 25-B: Record Marker Choice Task

Record choice of marker for both players.

This leaves user story (24), Recognizing a Win. This user story took the developers more time to break down than the other stories. You can see from the tasks that it appears that some design decisions were made here. There were considerable arguments about this fact. After trying different options it was agreed that it was better to halt the discussion and proceed with coding. Take a look at the way in which you broke down Recognizing a Win. Your tasks are probably different than those given below. You may have checked the whole board each time for winning configurations. You may have had row objects that represented rows, columns, and diagonals. You only needed to check completed row objects to see if they contained three of the same markers. You may have only kept track of those row objects that only contained one type of marker. As soon as a row contains one of each type of marker you no longer need to check to see if it's a winner. The point is that there are many ways to break down user story (24), Recognizing a Win.

Here's Jason and Kathy's solution.

Recognizing a Win **(24)**

A player wins the game when three of their markers form a line either horizontally (row), vertically (column) or diagonally, and the game ends.

Task 24-A: Checking Potential Wins Task

Determine if a given line contains three of the same marker.

Task 24-B: Finding Potential Wins Task

Determine which lines to check (i.e., those lines containing the last played marker).

Task 24-C: Recording a Win Task

Record a win for last player if a row returned from task 24-B is determined in task 24-A to contain three of their markers.

Task 24-B clearly stands out as suggesting a particular solution. Sometimes that is the case. eXtreme Programming doesn't forbid any design. It encourages you to design a little, test a little, and code a little. In this case the design decision may be changed later.

Stop: Look at the tasks and estimate how long each one will take using the units you used to estimate the entire stories before.

The Developers Estimate the Tasks

The developer team for this project is small. It's up to Kathy and Jason, the other developer, to estimate and claim responsibility for the tasks estimated in the previous section. Remember, Jason has been here all along; he's just been left out of the description. Each developer has ten units that they can spend in this estimation process. The developers bid on how long they think a task would take them with a partner. The low bid wins. You bid on stories until your allotment for the iteration is gone. You can not bid on more work than you can do. In a way, this simplified situation is a bit comical because when Kathy bids on a task, Jason will be her partner and when Jason bids on a task Kathy will be his partner. In other words, the same two people will be working on all of the tasks in this case. Nevertheless, it's a good idea to practice bidding and estimating tasks so they begin this phase of the planning game.

Jason begins by bidding one unit each on tasks 2-A and 2-B, the Board-GUI task and the Board-Model task. Kathy tells him that the tasks are his. She counters by bidding two units on 25-A and one unit on 25-B, the Choose Marker GUI task and the Record Marker Choice task. Jason tells her the stories are hers and he reconsiders his bid on 2-B, the Board-Model task. He says that he probably should change it to two units. Kathy tells him that he can if he wants. He decides not to. It turns out, as is often the case, that his instincts are correct. His bid is an underbid. If you worry that a bid is too low, have the confidence to change your bid. Although you are currently making a guess, you should make the most accurate guess you can.

Although you don't have to bid on tasks one story at a time, you do want to make sure that all of the tasks in a story are taken. The developers next looked at story (19), Make Move. Jason bids five units on 19-B and three on 19-C, the Place Marker task and the Ignore Bad Clicks task. Kathy thinks these estimates are very high. She counterbids four units on 19-B, Place Marker task and one on 19-C, Ignore Bad Clicks task. Jason thinks the bid on Place Marker task is okay but that the bid on 19-C, Ignore Bad Clicks task is quite low. He asked that Kathy reconsider her bid. She does, and decides she is fine. In this case, again, she may have wanted to reconsider the direction of the discussion. The person she would be pairing with was trying to indicate that he didn't think he could help finish this task in such a short time. The bidding in the planning game is more similar to two partners bidding in a game of Bridge than it is to two combatants bidding against each other for a chance at a job. The bidding is done openly and cooperatively.

Kathy also bids two units each on tasks 19-A and 19-D, Determine Marker task and Determine Current Player task. Jason counters with a bid of one unit on Determine Marker task. Kathy is overextended by one unit, but they agree to ignore this until after the bidding is done and then they'll redistribute the tasks if necessary. Kathy decides to let Jason have the Determine Marker task and Jason agrees that the Determine Current Player task is hers.

This leaves user story (24), Recognizing a Win. Kathy is still uncomfortable with the way the tasks have been written. Jason bids three units each on tasks 24-A and 24-B and one unit on 24-C, the Checking Potential Wins task, the Finding Potential Wins task, and the Recording a Win Task, respectively. Kathy considers the bids and tells Jason that the tasks are his. Here's a summary of the bidding.

	TASK #	TITLE	ESTIMATE (units)
Jason	2-A	Board-GUI	1
	2-B	Board-Model	1
	24-A	Checking Potential Wins	3
	24-B	Finding Potential Wins	3
	24-C	Recording a Win	1
	19-A	Determine Marker	1
Total			10
Kathy	19-B	Place Marker	4
	19-C	Ignore Bad Clicks	1
	19-D	Determine Current Player	2
	25-A	Choose Marker GUI	2
	25-B	Record Marker Choice	1
Total			10

You may notice that this totals to twenty units, although the client only selected nineteen units of stories. Because there was a small fudge factor built in, Jason and Kathy don't have to go back to the client and ask Steve to reorder his priorities. Story (24), Recognizing a Win, is now worth seven units and not six. If the task estimates had forced the total over twenty units, Jason and Kathy would have had to negotiate further with Steve. In this case, they are ready to begin the iteration.

REALITY CHECK

Halfway through the iteration, Kathy and Jason take a look at what they've accomplished. It took a little longer to set up their environment than they expected. Jason's estimate for 2-B, Board-Model task was too low. Kathy's estimate for 25-A, Choose Marker GUI, was a little low also. At the end of the first week they have completed all of stories (2), Board Setup, and (25), Choose Marker, as well as task 19-A, Determine Marker task. This leaves them with tasks 19-B, Place Marker task, 19-C, Ignore Bad Clicks task, 19-D, Determine Current Player task, and all of user story (24), Recognizing a Win. In terms of units, fourteen units remain to be done.

Jason smiles and says, "That's not so bad. There were problems starting up and some things took longer than they should. These next stories should go more quickly. We'll make it."

Kathy stops him and says, "No, we need to tell Steve."

Jason disagrees. "Steve doesn't need to know," he says. "By the time the week's over we'll be back on track, or pretty close. He'll never know the difference."

Kathy reminds Jason that telling the truth is fundamental to the process. "Maybe," she says, "Steve will agree that it's no big deal, but it is his call to make."

They agree to tell Steve. He's happy that two of the stories have been completed, but he's not happy to be eliminating more user stories so early in the project. He asks the developers if they need to reestimate their tasks given what they now know. They think about it and agree that their remaining estimates are still pretty accurate. The problem is that they aren't accomplishing nearly enough work. In the first week of the iteration they accomplished six units worth of work. Steve looks at the two stories left to complete. There are seven units remaining to be done in each.

Jason reminds Kathy that really he should have estimated one of the stories higher and that they could do seven units worth of stories this week. Kathy agrees with him. Although this seems plausible, it is dangerous to reassess what you should have estimated after the fact. Perhaps if they'd checked with Steve earlier they wouldn't have spent the one unit's worth of work on 19-A, Determine Marker task, and it would now be available. Steve considers his alternatives and decides that he'd like to see the team complete user story (19), Make Move.

Moving from One Iteration to Another

It's hard to know when summer ends and autumn begins. There is a transitional period where the seasons are muddied a bit. To make things easier, we have an agreed upon a date for the first day of autumn. It's the same way with iterations. An iteration ends on a particular day and yet some of the activities associated with preparing for the next iteration feel like the end of the last iteration while others feel like the beginning of the next.

As an iteration ends, you must again ask what you've accomplished. In this case Steve and Kathy completed tasks 19-B, Place Marker task, and 19-D, Determine Current Player task, but didn't quite complete 19-C, Ignore Bad Clicks task. From their perspective, they completed six units. They are allowed to commit to six units each week in the next iteration. This actually matches the reality of the first week in this iteration. Steve and Kathy completed six units each week during the iteration. Although they estimated that they would complete twenty units, they only completed twelve. This is an important and telling data point. They can bid on twelve units in the next iteration and have a fair amount of confidence that this is a more accurate estimate than twenty.

Take a minute to look at the situation from the client's point of view. Remember, the client doesn't care about tasks. The client cares about completed user stories. From that standpoint, only five units of user stories were completed in this iteration. Jason and Kathy are able to revise the estimate of user story (19), Make Move, to be one unit if they'd like because they've completed all but a task that they judged to be worth one unit.

They could also choose to reevaluate the time it would take to accomplish that task. It is likely that Steve will choose user story (19), Make Move, in the next iteration because he has so much invested in it already. For the marginal cost of one unit he gets eight units worth of value.

Before the next iteration begins, Steve needs to look at the remaining user stories and again group them according to their immediate importance to him. The developers need to estimate the stories that Steve sees as being the most important. Steve will then use these estimates to choose twelve units worth of user stories. The developers will break these stories, and a few more that don't make it into this stack, into tasks and estimate and sign-up for each task. Steve may then have to change his preferences and make choices based on these more recent estimates. The cycle continues until one side says *Stop*.

Chapter 13

Refactoring—Sharpening Your Knife

You and your partner write a test and quickly write the code that gets the test to compile and pass. Something just doesn't feel right. Maybe the problem is with a method. It could be too long, it could be misnamed, or it could belong in a different class. Maybe you've written a very similar method in another class and these methods belong in a common super class. Maybe as you look around the class you've been working with there is complicated conditional logic or duplicated code. For some reason the code doesn't seem as clean as it could be. Take a moment and clean it up. The subtitle of Martin Fowler's book, *Refactoring,* is "improving the design of existing code." You should own a copy of Fowler's book.

Refactoring may initially seem to be outside the scope of eXtreme Programming. After all, while you're messing around with code that already works you don't appear to be spending your time on a user story that the client has selected. You are taking a moment to sharpen your chef's knife so that the next time you need to use it you will be able to cut through food more quickly and more safely. You will return to this code at some point and not remember what you were thinking when you wrote it. If that's too close to home, you may visit code that someone else has written and not know what they were thinking when they wrote it. You'll wish they had taken the time to clean up the code to better communicate its meaning.

A comprehensive suite of unit tests is necessary for fearless refactoring. Unit tests let you know the code is working at all steps of your refactoring. You don't want to make the code prettier and break functionality. You only refactor working code. Your code should be passing all unit tests before you refactor it. As with other XP practices, you will refactor in very small steps, pausing to compile the code and run your unit tests after each small step. You should never need to resort to the debugger. All changes are small and reversible and the unit tests will point to where problems arise.

What if you have just written a unit test and you're about to write the code that makes it pass when you notice something that badly needs refactoring? You've noticed code that needs to be fixed but your unit tests aren't running at 100%. Comment out the test that you just wrote, run the tests, make sure they are all passing, then refactor the code. Now go ahead and uncomment the last unit test and continue coding. You'll most often notice code that needs refactoring when you're "in the neighborhood." Take care of it and move on.

Shouldn't existing code be clean when you get to it? Sure, and commercial software should be released bug free. Once code is working it's tempting to quickly move on to the next task. Also, right after code is written it may not occur to you that there is anything wrong with it. You'll also find that some members of your team are better at locating potential refactorings than are others. Some of this ability comes from their pet ways of accomplishing frequent tasks and some comes from a greater amount of experience in writing and reading code. Finally, clean code is in the eye of the beholder.

This chapter is not a comprehensive treatment of refactoring. You'll follow through a couple of examples to get the flavor of this practice. The idea is for you to see the benefits of refactoring your code. Often while pair programming, while your partner is driving, you'll see an opportunity to refactor. Suggest the refactoring to the driver. If the driver is busy getting code to work and you see a better way, refactoring allows you to wait until the tests pass before improving the code. You spend a lot more time reading and modifying code than you do writing it. The purpose of refactoring is to make code easier to read and easier to use and modify.

When you are first beginning, it is difficult to find opportunities to refactor. In this chapter, you'll focus on the most obvious way to refactor: replacing duplicated code, renaming methods, and splitting long methods. You may want to begin reading Fowler's book, especially the chapter he wrote with Kent Beck on recognizing when your code needs refactoring. They describe this as recognizing bad smells. Working with others and talking to coaches and mentors can help you develop this experience. Most students write a program and then move on. Because they don't have to wrestle with understanding or maintaining what they've written, they don't need to develop a sense of smell. In an extended project like the one in this course, you will revisit code and see the need to make it better. This project will help you develop your nose.

You should read and study Fowler's book, *Refactoring*. This chapter demonstrates a few refactorings but Fowler takes you carefully through the steps of performing a refactoring. He insists that you take very small, testable, reversible steps. Fowler has a companion web site, www.refactoring.com. You should also look at Joshua Kerievsky's work, *Refactoring to Patterns* available at www.industriallogic.com.

You don't need specialized tools to refactor but they make the job easier. The easier a process is, the more likely you are to follow it. Currently, Java IDEs such as JBuilder, IntelliJ, and Eclipse have support for refactoring and more are following suit.

EXAMPLE APPLICATION THE TETRIS GAME

Tetris is a favorite assignment in an introductory Java course. The game tends to be a familiar one and is surprisingly easy to program. Pieces that consist of four square blocks appear in the top center of the board and move downward in discrete time steps. The player can move the pieces right or left or rotate the pieces ninety degrees. Some homemade versions only allow rotations in one direction and some allow the player to press a key to have the piece drop down as far as it can on the board. Only one piece moves at a time. It is restricted from moving off of the board on the right or left and it can't move into a space occupied by other pieces. The moving piece finishes its turn when it can't move down any more. At that point any completed rows are eliminated and the rows above them move down to fill their void. If a new piece can enter the board then play continues, otherwise the game is over.

In a recent student assignment, the students were to create an abstract class named `Piece` and concrete subclasses for each of the classic shapes. These classes were called `StraightPiece`, `Square`, `Hill`, `LeftHook`, `RightHook`, `LeftRise`, and `RightRise`. In this chapter you'll see refactorings that were applied to the code that was turned in by students.

DUPLICATED CODE

One of the first smells you learn to look for is duplicated code. If you see the same code in more than one place, look for a way to collect the duplicated code. One advantage is that then changes to the code only need to be made in one place. Another advantage is that the code ends up where it wants to be. In the first example in this section, removing a student's duplicated code shows that the duplication was unnecessary and allows the rest of the method to dramatically simplify. In the second example, removing duplicated code in two classes leads to placing it in the common superclass and again simplifies the original classes.

Example: In a Single Method

The following method was used to initialize a new piece that was chosen at random from the seven possible types of concrete pieces. Although you could find other things to improve about this code, focus for a moment on the duplicated code highlighted below.

```
public void letsRoll(){
  switch ((int)(Math.random()*7)){
    case 0:
      activePiece = RightHook.getRightHook();
      ml = new MoveListener(activePiece);
      gameBoard.addKeyListener(ml);
      break;
    case 1:
      activePiece = LeftHook.getLeftHook();
      ml = new MoveListener(activePiece);
      gameBoard.addKeyListener(ml);
      break;
    case 2:
      activePiece = RightRise.getRightRise();
      ml = new MoveListener(activePiece);
      gameBoard.addKeyListener(ml);
      break;
    case 3:
      activePiece = LeftRise.getLeftRise();
```

```
      ml = new MoveListener(activePiece);
      gameBoard.addKeyListener(ml);
      break;
    case 4:
      activePiece = Hill.getHill();
      ml = new MoveListener(activePiece);
      gameBoard.addKeyListener(ml);
      break;
    case 5:
      activePiece = StraightPiece.getStraightPiece();
      ml = new MoveListener(activePiece);
      gameBoard.addKeyListener(ml);
      break;
    case 6:
      activePiece = Square.getSquare();
      ml = new MoveListener(activePiece);
      gameBoard.addKeyListener(ml);
      break;
    }
    gameBoard.setVisible(true);
  }
```

The same two lines appear in each of the seven `case` statements. The act of instantiating a `MoveListener` and registering it with the `gameboard` object is performed after the assignment of the `activePiece` in each case. Move these two lines outside of the `switch` statement and the code looks like this.

```
public void letsRoll(){
  switch ((int)(Math.random()*7)){
    case 0:
      activePiece = RightHook.getRightHook();
      break;
    case 1:
      activePiece = LeftHook.getLeftHook();
      break;
    case 2:
      activePiece = RightRise.getRightRise();
      break;
    case 3:
      activePiece = LeftRise.getLeftRise();
      break;
    case 4:
      activePiece = Hill.getHill();
      break;
    case 5:
      activePiece = StraightPiece.getStraightPiece();
      break;
    case 6:
      activePiece = Square.getSquare();
      break;
  }
```

```
    ml = new MoveListener(activePiece);
    gameBoard.addKeyListener(ml);
    gameBoard.setVisible(true);
  }
```

The code has gotten smaller, but the advantage is much greater than that. Now that you've moved the MoveListener code out of each case you can see that the switch statement is just assigning a random piece to the activePiece variable. You can create an array of Piece objects called pieceList as follows.

```
Piece [] pieceList = {RightHook.getRightHook(),
  LeftHook.GetLeftHook(), RightRise.getRightRise(),
  LeftRise.getLeftRise(), Hill.getHill(),
  StraightPiece.getStraightPiece(), Square.getSquare()};
```

Now you can get rid of the switch statement in letsRoll() like this:

```
public void letsRoll(){
  activePiece = pieceList[(int)(Math.random()*7)]
  ml = new MoveListener(activePiece);
  gameBoard.addKeyListener(ml);
  gameBoard.setVisible(true);
}
```

Compare this version to the original version of letsRoll() and you can see how much more readable this version is. The call to gameBoard.setVisible() looks misplaced. You need it the first time letsRoll() is called but not anytime after that. This call should be moved. A likely place for it is in the constructor of the GameBoard. That leaves us with this version of letsRoll().

```
public void letsRoll(){
  activePiece = pieceList[(int)(Math.random()*7)]
  ml = new MoveListener(activePiece);
  gameBoard.addKeyListener(ml);
}
```

The last two lines don't look right. Do you really want to create a new MoveListener every time a new piece starts to drop from the top of the board. Really only one piece moves at a time so you only need one MoveListener at a time. If you look at this code, it seems that the reason for creating a new instance of MoveListener is so that a pointer to the current active piece can be passed in. Add a setter for activePiece to MoveListener.

```
public void setActivePiece(Piece activePiece){
  this.activePiece = activePiece;
}
```

Also change the name of the MoveListener from ml, which doesn't communicate anything, to moveListener. Now you can change letsRoll() to the following:

```
public void letsRoll(){
  activePiece = pieceList[(int)(Math.random()*7)];
  moveListener.setActivePiece(activePiece);
}
```

This simplification was possible because you eliminated the duplicated code in each switch statement. Then it became clear what the switch statement was doing and it could be eliminated. Also you could then make changes to what was once the duplicated code in one place without having to change it in seven places.

The result is that the code communicates its intent much better. One reason that refactoring fits well with XP is that XP stresses communication. The team communicates with each other, pairs communicate as they program, and the team and the customer constantly communicate. The code should also communicate with the developers. If your code is hard to understand, it should probably be refactored.

You may want to refactor `letsRoll()` further. Create a private method called `nextPiece()`.

```
private Piece nextPiece(){
  return pieceList[ (int) (Math.random()*7)];
}
```

Now `letsRoll()` becomes the following:

```
public void letsRoll(){
  moveListener.setActivePiece(nextPiece());
}
```

You've added another method but `letsRoll()` is even easier to read. Whether or not you take this last step is a matter of taste. Your code is more flexible. Your assignment to `activePiece` is the result of a call to `nextPiece()`. If you decide to change the way pieces are selected you can just change the body of `nextPiece()`. You can change the collection type used for storing the pieces and call an iterator from `nextPiece()` that chooses the pieces in some particular way. On the other hand, you shouldn't code for features you don't need yet. If this final piece of the refactoring makes the code clearer to you, do it. Even if you decide not to add the `nextPiece()` method now, it will be simple enough to change later if you need to.

Example: In Two Classes

Often your head is down and you are working hard on your task and you don't notice duplicated code. Suppose your task is to get each of the pieces to move to the right one space, assuming that they can. First you try to get the `StraightPiece` to `moveRight()`. After writing the appropriate unit tests you end up with code that looks like this.

```
public class StraightPiece extends Piece{
  public void moveRight(){
    for (int i=0;i<4;i++){
      getBox(i).translate(1,0);
    }
  }
// rest of class omitted
}
```

Next, your task is to get the Square to moveRight(). You write the test and you know how to get it to pass: just use the same code that worked for StraightPiece. In this case, the following code will get your new test to compile and pass.

```
public class Square extends Piece {
  public void moveRight(){
    for (int i=0;i<4;i++){
      getBox(i).translate(1,0);
    }
  }
// rest of class omitted
}
```

Now your code is working, you notice the duplication and go about fixing it. Fowler refers to this refactoring as Pull Up Method. You could wait until you've provided each type of piece with the ability to move one square to the right, but the refactoring is calling out to you. Take the moveRight() method from Square and copy it into the Piece class. Remember that Piece is an abstract class that is the common superclass for Square and StraightPiece. Eliminate the moveRight() method from Square and compile the code and run the tests. Everything should pass. Comment out the moveRight() method in StraightPiece, compile, and run the tests. Everything should pass. Remove the code you just commented out in StraightPiece. Even though all you removed was commented out code, compile, and run the tests. This process of having the confidence to remove dead code is a direct result of having comprehensive unit tests. It is a goosebump producing experience.

When everything passes, you smile because you know how easy you've made this task. You can now write tests for each of the other pieces moving right and they should all compile and pass without writing any additional code in the subclasses. A moment spent refactoring has provided an immediate benefit. You can also see how easy it as to add the ability for each piece to move left one square.

Could you have refactored after writing the first class? Yes, but you may not have realized the code could be simplified. You could have reasoned from the beginning that moveRight() would be the same for each class and that it could be placed in Piece. Refactoring means that you can easily take advantage of this fact later if you weren't so clever to begin with. Unit tests mean that you are sure your refactoring behaved as it should. Also, as you saw in the test first tutorial, you will need to refactor your unit test code from time to time as well.

ALMOST DUPLICATED CODE

Duplicated code is easy to spot and usually not difficult to fix. If code is almost the same in two different places but not quite, it may be harder to locate and trickier to fix. In this section you'll see two quick examples of how you can extract the common behavior. In the first method, a helper method is created that each of the original methods can call. This allows you to remove the duplication without changing the interface. The second example shows the use of a template method to extract the common behavior from sibling classes into a parent and defer the class specific behavior to the subclass.

Example: In Different Methods of One Class

Continuing with the last example, once you have created the methods `moveLeft()`, `moveRight()`, and `moveDown()` in the Piece class, you'll notice that they're almost the same.

```
public void moveRight(){
  for (int i=0;i<4;i++){
    getBox(i).translate(1,0);
  }
}
public void moveLeft(){
  for (int i=0;i<4;i++){
    getBox(i).translate(-1,0);
  }
}
public void moveDown(){
  for (int i=0;i<4;i++){
    getBox(i).translate(0,1);
  }
}
```

They differ only in the direction the boxes are translated. Create a method called `move()` that takes the direction as parameters.

```
private void move(int x, int y){
  for (int i=0;i<4;i++){
    getBox(i).translate(x,y);
  }
}
```

Now you can change the original methods to call `move()`.

```
public void moveRight(){
  move(1,0);
}
public void moveLeft(){
  move(-1,0);
}
public void moveDown(){
  move(0,1);
}
```

Example: In Two Classes

If you have methods that are almost the same in sibling classes you can use Fowler's Form Template Method refactoring. In the game, all pieces moved left, right, and down in exactly the same way so it was easy to pull this behavior up to the superclass `Piece`. The details of rotating are different for each piece. A `StraightPiece` initially consists of four adjacent boxes in a single row. The standard rotation is such that the box that is one from the left side doesn't move. When `StraightPiece` is rotated, it uses the following code.

```
public boolean rotate(){
    prepareToMove();
    if (isHorizontal(tempBoxes)) {
      tempBoxes[0].translate(1,-1);
      tempBoxes[2].translate(-1,1);
      tempBoxes[3].translate(-2,2);
    } else {
      tempBoxes[0].translate(-1,1);
      tempBoxes[2].translate(1,-1);
      tempBoxes[3].translate(2,-2);
    }
    if (canMove()) makeMove();
    return canMove;
  }
```

A `Hill` initially consists of three adjacent boxes in a single row with the fourth box being right above the center box in the row of three. When this piece is rotated, it uses the following code:

```
public boolean rotate(){
   prepareToMove();
   switch (numberOfQuarterTurns(tempBoxes)){
     case 0:
       tempBoxes[0].translate(-1,1);
       tempBoxes[1].translate(1,1);
       tempBoxes[3].translate(-1,-1);
       break;
     case 1:
       tempBoxes[0].translate(1,1);
       tempBoxes[1].translate(1,-1);
       tempBoxes[3].translate(-1,1);
       break;
     case 2:
       tempBoxes[0].translate(1,-1);
       tempBoxes[1].translate(-1,-1);
       tempBoxes[3].translate(1,1);
       break;
     case 3:
       tempBoxes[0].translate(-1,-1);
       tempBoxes[1].translate(-1,1);
       tempBoxes[3].translate(1,-1);
       break;
   }
   if (canMove()) makeMove();
   return canMove;
 }
```

You'll notice that the steps are exactly the same. In this case the process is simplified by creating a template method in the class `Piece` that defers the actual rotation logic to the subclass. In `Piece` you will need the method `rotate()` along with an abstract method `rotateClockwise()`. A snippet looks like this:

```
public abstract Point[] rotateClockwise(Point[] tempBoxes);
public boolean rotate(){
    prepareToMove();
    tempBoxes = rotateClockwise(tempBoxes);
    if (canMove()) makeMove();
    return canMove;
  }
```

Now each concrete class can implement the `rotateClockwise()` method with the specific logic it needs. For example, `StraightPiece` would look like this:

```
public Point[] rotateClockwise(Point[] tempBoxes){
    if (isHorizontal(tempBoxes)) {
      tempBoxes[0].translate(1,-1);
      tempBoxes[2].translate(-1,1);
      tempBoxes[3].translate(-2,2);
    } else {
      tempBoxes[0].translate(-1,1);
      tempBoxes[2].translate(1,-1);
      tempBoxes[3].translate(2,-2);
    }
    return tempBoxes;
  }
```

In this way the structure of a rotation is in the `Piece` class and can be shared by all concrete subclasses while the details of the rotation that are specific to each subclass are in the `rotateClockwise()` method of that subclass. It is easier to see who's responsible for what by refactoring the code this way.

The steps of the refactoring are quite involved and you should check out the description in the Form Template Method section of Fowler's book. The template method is detailed in the Gang of Four book, *Design Patterns*. In XP, because you don't do big design up front, you often don't start by saying, "I'll use this design pattern here and that one there." Familiarity with design patterns will allow you to recognize when applying one is a refactoring that will greatly clean up your code. In this case, knowing about the template method made this refactoring straightforward. Joshua Kerievsky's book, *Refactoring to Patterns* presents code that can benefit from the introduction of a design pattern along with the mechanics of refactoring your code to reach that end.

WHAT'S IN A NAME

The name of a method or variable should clearly communicate what it does or what it is. There's a good chance that you won't get a name right the first time. If so, you should consider renaming it. Look at the first example of duplicated code. The name of the method is `letsRoll()`. What does it do? When you call it what is the expected behavior and do you expect a returned value? A more descriptive name might be `chooseNewPieceAndInitializeIt()` or `selectNewPieceAndStartItMoving()` or startNextPieceAtTop(). If you are new to Java you may be uncomfortable with such long method names. But, any time you invoke this method, it is clear what the resulting behavior will be. Fowler and Beck suggest that you turn the comment that you might include in describing the method into the name of the method. What if your method is too complicated to describe so simply? Perhaps your method does too much. You'll see an example of this in the next section.

Be careful to follow conventions. The names are intended to communicate meaning and there are standard naming conventions. For example, you wouldn't want to name this method getNewPieceAndInitializeIt(). Even though getNewPiece() and chooseNewPiece() seem synonymous, the former sounds like an accessor method that returns the value of the variable newPiece and the second sounds like a selection is being made. Similarly you wouldn't name the method START_NEXT_PIECE_AT_TOP(). Even though the parentheses indicate this is a method, at first glance it looks like a constant. The underlying assumption in this discussion is that you want your code to communicate and to help those reading your code. The person you may be helping most is yourself.

The following code is fairly easy to understand:

```
public boolean moveRightIfCan() {
  if ( piece.isAbleToMoveRight() ) {
    piece.moveRight();
    return true;
  } else return false;
}
```

You can see that the method isAbleToMoveRight() returns a boolean that you can guess indicates whether or not the object piece is able to move right one square or not. Similarly, you can guess that the method moveRight() actually performs the move. Now if someone else invokes the method moveRightIfCan(), they can guess that the behavior will be to move to the right if it is possible to do so. They may not anticipate that they get a boolean in return, but good naming has communicated a lot.

As code evolves methods no longer do what they once did. In the first iteration of Tetris the students had a method named rotateClockwise(). It was then discovered that pieces in one commercial implementation actually rotated counter clockwise. The body of the method was changed so that the pieces rotated counter clockwise and yet the original name remained. This method should probably have been renamed rotateCounterClockwise().

Suppose you decide to rename the method letsRoll() to startNextPieceAtTheTop(). You not only have to rename the method but you have to make sure that every place that you call letsRoll() is changed to an invocation of startNextPieceAtTheTop(). This part of the refactoring includes your unit tests. When you change the name of a method you also have to change the unit tests that use that method. In addition to this single instance of the method, you also need to see if you have overloaded the method, or if it overrides a method in a superclass that also needs to be renamed, or if it is overridden by a method in one or more subclasses that also needs to be renamed.

What seems to be a simple refactoring can be quite involved. Fortunately this is one of the first refactorings that tools support. Fowler calls this refactoring Rename

Method. In his Mechanics section, he describes a very conservative approach to implementing this refactoring. It is, of course, possible to combine steps but then if something goes wrong it is much harder to discover where to undo the damage you've caused.

You may just be tempted to change the name of the method and use compiler errors to find every place the method is called. Fowler suggests that you copy the method and change its name so that you have the old method and the new method. Compile and run your tests. Now change the old method so that it just calls the renamed method. Compile and run your tests. So far nothing should have gone wrong, you've just added an extra point of indirection. Find all of the references to the old method and change them to point to the new method. After each one, compile and run your tests. When you think you are done, comment out the old method. At this point you may discover references you haven't handled yet. Handle them and try again. The other thing that could go wrong at this point is that you're implementing an interface that requires this method signature. In that case, you can't comment out the method. Otherwise, you can eliminate the unused method.

Just as you can rename methods, you should take the time to rename variables that are poorly named. For private variables this should be easy, as all of your usage of the variable will be in the same class. One student named components numerically in the order that he thought of them. So for example, he may have a `JButton` named `one` and a `JTextField` named `two` and a `JMenuBar` named `three` and a `JPanel` named `four` and so on. You would then see calls such as `four.setBackground(Color.white)`. Code like this is very hard to read. It was as if the student had run his variables through an obfuscator to throw others off.

SPLITTING LONG METHODS

One of the most useful techniques in refactoring is to extract code and leave a descriptive name in its place that points somewhere else. You may have a complicated conditional in an if statement that can be cleaned up in this way. For example, consider this code for determining whether a piece can move:

```
private boolean canMove(){
  canMove = true;
  for (int i = 0; i< 4; i++){
    canMove = canMove &&
            tempBoxes[i].x < Config.NUMBER_OF_COLUMNS &&
            tempBoxes[i].x >=0 &&
            tempBoxes[i].y < Config.NUMBER_OF_ROWS  &&
            tempBoxes[i].y >= 0 &&
            gameBoard.getRow(tempBoxes[i].y).
              getCell(tempBoxes[i].x).isEmpty();
  }
  return canMove;
}
```

This isn't bad. But it might be clearer if you extracted the code that tells you whether the move would place the square off the board as well as the code that tells you whether the move would place the square into an occupied cell. Here is the refactored `canMove()` method:.

```
private boolean canMove(){
    canMove = true;
    for (int i = 0; i < 4; i++){
      canMove = canMove &&
                isTargetOnTheBoard(tempBoxes[i]) &&
                isTargetUnoccupied(tempBoxes[i]);

    }
    return canMove;
  }
```

It's much easier to read this `canMove()` method. You can see that for each box you're checking if the target is on the board and is unoccupied. You've pulled the logic into two utility methods.

```
private boolean isTargetOnTheBoard(Point thisBox){
   return (thisBox.x < Config.NUMBER_OF_COLUMNS &&
           thisBox.x >=0 &&
           thisBox.y < Config.NUMBER_OF_ROWS  &&
           thisBox.y >= 0 );
}

private boolean isTargetUnoccupied(Point thisBox){
  return  gameBoard.getRow(thisBox.y).
            getCell(thisBox.x).isEmpty();
}
```

The second method may be a bit puzzling. You took a single statement from the original code and extracted it into its own method. The resulting code isn't any shorter. One advantage is that you have documented the behavior with a descriptive method name. Now when it is called, it is clear to the reader what is being checked. A second advantage is that you have separated out the behavior of checking whether a cell is occupied.

A good place to use this technique, which Fowler calls the Extract Method, is when shortening a method that is too long. Contrary to popular belief, XP does not tell you not to comment your code. There is, however, a rule of thumb that when you are about to introduce a comment you may want to consider whether extracting the code you are about to comment on would be more helpful. Consider this code for setting up the `GameFrame`. It is long enough that the author thought that comments would be helpful (other authors might not have even included these comments):

```
public GameFrame()
  {
    // creating the components
    aFrame = new JFrame("Game Frame");
    gamePanel = new GamePanel();
    aMenuBar = new JMenuBar();
    optionsMenu = new JMenu("Options");

    // creating the action listeners
    resetGameAction = new ResetGameAction();
    pauseGameAction = new PauseGameAction();
```

```
    // adding components to the menubars and menus
    aMenuBar.add(optionsMenu);
    optionsMenu.add( resetGameAction);
    optionsMenu.add(pauseGameAction);

    // setting the layout and adding the
    // JMenubar, and JPanel. Also setting default
    // close operation to EXIT_ON_CLOSE
    aFrame.getContentPane().setLayout(new BorderLayout());
    aFrame.setSize(400,350);
    aFrame.setJMenuBar(aMenuBar);
    aFrame.getContentPane().add(gamePanel,
      BorderLayout.CENTER);
    aFrame.setVisible(true);
    aFrame.setDefaultCloseOperation(JFrame.EXIT_ON_CLOSE);
  }
```

The code could be refactored easily using the comments as guides.

```
public GameFrame(){
  initializeTheComponents();
  createTheActionListeners();
  setUpMenus();
  layoutTheFrame();
}
```

Other choices would accomplish the same result. Notice that now the constructor for `GameFrame` is readable. Each method contains very few lines that perform a task described by the method name. For example, `setUpMenus()` looks like this:

```
private void setUpMenus(){
  aMenuBar.add(optionsMenu);
  optionsMenu.add( resetGameAction);
  optionsMenu.add(pauseGameAction);
}
```

When you find long methods that require comments for understanding, you should consider using the extract method of refactoring.

FINAL THOUGHTS

Refactoring brings out the art in programming. You can see two paintings of the same setting and like one better than the other. Someone else may disagree with your choice. In XP the notions of writing the simplest thing that could possibly work and improving the design of code are subjective. There are some common notions of good and bad practices, but you will find many shades of gray. During this project play with refactoring and enjoy the security of having unit tests that allow you to change working code without worrying about breaking it.

Chapter 14

Customer Written Tests—

Automating the Acceptance Process

Your goal is to produce software that does what the customer asks for. There are many factors that make this difficult. There can be a gap between what the customer thinks is clearly being expressed and your understanding of their needs. Often, in the process of writing the software, you discover issues that were not made explicit. As the software evolves, the customer thinks of new requirements or wants to make adjustments to existing requirements.

Let's assume that if you could figure out what a customer wants then you could write the code to make it work. How can you be sure you understand what a customer wants? You and your client try to capture your common understanding in a sequence of activities called acceptance tests. The customer should write these tests. That doesn't mean that the client will be writing code. In the framework we'll explore in this chapter, the customer designs HTML tables and you provide a little bit of code to glue the tables to the parts of your application that the tables will be exercising.

Acceptance tests help the customer discover and the developers understand what is expected of a particular user story. In XP, we look at user stories as describing a conversation. They are not hard and fast requirement documents. Acceptance tests are a way of asking the customer how they will determine that you have satisfied the goals of the user story. As with all facets of XP, a customer can add acceptance tests to a story if they think the costs of doing so are justified.

Acceptance tests are more useful if they can be automated. You want to be able to run the tests all the time. Acceptance tests point you in the direction of tasks that can be used to split the user stories. You don't need to write your acceptance tests before you write your production code in the same way that you write unit tests first. Acceptance tests will, however, focus your efforts on the customer requirements.

In this chapter we'll work through a couple of examples of acceptance tests using the Fit framework. Even though it is early on in the life of this framework, there are compelling reasons for considering its use. Fit provides a format for acceptance tests with two chief advantages. First, customers are comfortable enough with spreadsheets and tables that they can write their own acceptance tests. Second, the approach is formal enough that developers can write the fixtures that tie the tests to the code being tested. In other words, with relatively little work on the part of customers or developers, acceptance tests can be written and run automatically so that both the customers and the developers can track the progress towards completing user stories.

THE FIT FRAMEWORK

There are four pieces to writing and automatically running acceptance tests.

- First, the customer has to write the acceptance tests. In the case of the Fit framework, the customer will be creating tables on a web page using either HTML or a Wiki.
- Second, the developers will write the code that makes the acceptance tests pass. This is the shipping code that the developers will release to the customers every couple of weeks.
- Third, the developers will need to write a little bit of code that maps from the tests the customers write to the application being tested. These fixtures will extend classes in the Fit framework and will exercise the shipping code according to the customer specifications.
- Finally, there needs to be a framework that parses the HTML or Wiki tables and makes the appropriate calls in the test fixtures created in the third step. These are provided by the Fit framework and can be run from the command line or remotely using scripts written in Perl, Python, Ruby, or other languages.

Writing Acceptance Tests as HTML Tables

There are several types of tests that can be run from the Fit framework. We'll take a quick look at three of them. Other types of tests are being developed for the Fit framework, but you can design a wide array of tests using a combination of the three basic types described in this section. In all cases the intent is that the tables express what the customer is interested in verifying in a form that is friendly to both customers and developers.

First, imagine that you've designed a new calculator program that you'd like to test. One test might be something like checking that 36 + 12 = 48. Suppose that you aren't really interesting in testing addition. This first test is designed to test the results of buttons being pushed and information being entered into text fields in a GUI.

enter	36	
Press	plusButton	
enter	12	
press	equalsButton	
check	result	48

A second test may be used when you need to quickly set some values and check the results of performing various actions. For example, we could set our first input to

36, our second input to 12, and then check what we get back for the sum, difference, product, and difference. We could then repeat the test when the values are 30 and 5. Here's what that test could look like in a table form.

firstNumber	secondNumber	sum()	difference()	product()	quotient()
36	12	48	24	432	3
30	5	35	25	150	6

Again, the test is easy to read. In this case the first two columns will be treated as input. The final four columns will call methods with the names that are specified in the first row of the table and the results will be compared with the values specified in the test data row.

A third type of test is used to look at the characteristics of an object. Perhaps you have an object that has been returned by a search and you want to check its state. As a simple example, suppose you have booked a flight from Cleveland to Seattle and have been given the flight locator id 123ABC. Then a table might look like this.

airline	id	departure City	destination City	flight Number	departure Date
BigAir	123ABC	Cleveland	Seattle	429	11/27/02

Of course your record contains more information. We didn't ask for all of the information available in this one table. We could also create a second table that queries some of the other information like this.

airline	id	departure Time	arrival Time	meal Served	movie	number Of Stops
BigAir	123ABC	11:30 EST	13:00 PST	lunch	none	none

These tests show that the name of the airline and the id should identify the record and that the rest of the information can be compared with the data stored in the object.

Supporting the HTML Tables with Fixtures

The next step is to process these tests so that the results can be reported back. To a computer there is no apparent difference between the tables for one type of test and those for another. In Fit, the code that is responsible for interpreting one or more tables is called a fixture. To map a table to a given fixture you'll list the Java class used to process the table in the first row of the table. For example, a subclass of `ColumnFixture` is required to process the calculator example that adds, subtracts, multiplies, and divides. Suppose that this class is called `CalculateThis` and that it is part of the `answers` package. Then your table would look like this.

answers.CalculateThis					
firstNumber	**secondNumber**	**sum()**	**difference()**	**product()**	**quotient()**
36	12	48	24	432	3

The `CalculateThis` class will need to have public variables `firstNumber` and `secondNumber`. In our example, we can declare these variables to be `ints`. `CalculateThis` will also need public methods named `sum()`, `difference()`, `product()`, and `quotient()`. The variables don't take any arguments and they return `ints` that can be compared with the values in the table.

The first calculator example will use the `ActionFixture` class that comes with the framework. The `ActionFixture` class uses the keywords start, press, enter, and check. The start keyword points to the class that understands the method names that are in the second column after the words Press, enter, and check. Let's assume that the class in our example is `CalculateGUI` in the `answers` package. We have to give names to the methods accepting entered input. Now the table looks like this.

fit.ActionFixture		
start	answers.CalculateGUI	
enter	number	36
press	plusButton	
enter	number	12
press	equalsButton	
check	result	48

The `CalculateGUI` class then would need no argument methods such as those named `plusButton` and `equalsButton`. It would also need a method named `number` that accepts, in this case, an `int`. Finally, the `result` method needs to return an `int`.

Together the tables and the corresponding classes combine to define the acceptance tests. The fixtures should contain little more than the calls into the production code. The next step is to write the functionality into your application.

Writing the Code to Pass the Tests

Remember that the focus of your efforts is still delivering working code that meets the customer's requirements. The Fit framework is designed to make it easy to write the acceptance tests that call into your code in the same way that JUnit is a framework that allows you to easily write unit tests. Once you are accustomed to the Fit framework, it won't take you long to extend a column or row fixture or to write the code that you need to get an action fixture working.

Acceptance tests should not change the way you write the actual code. Acceptance tests will help you partition the user stories into tasks. Pairs of developers can work on these tasks by writing unit tests and then the code that makes the unit tests pass. Often the acceptance tests can help suggest unit tests that you might write. The fixtures should not determine the interface of the code being tested in the same way that unit tests do. When it is time to deploy your code, you will strip out the acceptance test HTML, Java source, and Java class files.

Running Acceptance Tests with Fit

You need to process your acceptance tests by passing them as input into an application. The runner we'll use in this chapter is `FileRunner`. You'll run it from the command line by making sure that `fit.FileRunner` and the classes in your fixture are in the classpath.

You'll also need to pass in the path to the input and output files. We'll look at the actual syntax in depth later in this chapter.

You'll get an indication of the results of processing the tests in the Terminal window. Exceptions often indicate that a variable, method, or class required by the table isn't provided or accessible. The problem also might be with the type returned by the method. You should check that your classpath has been set correctly and make sure that you have compiled your fixture. When bouncing between Java code and HTML, it's easy to forget that HTML only needs to be saved while Java code needs to be both saved and compiled.

The results of running the acceptance tests should be easy to read. The resulting HTML file is color coded to highlight areas that you need to address. Yellow areas are intended for developers. This is where you'll see warnings that certain parts of the acceptance tests haven't been implemented in the fixtures. Red highlighting indicates that the tests ran without exception but that the results weren't what was expected. Not only will the cell be highlighted in red, but you also will see a report that tells you what the actual result was and what the expected result was. Green highlighting is reserved for tests that ran without any problems and returned the expected result.

Exploring Fit

You'll find the Fit wiki at http://fit.c2.com. A wiki is a special web site where every page is editable by anybody. This means that as the community gains more experience with Fit, more examples and helpful observations are added to the site. Page through the site and explore the different styles of acceptance tests that you can write using Fit. On the DownloadNow page, early downloads support Java, .Net, and Python with plans to support Lisp, Ruby, Perl, and C++. In addition, Bob and Micah Martin have released Fitnesse at www.fitnesse.org. Fitnesse provides a wiki framework for easily writing and running acceptance tests.

For this chapter you'll need the Java version of the framework. Download it and expand it. You only need the fit.jar file to run the framework, but you'll find the supporting documentation helpful. Source files are included for the framework in the fit package and for several of the examples that you'll find on the site in the eg package. Under the Documents directory you'll find some of the pages that can also be found on the site. Because the on-line site is a wiki, the pages you download are a snapshot of the site at a given time. The Reports directory contains some of the acceptance test pages from the wiki. These can be processed locally from the command line. On the wiki, the tests can be processed by clicking a hyperlink to a CGI script.

While on-line, follow the Cook's tour for developers. Get a quick view of the Row, Column, and Action fixtures. Take a moment to look at the *Field Guide To Fixtures* to figure out which fixtures are best suited to different tasks that you are trying to accomplish. You'll notice that the advice for *Making Fixtures* is similar to the advice for using JUnit to write test first code. The ideas in Fit and JUnit are different but related. With JUnit you write the test first and then write the code that makes the test code compile and then pass. With Fit your customer writes the test. You write the fixture that makes the test not throw any exceptions. Then you write the code that gets the tests to pass. The differences in intent and practice will become more evident as you play with the two testing frameworks.

FROM USER STORIES TO ACCEPTANCE TESTS

Because we haven't had a way of automating acceptance tests, until now, much of our experience has been with customers playing with the application and saying, "That looks right." Sometimes the customer is able to formalize the steps we need to take to test the code. Even in these cases, because the tests needed to be run manually, they weren't run frequently.

Fit allows us to automate the processing of our acceptance tests. This means that the developers can run the tests while working on a user story to help measure progress. A customer can also either run the tests or view the results of the most recently generated tests. You'll run the tests by passing arguments to the Java class `fit.FileRunner` to specify the input HTML file and the corresponding location and name of the output file.

Test results can be easily published. Since you are generating HTML files, these can be shared with the customer by putting them on a web site or attaching them to or including them in an e-mail. You can also customize a CGI script or create a Java server page (JSP) or servlet to allow the developers or the customers to run the acceptance tests remotely by clicking a link on a web page. As the community explores Fit, more of this will be available to you in an easily downloadable form.

Our First Example User Story

Let's begin with a user story that tests that the value returned in a transaction is correct. Our customer is Brian, the information technology (IT) manager of a fictional grocery chain called Cheaper Buy the Dozen. Brian has explained that each item in the story has a unit amount. Any time a customer buys twelve of any item, they get a 5% "case" discount on that set of twelve items.

Brian captures this as the following user story.

Case Discount

The price for multiple copies of the same item is the number of items multiplied by the unit cost with a 5% discount on any set of twelve purchased.

Initial Acceptance Tests for the Case Discount Story

We think we know what Brian means, but we ask him to come up with acceptance tests that will tell him that we've done what he wants. He thinks a moment, and says, "Let's say that a pound of coffee costs $8.00. If I buy one pound then the item total should be $8.00. If I buy five pounds then the item total should be $40.00. If I buy twelve pounds then we need to figure out the discount. Multiplying $8.00 times twelve gives us $96.00. Now 5% of $96 is $4.80. This means that the price for a dozen pounds of coffee is $96 minus the $4.80, or $91.20."

"Okay," you suggest, "Why don't we summarize your requirements in this table."

Unit Price	Number of Items	Item Total
$8.00	1	$8.00
$8.00	5	$40.00
$8.00	12	$91.20

"That's nice," says Brian. "Now that I see it like this, I think there's a couple of cases I'd like to add."

"Like what?" you ask.

"Well, if I buy more than one dozen but less than two dozen, I want to make sure I only get a discount on the first dozen. So if I buy seventeen pounds of coffee I should get $131.20—the price with a discount for the first dozen plus the price for the next five pounds."

"What else?" you prompt.

"Well, I want to make sure that I get discounts correctly calculated if I buy two dozen or more. So let's check that the price for two dozen pounds is twice $91.20, or $182.40, and that the price for twenty-nine pounds is $40 more than that, or $222.40. While we're at it, lets check that the price for one hundred dozen pounds is $9,120.00. It's kind of ridiculous—we'd never sell this quantity out of our stores but it will make me feel better that we're getting the calculation correct."

"Great," you agree, "This will check our logic on the dozen discounts pretty thoroughly."

"There's one more case I'd like to check," says Brian.

"What's that?" you ask.

Brian answers, "I'd like to see what happens if 5% of the unit price is a fraction of a cent. Let's say I sell candy corns at five cents a piece. A dozen of them would be $0.60 minus the 5% discount of $0.03. Oh, I guess that's okay."

"No," you chime in, "I see where you're going. If you sell them for four cents a piece, then a dozen of them would be $0.48 minus the 5% discount of $0.024. Now you'd end up pricing them at $0.456 per dozen."

"Right," answers Brian, "I'd really like them to be priced at $0.46 per dozen. It sounds small, but these differences add up."

"So," you summarize, "if all of your prices end in a five or a zero this will never happen, but if they end in other digits then we'll have to deal with these fractions of a penny."

Brian thinks another moment and answers, "I want to leave flexibility in pricing, so let's add your case in as a test case. Whenever we get a fraction of a penny, I'd like to round up."

"Okay," you agree, "would you mind if we give prices in terms of pennies in our tests?"

"No, that's fine," says Brian. You present him with the following updated table.

Unit Price in Pennies	Number of Items	Total Price in Pennies
8 00	1	8 00
8 00	5	40 00
8 00	12	91 20
8 00	17	131 20
8 00	24	182 40
8 00	29	222 40
8 00	1200	9 120 00
4	12	46

Benefits of Having Acceptance Tests

Compare your current understanding of what Brian wants with what you understood when you first saw this user story.

Case discount

The price for multiple copies of the same item is the number of items multiplied by the unit cost with a 5% discount on any set of twelve purchased.

Armed with Brian's tests, you now have a much better idea of how the case discount should apply in his stores. More than that, you now have an agreement with him that when you have passed all of these tests, he will consider this story completed. As with all other aspects of XP, Brian can change the requirements or add to the tests, but he will take the costs into consideration before doing so.

The table also helps Brian understand what he needs to see in order to consider this user story complete. If he can quickly look at this table and see which of these cases are passing and failing, he'll have a good indication of the status of this user story. We used JUnit to run our unit tests and indicate which tests failed and why. As smart as Brian is, he's not a developer. We should be able to present the results to him in a customer-friendly way. The strategy of the Fit framework is simple. If a result is correct, it is colored green. If it is incorrect it is colored red and the returned and the expected values are displayed for the customer to inspect. If the fixture isn't yet in place to support the acceptance tests then the cell will be colored yellow with a message designed for developers not customers. We'll see examples of all three of these test results soon.

FORMALIZING THE ACCEPTANCE TESTS

The Fit framework is designed to take tables like the one we created in the last section as input. There are several types of fixtures used to process tables differently. We'll begin with the column fixture. We'll tweak the table we created so that we can process it using the Fit framework. We'll then begin to process the table and create the fixture needed to respond to these inputs.

Mapping to the Fixture

The main advantage of the table we set up with Brian is that it clearly communicates to him and to us what his requirements are. In the table the first column is an integer that represents the price of a single unit and the second column is an integer that represents the number of units purchased. You can view the contents of these columns as inputs into some method responsible for determining the total cost for that item. The third column is a bit different. It contains the expected value of the total cost for the item. You can think of it as the expected return value for the method.

For the column fixture, these are the two types of columns. Either a column corresponds to a variable in the corresponding Java class or it corresponds to a method. The values of the variables are read from the table. The values in the method column are read from the table and compared with the value of the corresponding methods. We indicate methods by ending their names with parentheses.

In our example, let's create an HTML file called CaseDiscountFitTest.html. Let the corresponding Java class be called CaseDiscountFixture.java and place it in a package called register. It is possible that several tables use the same fixture or that a single HTML file contains more than one table that uses different fixtures. Each table needs to contain identification of the fixture that is intended to process it. The top line of a table is the name of the fixture used to process it. To make it look nicer, we use the `colspan` attribute to force the top row to span all of the columns. Our current example looks like Figure 14-1.

Acceptance Tests for User Story: Case Discount

The price for multiple copies of the same item is the number of items multiplied by the unit cost with a 5% discount on any set of twelve purchased.

register.CaseDiscountFixture		
unitPrice	numberPurchased	itemTotal()
800	1	800
800	5	4000
800	12	9120
800	17	13120
800	24	18240
800	29	22240
800	1200	912000
4	12	46

Figure 14-1 Acceptance Tests for User Story: Case Discount

Notice that the first line of the table includes the qualified name of the Java class, `register.CaseDiscountFixture`. The first two columns are labeled `unitPrice` and `numberPurchased` and, therefore, correspond to public variables in the `CaseDiscountFixture` class. The third column is labeled `itemTotal()` and corresponds to a public method in the `CaseDiscountFixture` class.

The client is expected to be able to produce these tables. They can use a spreadsheet program or word processor to produce the tables and export the HTML. They can write the actual HTML itself. Even the most nontechnical clients can easily follow the template to create their own tables. In our case, Brian quickly created the following HTML that generated the page in Figure 14-1.

```
<html>
  <head>
    <title> Acceptance Tests User Story: Case Discount </title>
  </head>
  <body>
    <h1> Acceptance Tests for User Story: Case Discount </h1>
    <p> The price for multiple copies of the same item is the
        number of items multiplied by the unit cost with a 5%
         discount on any set of twelve purchased.
    </p>
    <table BORDER>
      <tr>
        <td colspan = 3> register.CaseDiscountFixture </td>
      </tr>
      <tr>
        <td> unitPrice </td>
        <td> numberPurchased </td>
        <td> itemTotal() </td>
      </tr>
      <tr>
        <td> 800 </td>
        <td>  1 </td>
        <td> 800 </td>
      </tr>
      <tr>
        <td> 800 </td>
        <td>  5 </td>
        <td> 4000 </td>
      </tr>
      <tr>
        <td> 800 </td>
        <td>  12 </td>
        <td> 9120 </td>
      </tr>
      <tr>
        <td> 800 </td>
        <td>  17 </td>
        <td> 13120 </td>
```

```
    </tr>
    <tr>
      <td> 800 </td>
      <td>  24 </td>
      <td> 18240 </td>
    </tr>
    <tr>
      <td> 800 </td>
      <td>  29 </td>
      <td> 22240 </td>
    </tr>
    <tr>
      <td> 800 </td>
      <td>  1200 </td>
      <td> 912000 </td>
    </tr>
    <tr>
      <td> 4 </td>
      <td>  12 </td>
      <td> 46 </td>
    </tr>
  </table>
</body>
<html>
```

Running the Tests

We will process the HTML file by running the `FileRunner` class in the `Fit` package. We can do this from the command line or from within an IDE. When you first downloaded the Fit framework, you should have run the setup tests specified on the `RunMeFirst` page of the Wiki. To run FileRunner you had to specify the classpath and an input file and an output file. Let's look at each of those parts in turn.

We'll begin by creating a directory named "dozen." Inside of this new directory we'll copy the fit.jar file and create additional directories labeled classes, docs, src, and tests. All source files are compiled into the classes directory. Within the tests directory we'll create subdirectories labeled acceptance and unit to hold the source files. At this point we only created a single file named CaseDiscountFitTest.html. Place it inside of /dozens/tests/acceptance/testsource. Our dozen directory should look like Figure 14-2.

Your classpath needs to include two things. First it must point to the classes that make up the Fit framework. In the `RunMeFirst` example you just pointed at the Classes directory. You could also just use the fit.jar file and include it in the classpath. The classpath must also include the fixtures used to process the tables. In this setup, the classpath should just include fit.jar and the classes directory.

The input file is CaseDiscountFitTest.html. We'll start by running the acceptance tests from the command line just inside the dozen directory. This means that the path to the input file is tests/acceptance/testsource/CaseDiscountFitTest.html. We'll write the output to a file of the same name in the testresults directory. This means that the path to the output file is tests/acceptance/testresults/CaseDiscountFitTest.html.

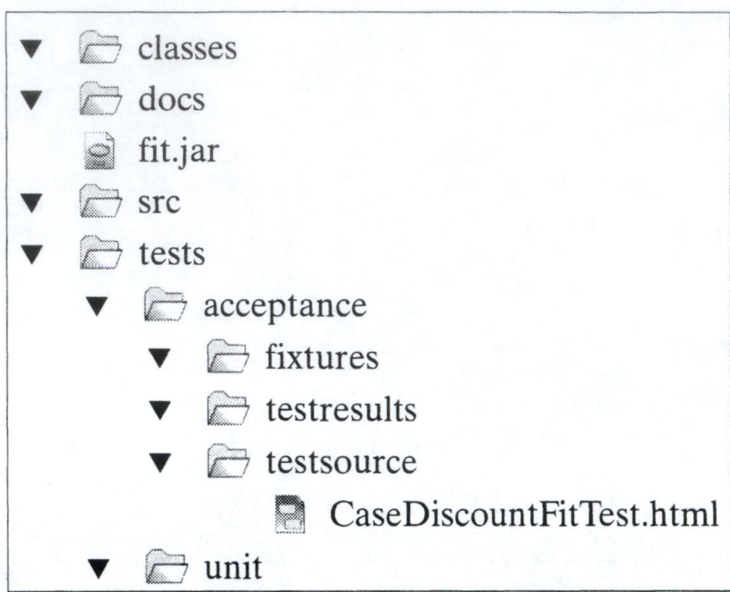

Figure 14-2 The Dozen Directory

Now we can run the acceptance tests. Open a terminal window and navigate inside of the dozen directory. Run the acceptance tests with this command:

```
java -classpath fit.jar:classes fit.FileRunner
  tests/acceptance/testsource/CaseDiscountFitTest.html
  tests/acceptance/testresults/CaseDiscountFitTest.html
```

On a Windows machine replace : with ; and replace / with \. We get the following feedback in the terminal window.

```
0 right, 0 wrong, 0 ignored, 1 exceptions
```

This doesn't surprise us. The table specifies that the fixtures needed to run the tests are found in the class `register.CaseDiscountFixture`. So far, this class does not exist. In fact, if we look at the generated HTML file in the testresults directory, we can see that it provides us with this information (see Figure 14-3).The top row of the table is presented with a yellow background color to indicate to developers that something hasn't yet been implemented. In this case a `ClassNotFoundException` is reported because the framework can't find the class `register.CaseDiscountFixture`. Our next step is to take care of this exception.

Creating a Stub Fixture

As a first step, inside of the /tests/acceptance/fixtures directory create a subdirectory named register. Inside of this register directory, create a file CaseDiscountFixture.java. The class `CaseDiscountFixture` needs to extend the class `fit.ColumnFixture` in order to properly process our table. Our first version of CaseDiscountFixture.java looks like this.

register.CaseDiscountFixture		
java.lang.ClassNotFoundException: register.CaseDiscountFixture at java.net.URLClassLoader$1.run(URLClassLoader.java:195) at java.security.AccessController.doPrivileged(Native Method) at java.net.URLClassLoader.findClass(URLClassLoader.java:183) at java.lang.ClassLoader.loadClass(ClassLoader.java:294) at sun.misc.Launcher$AppClassLoader.loadClass(Launcher.java:281) at java.lang.ClassLoader.loadClass(ClassLoader.java:250) at java.lang.Class.forName0(Native Method) at java.lang.Class.forName(Class.java:115) at fit.Fixture.doTables(Fixture.java:69) at fit.FileRunner.process(FileRunner.java:29) at fit.FileRunner.run(FileRunner.java:22) at fit.FileRunner.main(FileRunner.java:17)		
unitPrice	numberPurchased	itemTotal()
800	1	800
800	5	4000
800	12	9120
800	17	13120
800	24	18240
800	29	22240
800	1200	912000
4	12	46

Figure 14-3 Message Not Created Yet

```
package register;
import fit.ColumnFixture;
public class CaseDiscountFixture extends ColumnFixture {
}
```

Compile CaseDiscountFixture.java so that the .class file is written to the classes directory. Now we can rerun the Fit framework as before. This time the results are a bit different. You can view the generated HTML page for more details on the test results, but you should see this display in the terminal window.

```
0 right, 0 wrong, 24 ignored, 3 exceptions
```

It may seem that things are getting worse—but we are actually making progress. Before creating the `CaseDiscountFixture` class we had no ignored tests and now there are twenty-four. This actually indicates that now the tests are being found. Earlier there was one exception and now there are three. The initial version of `CaseDiscountFixture` also addressed the `ClassNotFoundException`. Now we have one `NoSuchFieldException` for both `unitPrice` and another for `numberPurchased`, and a `NoSuchMethodException` for `itemTotal()`.

As a next step, let's add variables for `unitPrice` and `numberPurchased`. The variables need to be public as they are being called from outside of the register package. They need to be compatible with `ints` because we're passing in integral values. Add the highlighted lines to CaseDiscountFixture.java.

```
package register;
import fit.ColumnFixture;
public class CaseDiscountFixture extends ColumnFixture{
  public int unitPrice;
  public int numberPurchased;
}
```

Now, compile the code as before and rerun the Fit framework. This time the results reported in the terminal window are predictably better.

```
0 right, 0 wrong, 8 ignored, 1 exceptions
```

As before, the generated HTML page contains more details if you need them. The `itemTotal()` cell is colored yellow and contains the stack trace for the `NoSuchMethodException`.

What remains is to address the `NoSuchMethodException`. You could make a good argument in favor of doing this now or leaving it for later. On the side of leaving it as is, the developers and the client can clearly see by this report that `itemTotal()` has not been implemented yet. No one needs to be worried about tests that pass or fail, because we haven't gotten around to this task yet. On the other hand, we could create a trivial version of `itemTotal()` and most or all of the tests would fail. Failing tests also indicate an area that needs to be addressed.

Stubbing out `itemTotal()` shouldn't take us very long. In one sense, it's as simple as creating a public method named `itemTotal()` that takes no parameters and returns an int. We do want to be careful to make sure that we aren't putting in the logic to make these tests pass. The `CaseDiscountFixture` class is part of the testing framework. It should defer the programming logic to classes that will become part of the production code. As Bob Martin notes on the Fit framework Wiki, acceptance tests are not the same as unit tests. Our task in the fixture isn't to get one after another of the acceptance tests running. For now we'll return the number –1 from `itemTotal()`. Here's the new version of CaseDiscountFixture.java.

```
package register;
import fit.ColumnFixture;
public class CaseDiscountFixture extends ColumnFixture{
  public int unitPrice;
  public int numberPurchased;
  public int itemTotal(){
    return -1;
  }
}
```

Again, compile the revised version of CaseDiscountFixture.java and run the acceptance tests. This time this message in the terminal window lets us know that all of the tests are run, there are no exceptions, and that all of the tests have failed.

```
0 right, 8 wrong, 0 ignored, 0 exceptions
```

The generated HTML file shown in Figure 14-4 highlights all of the entries in the third column in red. You can see that each of the cells in that column is split into two pieces: one for the expected result that was entered in the table and the other for the actual result that was returned from the method.

Writing the Production Code

All of the production code that you write should have a written test first. This means that you'll need to write unit tests in addition to the acceptance tests. Unit tests specify the interface of the code being tested in a way that isn't possible or desirable with acceptance tests. You don't want to allow your customers to make technical decisions about how the code should be written. These decisions often come out of a suite of unit tests. Your customer is making business decisions about what your software should do. You should consult the unit-testing tutorial in Chapter 10 for more details on that process.

In this case, the acceptance tests suggest something about the structure of the code. The tests themselves lead us to unit tests that we might write. Also, the acceptance test fixtures need to call into the production code somewhere. You'll find it best if the test fixture is in the same package as the code it's calling into. This means that you will minimize the number of changes to the access level of methods being called.

Let's create the class `ItemTest` inside of the `register` package. We'll create a new object of type `Item` that has a `unitPrice` of 800 pennies just as in our acceptance tests. We'll add one item to our purchases and verify that the total price for this item is 800. Here's the code for ItemTest.java.

```
package register;
import junit.framework.TestCase;
public class ItemTest extends TestCase{
  public void testCostOfSingleItemIsUnitPrice(){
    Item item = new Item(800);
    item.addToOrder(1);
    assertEquals(800,item.totalItemCost());
  }
}
```

We go through the usual steps of writing enough code until this class compiles. This requires that we create an `Item` class that has a constructor that takes an `int` representing the unit price as a parameter. It also requires that we create an `addToOrder()` method that takes an `int` representing the number purchased as a parameter. Finally, this unit test implies that there must be a method called `totalItemCost()` that has no parameters and returns an `int` representing the total cost of purchasing the prescribed number of copies of this particular item. After a little refactoring, the code for Item.java looks like this:

```
package register;
class Item {
  private int unitPrice;
  private int numberPurchased;
  Item(int unitPrice) {
```

register.CaseDiscountFixture		
unitPrice	numberPurchased	itemTotal()
800	1	800 *expected* -1 *actual*
800	5	4000 *expected* -1 *actual*
800	12	9120 *expected* -1 *actual*
800	17	13120 *expected* -1 *actual*
800	24	18240 *expected* -1 *actual*
800	29	22240 *expected* -1 *actual*
800	1200	912000 *expected* -1 *actual*
4	12	46 *expected* -1 *actual*

Figure 14-4 Initial Failing Tests

```
    this.unitPrice = unitPrice;
  }
  void addToOrder(int numberOfAdditionalItems){
    numberPurchased += numberOfAdditionalItems;
  }
  int totalItemCost() {
    return numberPurchased * unitPrice;
  }
}
```

Tying the Fixture to the Production Code

Now that we are passing one unit test, our `Item` class has taken shape enough that we can tie our acceptance test fixture to it. We could have waited until this point to fill out the `itemTotal()` method in `CaseDiscountFixture` instead of having returned a –1 to avoid the `NoSuchMethodException`. Now that we know how to fix `itemTotal()`, we initialize a new `Item`, add to the number of items purchased, and then return the total price for that item as calculated by the instance of `Item`.

It is important to note that the `ColumnFixture` class is very thin. Its job is to call into the main codebase. This should feel like writing a good GUI for a program. Very little of the business logic should sit in the GUI. A second note is that if you find yourself needing to place some amount of logic in the fixture, then you need to write this code test first as well.

We've now tied the acceptance test through its fixture to the production code. The altered code is highlighted below.

```
package register;
import fit.ColumnFixture;
public class CaseDiscountFixture extends ColumnFixture{
  public int unitPrice;
  public int numberPurchased;
  public int itemTotal(){
    Item item = new Item(unitPrice);
    item.addToOrder(numberPurchased);
    return item.totalItemCost();
  }
}
```

Now when you rerun the acceptance tests, you'll see that two of the acceptance tests are now passing. Here's the message in the terminal window.

```
2 right, 6 wrong, 0 ignored, 0 exceptions
```

Figure 14-5 shows the results that you can see in the generated HTML file. Now the tests that passed have a green background while the tests that failed have a red background and list the expected and actual values.

Passing More Acceptance Tests

We can see from the acceptance test results that we are only passing those tests when we purchase fewer than a dozen items. We need to create a more complex pricing

register.CaseDiscountFixture		
unitPrice	numberPurchased	itemTotal()
800	1	800
800	5	4000
800	12	9120 *expected* 9600 *actual*
800	17	13120 *expected* 13600 *actual*
800	24	18240 *expected* 19200 *actual*
800	29	22240 *expected* 23200 *actual*
800	1200	912000 *expected* 960000 *actual*
4	12	46 *expected* 48 *actual*

Figure 14-5 Test Indicates What Needs Fixing

scheme than just returning the product of the unit price and the number of items purchased. Of course, before we add any production code we have to write another unit test. Let's just see what will happen if we buy a dozen of an item. We'll add that test to `ItemTest.java` and refactor the test code a little by adding a `setUp()` method. Here's ItemTest.java.

```
package register;
import junit.framework.TestCase;
public class ItemTest extends TestCase{
  private Item item;
  protected void setUp(){
    item = new Item(800);
  }
  public void testCostOfSingleItemIsUnitPrice(){
    item.addToOrder(1);
    assertEquals(800,item.totalItemCost());
  }
  public void testCostOfADozenIsDiscounted(){
    item.addToOrder(12);
    assertEquals(9120,item.totalItemCost());
  }
}
```

Everything compiles and runs, but the second test fails. The discounted cost should be 9120 but the calculated cost remains 9600. We return to `Item` and add the logic to factor in the discount. We quickly get the test to pass and then refactor the code so that it looks like this:

```
package register;
class Item {
  private int unitPrice;
  private int numberPurchased;
  private double percentDiscount = .05;
  Item(int unitPrice) {
    this.unitPrice = unitPrice;
  }
  void addToOrder(int numberOfAdditionalItems){
    numberPurchased += numberOfAdditionalItems;
  }
  int totalItemCost() {
    return totalCostWithoutDiscount()
           - discountForDozensPurchased();
  }
  private int numberPurchasedByTheDozen() {
    return 12 * ((int) (numberPurchased/12) );
  }
  private int totalCostWithoutDiscount(){
    return unitPrice * numberPurchased;
  }
  private int discountForDozensPurchased(){
    return ( (int) (unitPrice
                 * numberPurchasedByTheDozen()
                 * percentDiscount));
  }
}
```

Notice that `Item` has no public methods or variables. In fact, `Item` itself isn't public and doesn't have a public constructor. We can expose this class and its methods later if the need arises. The classes used by JUnit and Fit have to be public. The Fit variables and methods that are referenced by the HTML tables also must be public. By placing the class that extends the `ColumnFixture` class in the same package as `Item`, we aren't required to expose very much of the class being tested. At this point our directory structure looks like that shown in Figure 14-6.

With test-driven development we run unit tests all the time. We write a little code, compile, and then run the unit tests continuously. How often should we run the acceptance tests? The advantage of having automated acceptance tests is that we can run them frequently. We have a suspicion that by passing the last unit test, we've probably passed all but the last acceptance test. When we run the acceptance tests to check where we are we get the following surprising result.

```
8 right, 0 wrong, 0 ignored, 0 exceptions
```

In the `discountForDozensPurchased()` method we inadvertently rounded the amount of the discount down to the nearest penny when casting the calculated value back to an int. This had the effect of rounding the total item cost up to the nearest penny as Brian had specified. By running the acceptance tests we saved ourselves some time and work by creating functionality that already existed.

The Client and the Acceptance Tests

We have completed our work on Brian's first user story and can demonstrate our success. We can now go back to Brian and show him his acceptance tests running. He accepts that somehow we've taken care of all of his goals in this particular user story. If he'd like, he can add another test or two if he feels there's some area of this story that he's left unexplored. For now, he accepts that we've done what we promised, but he doesn't seem satisfied.

"What's wrong?" you ask.

"I don't know," Brian answers, "it just feels like magic."

"What do you mean?"

"Well," says Brian, "I came up with some tests and you said you'd make them all pass. Now you show me a third column colored green and tell me that you've made them all pass. How do I know you didn't just color the third column green?"

"Well, I could change the code back to when everything was breaking," you suggest.

Brian isn't satisfied with this answer. "No," he says, "that wouldn't help. I want a test that convinces me the system really is calculating the values correctly."

It's hard not to take Brian's objection personally. It sounds as if he's saying that he doesn't trust you. He's not saying that—he's saying that the passing acceptance tests you showed him aren't convincing him right now. He needs reassurance that this process really is testing what you say it's testing. Brian is an expert in his domain. You've asked him to sign off on a user story when his acceptance tests are passing and it is the automation that is giving him pause.

Let's look back at how we got to this point. You asked Brian to come up with test cases that would show that you were correctly calculating the cost of one or more of a

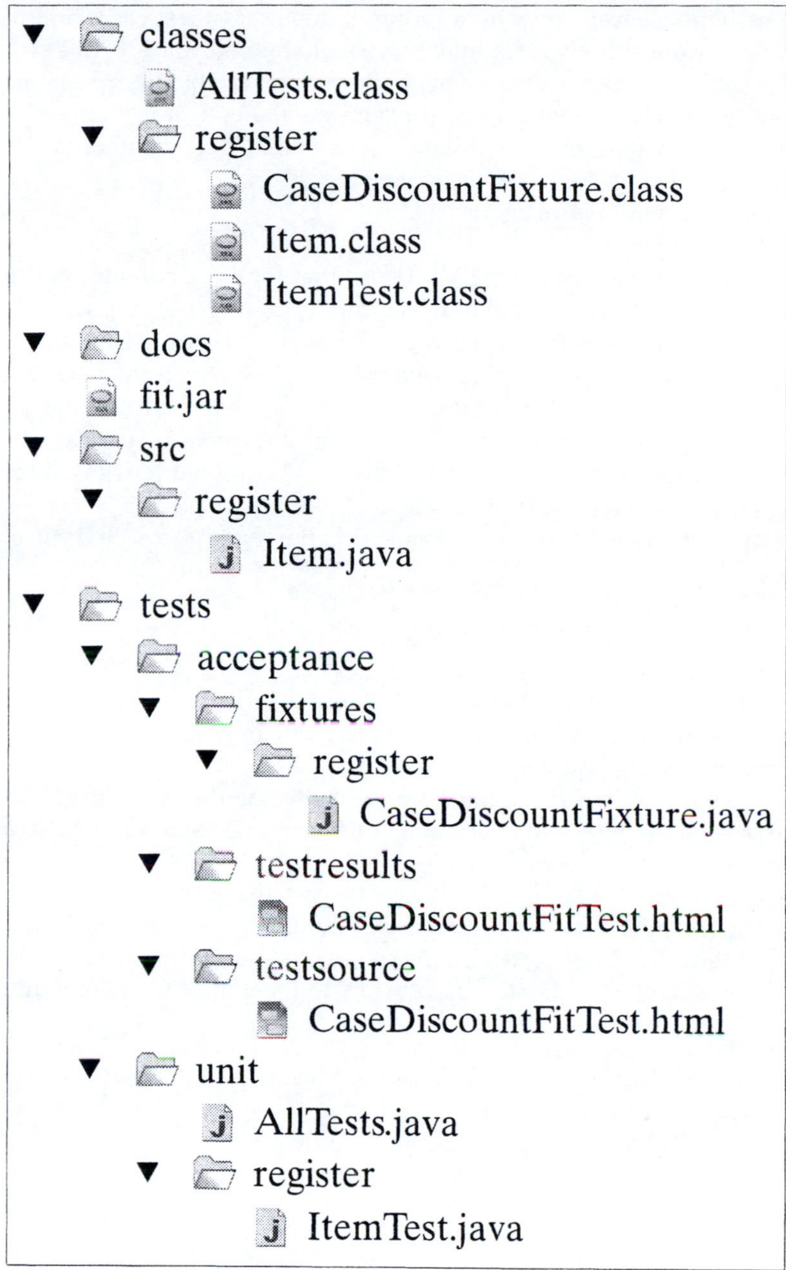
classes
AllTests.class
register
CaseDiscountFixture.class
Item.class
ItemTest.class
docs
fit.jar
src
register
Item.java
tests
acceptance
fixtures
register
CaseDiscountFixture.java
testresults
CaseDiscountFitTest.html
testsource
CaseDiscountFitTest.html
unit
AllTests.java
register
ItemTest.java

Figure 14-6 Directory Structure

particular item. He came up with a representative set of test cases and then you told him that you would run them for him. This should remind you a bit of a strategy we employed when unit testing. Often we need to see a test fail before we can make it pass—just to have confidence that the test is exercising the code it is intended to test. Brian never got to see failing tests. We'll show Brian a failing test and then we'll set up a system that will help him see tests during the process.

You tell Brian, "I have an idea."

"What?" he asks.

"What if you change the HTML file so that the third column isn't the value you expect. Then the tests should fail in those rows."

"That's great," says Brian. "I can change the HTML myself and then we'll run the tests. Let's change the first three. Coffee still costs 800 pennies for one pound. When I buy one pound let's change the third column to say that the total cost should be 100, and when I buy five pounds let's change the third column to 500. Then let's leave the total amount alone in the third row, but change the amount purchased to three dozen pounds. Now let's rerun the tests."

You open up a terminal window and rerun the tests. As expected you get this result.

```
5 right, 3 wrong, 0 ignored, 0 exceptions
```

"Whoa," says Brian. "That's really nice."

"What do you mean?" you ask.

"That summary. I've never seen it before."

"I've shown you the web page where you can look for green and red to see which tests pass."

Brian says, "That's great, but I'd also like to see the summary. Eventually we're going to have a lot of tests. If everything is passing, I'd rather not have to look through all of the tables."

"Okay," you answer, "it's actually pretty easy to do. We just need to add a table to the end of the page with a single cell that contains `fit.Summary`. When the page is processed this will be replaced with the summary data for this page."

Brian adds the highlighted lines below to the end of CaseDiscountFitTest.html.

```
    </table>
    <h1> Summary of tests run on this page </h1>
    <table BORDER>
      <tr>
        <td> fit.Summary </td>
      </tr>
    </table>
  </body>
<html>
```

We rerun the tests and view the resulting web page (see Figure 14-7). Brian is beaming. The three incorrect values are highlighted in red, as he wanted. He can see the difference between the actual and expected values for the first three rows. The third row also correctly lists the total expected for three dozen pounds, even thought that's not a value he had originally tested. At the bottom of the page is the summary that he requested.

Summary of tests run on this page

fit.Summary	
counts	5 right, 3 wrong, 0 ignored, 0 exceptions
input file	/Users/daniel/Dev/dozen/tests/acceptance/testsource/CaseDiscountFitTest.html
input update	Tue Nov 26 10:19:18 EST 2002
output file	/Users/daniel/Dev/dozen/tests/acceptance/testresults/CaseDiscountFitTest.html
run date	Tue Nov 26 10:19:25 EST 2002
run elapsed time	0:00.17

Figure 14-7 Summary of Tests Run on This Page

"Really," says Brian, "I'd like the summary at the top of the page." You start to explain to him that this won't work and then stop. Let him try it. You know that he'll be more convinced that the framework is doing something by exploring a bit. He moves the `fit.Summary` table to the top of the page and gets the results that there were 0 right, 0 wrong, 0 ignored, and 0 exceptions.

"Hang on," says Brian, "it doesn't look like anything ran." He thinks for a moment and then gets it. "I can't have the summary before the tests are run because at that point nothing has run. There are no results to report."

Brian then puts the HTML file back in order. He corrects the table entries so that the values are correct and he puts the `fit.Summary` table back on the bottom. He reruns the tests and sees that all of the tests have passed. With this summary he can tell how recently the tests were run and what the current status of this story is.

Brian asks you to run the tests once a day and post the HTML files to a web site that he's set up. We agree that any time new code is integrated, we'll run the acceptance tests and that once a day we'll post the results to his web site. We also make a note to either use a variant of the CGI script on the Fit wiki site or a JSP page or servlet to allow Brian to process the tests remotely whenever he likes.

TESTING GUIs

"Now," says Brian, "let's work on the actual register. For the most part the cashiers will be scanning the items in and the register will be keeping a running record. If a cashier scans in an item that the register doesn't recognize, then the cashier needs to be able to enter the unit price and the number of items purchased."

"Actually," you respond, "that sounds like two stories. Story one has to do with having some list that matches bar codes, item numbers, and unit prices so that the register can scan a bar code and know the item and its price. Story two has something to do with items not on the list being manually entered."

"Maybe," says Brian, "but I would think there are more stories than that. I'd like to keep the list that matches bar codes to items separate from the list that matches items to prices. I may be updating the price list pretty regularly. Then I want to give the cashier some indication if either the item can't be scanned or it can be scanned but there's no price on file for it. Finally, I want to allow the cashier to manually enter prices for any item."

"That seems like a lot," you say.

"It is," agrees Brian. "Let's start with the last one. If everything else fails, I can still provide each cashier with a price list on paper and let them enter the amounts by hand." He writes down this user story.

Miscellaneous Item

A user can enter an item by hand by pressing the "MISC" button and then entering the unit price and number of items purchased.

Designing the Acceptance Tests

With this starting place, you are ready to have Brian flesh out the acceptance tests. Then you can write the fixtures and the code that will make them pass. Remembering your earlier experience, you are careful to involve Brian in this process.

"Describe the process to me," you prompt.

"Well, they will hit the 'Misc' button and they will see a prompt that says 'Enter Unit Price'. They will then enter the unit price. The display will reflect this unit price. Next, they'll press the 'Enter' button. They'll then see a prompt that says 'Enter number of items.' They will then enter this number. The display will reflect this number. Then they'll press the 'Done' button."

"Then what?"

"Then, they'll see the total cost for that item. Then they can enter another item or finish the transaction by pressing the 'End' button."

You show him a table that you think captures what he just said.

Press	miscButton	
Check	display	Enter Unit Price
Enter	unitPrice	800
check	display	800
press	enterButton	
check	display	Enter number of items
enter	numberOfItems	
check	display	5
press	doneButton	
check	display	4000
check	totalCost	4000
press	endButton	

Brian thinks that the table looks pretty good. He suggests two changes. First, he would like a running total to be available in a separate display and second, he wants to make sure you can handle more than one item in a transaction and more than one transaction.

You and Brian reread the user story.

Miscellaneous Item

A user can enter an item by hand by pressing the 'MISC' button and then entering the unit price and number of items purchased.

You and Brian agree that this story is about entering a single item and defer the additions that have to do with handling more than one item in a transaction and keeping track of a running total.

Stubbing Out a Fixture for the Tests

You can see that this table is different than the one we worked with earlier. In that one each column corresponded to variables that would be input into the system being tested and methods that included the value that we expected to be returned from the method. In this one the first column consists of one of four keywords: start, press, enter, or check.

The start keyword is accompanied, in the second column, by the name of a class that is instantiated. The rest of the commands will be handled by this instance of the class. The press keyword is meant to simulate a button press. The second column contains the name of the method called by the press. The enter keyword is meant to simulate entering values into a GUI via a text field. The second column contains the name of the method corresponding to the text field and the third column contains the value being entered. Finally, the check keyword indicates that this row is being tested against a value returned by the fixture. The second column contains the name of the method that will return the value and the third column contains the value being compared.

Our first step is to make a few adjustments to the table. With Brian's help, we add the two lines at the top of the table to specify the class used to process the table and the class that is instantiated to run the methods listed in the table. Brian also decides to tweak the process a little bit. The revised table looks like this.

fit.ActionFixture		
start	register.MiscItemFixture	
press	miscButton	
check	display	Enter Unit Price
enter	unitPrice	800
check	display	800
press	enterButton	
check	display	Misc Grocery 800

press	timesButton	
check	display	Enter number of items
enter	numberOfItems	5
check	display	5
press	doneButton	
check	display	4000
check	totalCost	4000

We'll create the file MiscItemFixture.java in the /tests/acceptance/fixtures/register/directory. It must extend the `Fixture` class in the `fit` package. We can quickly stub it out with the methods that it needs to contain. You can read those off of the table one at a time.

```
package register;
import fit.Fixture;
public class MiscItemFixture extends Fixture {
  public void miscButton(){}
  public void enterButton(){}
  public void doneButton(){}
  public void timesButton(){}
  public int totalCost(){
    -1;
  }
  public String display(){
    return "";
  }
  public void unitPrice(int unitPrice){}
  public void numberOfItems(int numberOfItems){}
}
```

Compile this class and run the acceptance tests in the file MiscItemFitTest.html. The report is that none of the tests are right, seven of them are wrong, and that no exceptions were thrown. In an `ActionFixture` the tests correspond to the rows that begin with the keyword check. Our next step is to write the code that gets these tests to pass.

Problems Passing the Acceptance Tests

We'll pass the acceptance tests in a way that has problems not caught by these tests. Don't skip to the next section where a more correct solution is presented. It's important to see the problems that can arise when you take care of programming logic in your acceptance test fixtures.

Let's first look at the production code class `ManualEntry`. It was written using the test first method to take care of many of the tasks specified in the acceptance tests. Only the highlighted areas are used for real input or calculation. Everything else is used to set the display or access variables.

```
package register;
class ManualEntry {
```

```
    private String display;
    private Item currentItem;
    ManualEntry(){
      setDisplay("Enter Unit Price");
    }
    void setDisplay(String display){
      this.display = display;
    }
    String getDisplay(){
      return display;
    }
    void createItemWithPrice(int price){
      currentItem = new Item(price);
      setDisplay("Misc Grocery " + price);
    }
    void buyMoreThanOne(){
      setDisplay("Enter number of items");
    }
    void setNumberOfItems(int numberPurchased){
        currentItem.addToOrder(numberPurchased);
        setDisplay(""+ getTotalCost());
    }
    int getTotalCost(){
      return currentItem.totalItemCost();
    }
  }
```

Here's the test fixture that calls into `ManualEntry`. Notice that it does a little more than it should. Here's the code for MiscItemFixture.java.

```
package register;
import fit.Fixture;
public class MiscItemFixture extends Fixture{
  private ManualEntry manualEntry;
  private int unitPrice;
  private int numberOfItems;
  public void miscButton(){
    manualEntry = new ManualEntry();
  }
  public void enterButton(){
    manualEntry.createItemWithPrice(unitPrice);
  }
  public void doneButton(){
    manualEntry.setNumberOfItems(numberOfItems);
  }
  public int totalCost(){
    return manualEntry.getTotalCost();
  }
  public String display(){
    return manualEntry.getDisplay();
```

```
  }
  public void unitPrice(int unitPrice){
    this.unitPrice = unitPrice;
    manualEntry.setDisplay(""+unitPrice);
  }
  public void numberOfItems(int numberOfItems){
    this.numberOfItems = numberOfItems;
    manualEntry.setDisplay(""+numberOfItems);
  }
  public void timesButton(){
    manualEntry.buyMoreThanOne();
  }
}
```

All of the tests pass. The unit tests pass and the acceptance tests pass. For the most part, the acceptance tests call into the class being tested. There are two main exceptions. Consider the code for the methods `unitPrice()` and `numberOfItems()`. They both do two things that should raise a red flag: they set the value of an instance variable and they explicitly set the value of a variable instead of calling methods in the `ManualEntry` class. The acceptance test has separated the steps of typing in the unit price and pressing the enter button. These steps should be handled in our production code and not in our test fixture.

This example along with its mistakes may seem a little artificial. Of course, you reason, the functionality of those methods has to be in `ManualEntry` and not in the fixture. On the other hand, it is easy to make this mistake. You need to be vigilant and keep any logic that belongs in your production code out of your test code.

The Revised Fixture and Production Code

Before reading the code presented in this section, try to refactor MiscItemFixture.java to eliminate the instance variables `unitPrice` and `numberOfItems`. One technique is to comment out `unitPrice` and see what else needs to change. You'll see that you have to change the way you implement the methods `enterButton()` and `unitPrice()`. Similarly, when you comment out `numberOfItems` you'll find that you need to change the way you implement the methods `doneButton()` and `numberOfItems()`. Here's one possible refactoring of MiscItemFixture.java:

```
package register;
import fit.Fixture;
public class MiscItemFixture extends Fixture {
  private ManualEntry manualEntry;
  public void miscButton(){
    manualEntry = new ManualEntry();
  }
  public void enterButton(){
    manualEntry.createItemWithPrice();
  }
  public void doneButton(){
```

```
    manualEntry.setNumberOfItems();
  }
  public int totalCost(){
    return manualEntry.getTotalCost();
  }
  public String display(){
    return manualEntry.getDisplay();
  }
  public void unitPrice(int unitPrice){
    manualEntry.enterUnitPrice(unitPrice);
  }
  public void numberOfItems(int numberOfItems){
    manualEntry.enterNumberOfItems(numberOfItems);
  }
  public void timesButton(){
    manualEntry.buyMoreThanOne();
  }
}
```

Now the acceptance test fixture is thin. It just delegates all calls into the class being tested. The downside is that these two classes are highly coupled. This means that changes to `ManualEntry` may require changes to `MiscItemFixture`. In this case, we've made changes in `MiscItemFixture` that require changes to `ManualEntry`. You should make the changes by writing unit tests for `ManualEntry`. The tests will check some of the behavior specified by the acceptance tests.

Here's one possible version of ManualEntry.java. Most of the changes have been highlighted.

```
package register;
class ManualEntry {
  private String display;
  private Item currentItem;
  private int numberOfItems;
  private int unitPrice;
  ManualEntry(){
    setDisplay("Enter Unit Price");
  }
  void setDisplay(String display){
    this.display = display;
  }
  String getDisplay(){
    return display;
  }
  void createItemWithPrice(){
    currentItem = new Item(unitPrice);
    setDisplay("Misc Grocery " + unitPrice);
  }
  void buyMoreThanOne(){
    setDisplay("Enter number of items");
```

```
    }
    void setNumberOfItems(){
        currentItem.addToOrder(numberOfItems);
        setDisplay(""+ getTotalCost());
    }
    int getTotalCost(){
      return currentItem.totalItemCost();
    }
    void enterNumberOfItems(int numberOfItems){
      this.numberOfItems = numberOfItems;
      setDisplay(""+ numberOfItems);
    }
    int getNumberEntered(){
      return numberOfItems;
    }
    void enterUnitPrice(int unitPrice){
      this.unitPrice = unitPrice;
      setDisplay(""+ unitPrice);
    }
    int getUnitPrice(){
      return unitPrice;
    }
  }
```

Now the changes to what is displayed are in the production code and not in the test fixture.

RUNNING ALL OF THE TESTS

As your suite of acceptance tests grows you will want a way of running all of them, all of the time. One method is to put them all in a single HTML file. Although allowable, this is an unwieldy solution. You and your customers will need to scroll down through extremely long files looking for particular results. Another solution is to create a test that calls all of the other tests and reports back the results. If you need more details, you can look at the particular tests that returned incorrect results.

The AllFiles Fixture

Several fixtures have been created for running more than one test file. We'll use the `AllFiles` fixture that is included in the `eg` package. Note that this means that `AllFiles` is not included in the fit.jar file. In order to use `AllFiles` you need to add it to your classpath. You can create a jar file eg.jar that contains the `eg` package or you can just add the Classes directory in the Fit distribution to your classpath. Because `AllFiles` is not currently part of the framework, you'll need to check that it is still in the distribution.

Create an HTML file named AllTests.html and place it in the tests/acceptance/test-source directory. This time you'll include a row with the path to any HTML file containing acceptance tests that you want to run as part of this suite. You are allowed to use wild cards to include all of the files in a certain location or with a certain naming pattern. For example, we can run both the CaseDiscountFitTest.html and the MiscItemFitTest.html by specifying that we are running *FitTest.html. Here's the AllTests.html file.

```
<html>
  <head>
    <title> Acceptance Tests for all User stories</title>
  </head>
  <body>
    <h2> Acceptance Tests for all User stories:  </h2>
    <table BORDER>
      <tr>
        <td colspan = 2>
          eg.AllFiles
        </td>
      </tr>
      <tr>
        <td colspan = 2>
          tests/acceptance/testsource/*FitTest.html
        </td>
      </tr>
    </table>
    <h2> Summary of tests run on this page </h2>
    <table BORDER>
      <tr>
        <td> fit.Summary </td>
      </tr>
    </table>
  </body>
<html>
```

Notice that we've also included a call to `fit.Summary` in a second table. This provides a more informative summary of the tests run by the call to `AllFiles`.

Results of Running the AllFiles Fixture

You need to know what you do and don't get from running this fixture. You do get a comprehensive report as shown in Figure 14-8.

The top table in Figure 14-8 lists the results for each of the files matched by the expressions you input. One advantage of running this test suite is that while you have your heads down and are focused on the tests in MiscItemFitTest.html you can make sure you aren't breaking anything anywhere else.

The bottom table lists the total files run in the counts variable and the summary results for tests in the counts run variable. The number of tests run should continue to climb. It's a matter of taste, but the number ignored and the number that appears in the exceptions should never be nonzero for very long. The ratio of right to wrong should increase. You can't insist that acceptance tests run at 100% all of the time. With unit

Acceptance Tests for all User stories:

eg.AllFiles	
tests/acceptance/testsource/*FitTest.html	
CaseDiscountFitTest.html	8 right, 0 wrong, 0 ignored, 0 exceptions
MiscItemFitTest.html	7 right, 0 wrong, 0 ignored, 0 exceptions

Summary of tests run on this page

fit.Summary	
counts	2 right, 0 wrong, 0 ignored, 0 exceptions
counts run	15 right, 0 wrong, 0 ignored, 0 exceptions
input file	/Users/daniel/Dev/dozen/tests/acceptance/testsource/AllFiles.html
input update	Thu Nov 28 07:15:42 EST 2002
output file	/Users/daniel/Dev/dozen/tests/acceptance/testresults/AllFiles.html
run date	Thu Nov 28 07:15:59 EST 2002
run elapsed time	0:00.25

Figure 14-8 Acceptance Tests for All User Stories

tests, everything stops until you fix a broken test. But you also don't write code until you write a test that breaks. Acceptance tests communicate customer requirements. It is not unexpected that when a customer contributes a new set of requirements that many of the acceptance tests won't work.

Running this fixture does not generate new HTML files for each of the files for which tests are run. You can see the summary results here. If you then decide to look at the latest information in the tests/acceptance/testresults/MiscItemFitTest.html you'll notice that this is still the same version. If you want details for failing tests, you need to process that individual page. The comprehensive tests point you in the direction of files that need to be looked at further.

Next Steps

Now create your own tests and add them to the AllTests.html file. In this tutorial we've explored examples of column fixtures and action fixtures. You can now create a row fixture and see how it is different from the other two. Work with your customer to help create tables that capture their requirements. Automate the testing process in a way that allows you to provide feedback to your customer, your instructor, and the other developers on your team.

Finally, it may feel as if you have devoted a lot more effort to testing than to writing the application code. It is true that between unit tests and acceptance tests you may actually end up with more lines of code used in testing than in your application. Your application will tend to be more directed, lean, and modular. The test code will benefit the application you are building. In addition, you should know that in an actual commercial development environment your application would still require more testing, which is often created by an independent team.

Chapter 15

Development Mechanics—Organizing Your Project

There are activities you participate in during a long project that may be unfamiliar if you've only worked by yourself on small projects. In this chapter, you'll look at a few of them. These are not necessarily XP-specific skills, but they will come in handy during the course of this semester. Treat this chapter as a buffet—read the sections that interest you and pass the others by. These are the items that are requested most frequently.

PACKAGES

Typically, when you write a small project, all of your files can go in the same directory. For larger projects, you'll find it easier to work with the project if you first organize your classes into packages. Think of it this way. Suppose you are writing a short essay and have prepared five index cards full of information. You can spread these out on your desk next to your computer. As you need a fact, you can quickly scan over the cards and find the one with the information you need. Imagine instead that you are writing a book on creating a software-engineering course that uses XP. Now you have several hundred index cards. You can still just spread them out on your desk, but what are your hopes of locating the information you need quickly? It is more likely that you will create a stack of cards on testing first and another stack on refactoring. When it becomes time to write the section on refactoring, you could spread those cards out. If there are too many cards in the refactoring stack you may organize them into subcategories that are paper clipped together. Some of the cards might be in a substack on eliminating duplicated code, while others may be in a substack on refactoring to improve communication.

It is more work to set up these categories and to impose this order, but it makes the cards much more usable. Also, you don't necessarily create the categories up front. You may have a refactoring category with everything mixed together. After a while you notice that it is getting a little large and you create the subcategories. Notice that these subcategories are logical units. When someone asks a question on combining methods to remove repetition, you know where to look. In fact, you may pass them the entire substack on "refactoring to avoid duplicate code." As you develop your applications, you may move from programs that had five classes to those that have dozens of classes. It will become easier for both you and others to navigate these classes if some order is provided. Order is achieved by organizing the cards in stacks and substacks. For files, this is done by setting up directories and subdirectories. The Java programming construct that corresponds to this hierarchy is a package. Each directory is a package. A subdirectory is a subpackage. If you place the file AClass.java inside the directory `inner` that is itself inside the directory `outer` then the class `AClass` belongs to the package `outer.inner`.

The category of an index card can be changed by moving it from stack to stack. You can also just move a Java source file from one directory to another, but you have to make sure that the appropriate changes are made. Java classes look for each other based on the packages that have been imported. If AClass.java is moved into the directory `alsoInner`, which is also a subdirectory of `outer`, then the class `AClass` now belongs to the package `outer.alsoInner`. Any other class that tries to import `AClass` with the statement `import outer.inner.AClass` must be changed to import `outer.alsoInner.AClass`. Suppose BClass.java is in the package `outer.inner`. Once `AClass` is moved, then the protected methods in `AClass` are no longer visible in `BClass`. You are probably familiar with the rules of access modifiers such as public and private, but you may not yet have had to package your own applications.

A Two Class Example

Let's start with two classes. Create a directory called example. Inside of `example` you save the file Caller.java that contains this code:

```
public class Caller {
  void call(Responder responder){
    System.out.println("I'm calling you.");
    System.out.println(responder.respond());
  }
  public static void main( String[] args){
    Caller caller = new Caller();
    caller.call(new Responder());
  }
}
```

Also inside of `example` save the file Responder.java containing the following code.

```
public class Responder {
  String respond(){
    return "You've been responded to.";
  }
}
```

Open up a terminal window and navigate inside of `example`. Compile the code by typing the following.

```
javac *.java
```

Run the application by typing this code.

```
java Caller
```

You should see the following output.

```
I'm calling you.
You've been responded to.
```

Now, let's see what happens when we change the packaging. Delete the two generated class files, Caller.class and Responder.class. Create two subdirectories of `example`. Name one `call` and name the other `response`. Place Caller.java inside of `call` and Responder.java inside of `response`.

When the file compiles, you will receive several error messages. First, you need to make sure that your packaging matches your directory structure. This means that Caller.java must begin with the following:

```
package call;
```

and Responder.java must begin with:

```
package response;
```

Second, let's be clear on which source directory you are compiling from. You're still inside the `example` directory but outside the `call` and `response` subdirectories. You can compile Caller.java as follows:

```
javac call/Caller.java
```

Similarly compile Responder.java as follows:

```
javac response/Responder.java
```

You should still get a compiler error because `Responder` is in a different package than `Caller`, so when you try to create a new `Responder` from inside of `Caller` the compiler has no idea what you mean by `Responder`. Add this `import` statement to Caller.java after the `package` statement.

```
import response.Responder;
```

You'll still get a compiler error because `respond()` inside of Responder.java isn't a public method and can't be called from a different package. Change the access on `respond()` to `public`. This time the two files should compile with no problem. To run the applications use this command:

```
java call.Caller
```

Adding a Main Class

It isn't obvious to someone else how to run your application. As a rule, use either a class named `Main` or a class with the same name as the top package but beginning with an uppercase letter. Create this file, called Main.java, inside of the `example` directory.

```
package example;
import example.response.Responder;
import example.call.Caller;
```

```
public class Main {
  public static void main( String[] args){
    Caller caller = new Caller();
    String conversation = caller.call(new Responder());
    System.out.println(conversation);
  }
}
```

The class `Caller` is now inside of the directory `call`, which is inside of the directory `example`. `Caller` now must be changed so that it can still access `Responder`.

```
package example.call;
import example.response.Responder;
public class Caller {
  public String call(Responder responder){
    return "I'm calling you.\n" + responder.respond();
  }
}
```

Notice that this time `call()` had to be made public so that it could be called from `Main`. Also, it now returns a `String` that is printed inside of `main()`. Here is the, mostly unchanged, version of `Responder`.

```
package example.response;
public class Responder {
public  String respond(){
    return "You've been responded to.";
  }
}
```

Compile the files by moving outside of `example` and entering this.

```
javac example/*.java
```

If you have to explicitly compile the other classes, from the same location type

```
javac example/call/Caller.java
```

and

```
javac example/response/Responder.java
```

Now run the application with this command.

```
java example.Main
```

A Sample Hierarchy

A package should correspond to some logical unit of functionality. For example, in Chapter 10 you looked at Conway's Game of Life. You might imagine separating the GUI from the model of the game underneath into separate packages. Remember from the index card example that organizing the files will help locate the files you want. All of the GUI files will be together. If the GUI contains a `Jframe` that has a complicated menu bar then perhaps there will be a package for all of the menus and menu items.

In an actual student group's implementation there was a parent directory called `life`. Inside of `life` were the file Main.java and two subdirectories: `cells` and `gui`. Inside of `cells` were the files Cell.java, CellManager.java, CellType.java, CellWalker.java, DeadCell.java, and LiveCell.java. Inside of the `gui` subdirectory were the files BoardPanel.java, CellPanel.java, and LifeFrame.java. Notice that the GUI files are grouped together and the model files are grouped together.

Again, this directory structure must map completely to the package structure. For example, suppose Main.java begins with the following line:

```
package life;
```

This means that each of the files inside of the `gui` subdirectory must begin with this line.

```
package life.gui;
```

In addition, each of the files inside of the `cells` subdirectory must begin with this line:

```
package life.cells;
```

It may seem silly, but if an object of type `CellPanel` needs to communicate with an object of type `Cell`, you need to include the statement `import life.cells.Cell` in CellPanel.java. Even more difficult is trying to remember that because `CellPanel` doesn't extend `Cell` and isn't in the same package, you can't access any of `Cell`'s methods from `CellPanel` unless they are `public`.

PREPARING YOUR FILES FOR A RELEASE

Releases in this project will be a bit different from those you might remember from other computer science courses. In those classes, the professors expected to see the source code. They may have ignored the compiled code and recompiled the code from the source you submitted. Even if they ran the versions you submitted, much of your grade was based on the code that you wrote. Running and meeting the functional requirements were just part of the standards used to evaluate you.

In this project, your professor may still want to see the source code. Your grade may depend in part on the quality of the code. For the most part, however, your client won't care about anything except what the application actually does. Clients may want a copy of the source code in case they want someone else to someday continue development on your project. This can be delivered separately along with the final release. The release only needs to contain executable programs. Perhaps you want to deliver class files neatly packaged up with a shell script or batch file. Maybe you want to provide a jar file or want to use a more sophisticated application (for example, MRJAppBuilder on Mac OS X, or InstallAnywhere from ZeroG on any platform) to build an installer for your program. In any case, you can begin to prepare for release by keeping your files nicely separated.

When you use an IDE, you are often prompted to set up a `src` directory for the source files and a `classes` directory for the compiled files. Some IDEs also create a directory in which to keep backups of altered source files and a `docs` directory to contain the generated JavaDocs, manuals, installation notes, and README files. Keep your project organized like this. It makes the distribution easier.

Separating Source and Class Files

Let's continue to work with the sample project begun in the last section. You're going to create a new directory for this project. For definiteness, call it `SampleProject`. Inside of `SampleProject` create the subdirectories `src`, `classes`, `docs`, `backup`, and `tests`. Include the `example` subdirectory you created in the previous section inside of `src`. If you'd like, delete all of the `.class` files inside of `example`.

You'll still want to compile the source files from just outside of the `example` directory. This time, however, you want the generated files to be saved inside of the `classes` directory. The `example` directory is inside of the `src` directory, which is one of `classes`' siblings. So you use the `-d` flag when you compile to indicate the target for the `.class` files. In this case the command would be the following:

```
javac -d ../classes example/*.java
```

As a result, `example` is created as a subdirectory of `classes`. It contains Main.class and the further subdirectories `call` and `response`, which contain Caller .class and Responder.class respectively. Now the class files are all contained in the example directory inside of the classes directory. You can simply distribute these files with a platform-specific, double-clickable file that runs the application.

Jar-ing Up the Results

You have a free zip tool available to you as part of the standard Java distribution. Use it to create an archive of your `.class` files using the jar (Java Archive) tool. Navigate inside of the `classes` directory. You want to zip up everything in the `example` directory. Suppose you want to save it as assignment.jar. You would type this:

```
jar cvf assignment.jar example
```

Here the `c` flags that you are creating an archive, `v` indicates you want verbose output that chronicles the whole process and `f` signifies that you are providing the file name. You can see all of the available options by just typing `jar`. You will see that you have created a new file named assignment.jar containing the directories and files contained in `example`. You'll also see how much the jar tool was able to deflate the files when archiving them. You can run the application with the following command:

```
java -classpath assignment.jar example/Main
```

In other words, you need to make sure that the contents of assignment.jar are visible in the classpath and then you just specify the class that contains the `main()` method. Here you could just distribute a single file instead of many. In addition, you will distribute your batch file or shell script for executing this single jar file.

You can actually do better by adding the information about the class containing `main()` to a file that is included in the jar called the manifest. Create a text file called setMain.txt (or some such name) that contains the following line as its only content:

```
Main-class: example/Main
```

This line must contain a return character after `example/Main`. Save this file inside of the `classes` directory along with assignment.jar and add its contents to the manifest included in assignment.jar with this command:

```
jar umvf setMain.txt assignment.jar
```

Here the flag `u` indicates that you are updating a jar and `m` indicates that the file setMain.txt contains additional information for the manifest. You will get confirmation that the manifest is updated and can now run the jar by just typing this:

```
java -jar assignment.jar
```

The jar file now contains information about the class containing `main()` so it can execute in response to this command. Even better, you've actually created a double clickable jar file. Click on it twice and it should execute.

PACKAGING YOUR UNIT TEST FILES

In a standard XP project you would have written tests before you wrote the code. Let's look at that code and where you might put it. Generally, you will need to access both public- and package-accessible methods. This means that the test class must be in the same package as the class that it is testing. When you've finished your directory may look like that shown in Figure 15-1.

As you saw in the last section, you should be creating these files in the src directory and compiling them to the classes directory.

The Tests

To begin, create the file AllTests.java and place it in the `example` directory along with Main.java.

```
package example;
```

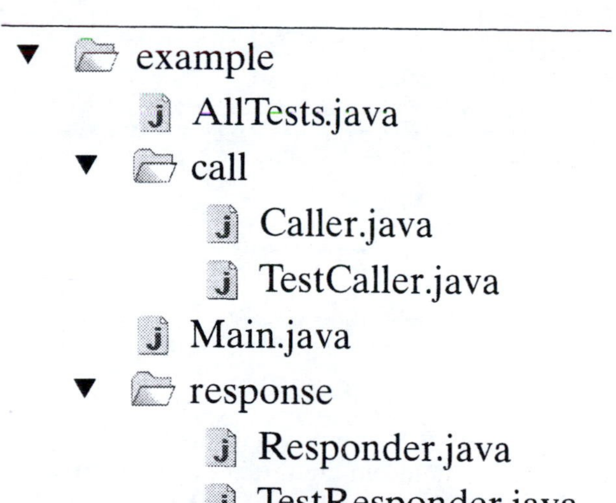

Figure 15-1 Directory Organization

```
import junit.framework.Test;
import junit.framework.TestSuite;
public class AllTests {
  public static void main (String[] args) {
    junit.textui.TestRunner.run (suite());
  }
  public static Test suite ( ) {
    TestSuite suite = new TestSuite("All JUnit Tests");
    suite.addTest(new TestSuite(example.call.TestCaller.class));
    suite.addTest(new TestSuite(example.response.TestResponder.class));
    return suite;
    }
}
```

The TestResponder.java file is in the `response` subdirectory of `example`. It contains a single test method for the `respond()` method in `Responder`.

```
package example.response;
import junit.framework.TestCase;
public class TestResponder extends TestCase {
  public TestResponder(String name){
   super(name);
  }
  public void testRespond(){
    Responder responder = new Responder();
    assertEquals(responder.respond(), "You've been responded to.");
  }
}
```

Similarly, TestCaller.java is in the `call` subdirectory of `example`. It also contains a single test method for the `call()` method in `Caller`.

```
package example.call;
import junit.framework.TestCase;
import example.response.Responder;
public class TestCaller extends TestCase {
  public TestCaller(String name){
    super(name);
  }
  public void testCall(){
    Caller caller = new Caller();
    assertEquals(caller.call(new Responder()),
      "I'm calling you. \nYou've been responded to.");
  }
}
```

You can compile these files and run the test suite as described in the test first tutorial in Chapter 10. You should get a report that both tests passed.

Separating the Test Files

There are several problems with where you've placed the test files. First, your test files are stored in the same directories as the code that you intend to distribute. If you produce JavaDocs, you will get documentation for both types of files. Second, your compiled files will be compiled together into the same directories. Do you really want to distribute the test code as part of your application? This is a particular problem if you are deploying an application to a device that may have memory constraints.

On the other hand, in general your test files do need to be in the same package as the classes they are exercising. The key here is that this doesn't mean that they have to physically be in the same directory. This is a bit confusing. You learned in the first section of this chapter that the physical file structure has to correspond to the packaging scheme. Now you are going to move the test files so the directory structure looks like Figure 15-2.

Notice that within the `src` and `tests` directories are parallel directory structures. The idea is that if `src` and `tests` are in the classpath then AllTests.java and Main.java are viewed as if they were in the same package. Relative to the classpath they are both inside of the `example` directory.

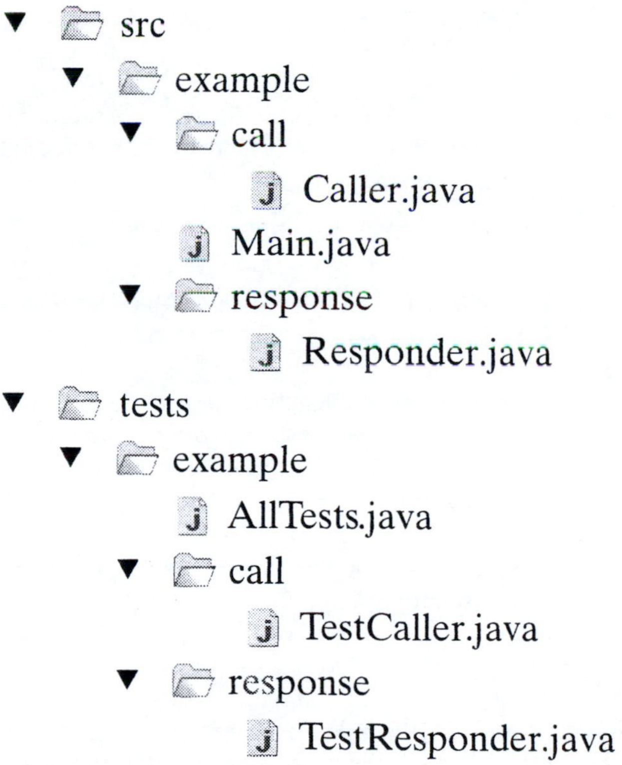

- src
  - example
    - call
      - Caller.java
    - Main.java
    - response
      - Responder.java
- tests
  - example
    - AllTests.java
    - call
      - TestCaller.java
    - response
      - TestResponder.java

Figure 15-2 Tests in the Directory Structure

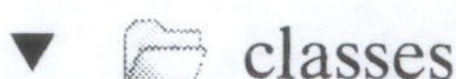

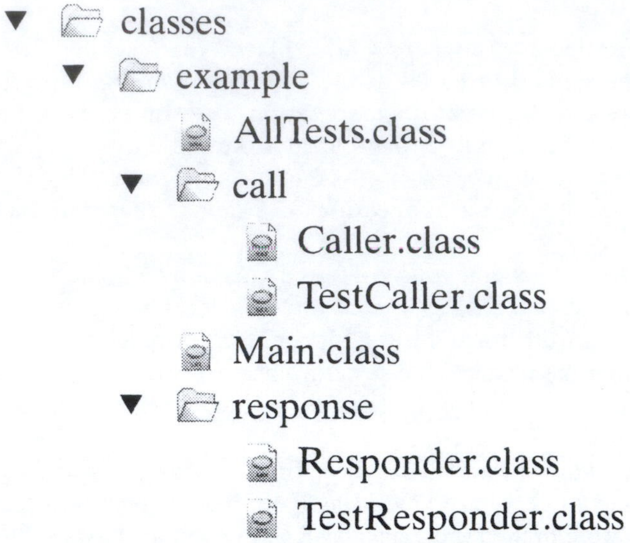

Figure 15-3 The Classes Subdirectory

Get rid of the contents of the `classes` directory and any residual class files that you may have in the `src` or `tests` directory. Compile the code in two steps. Compile the contents of `src` by navigating inside of the `src` directory and entering the following:

```
javac -d ../classes example/*.java
```

You did this step before. Next, navigate inside of the tests directory and compile the test files. You'll need to add junit.jar to your classpath as well as adding the `src` directory. Here's a template for the command.

```
javac -classpath ../src:.:<path to junit install>/junit.jar -d ../classes
example/*.java
```

You'll replace *<path to junit install>* with the actual path on your machine. After you have compiled the contents of your `tests` and `src` directories, your `classes` directory should look like Figure 15-3.

You can now run the application by executing `Main` or the tests by executing `AllTests`. If you don't want to distribute your test files, you can now easily not do so. Just clean out your existing class files and compile the contents of the `src` directory.

As you add acceptance tests to your project you may want to further divide the `tests` directory. You can see descriptions of this in the acceptance test tutorials. One alternative is to create `unit` and `acceptance` subdirectories for `tests` and structure `unit` as was described for `tests` in this section.

JAVADOCS

One of the great misconceptions of XP is that documentation is somehow prohibited in the methodology. Ron Jeffries has written quite a bit about this in *XP Magazine*. In his article entitled "Misconceptions about XP" (www.xprogramming.com/xpmag/

Misconceptions.htm), he provides a nice summary. He explains that much of the misunderstanding comes from repeated assertions in the XP literature that developers who pair and are located near the other developers on the team tend to need fewer documents for themselves. Documentation can be split into two categories based on the intended audience.

If a customer requires documentation, then providing it is a business decision. The customer decides whether the programmers need to spend time on this sort of documentation in the same way that the customer gets to assign the other business priorities. As Jeffries writes in his article "Essential XP:Documentation" (www.xprogramming.com/xpmag/expDocumentationInXP.htm), if "there is a need to communicate outside the team, and it can't be done by coming together, then of course it is just fine to write something. That just makes good sense. We're Extreme, not stupid."

You also may need internal documentation to communicate with other developers as you work on the project. Remember, however, that as you saw in the refactoring tutorial in Chapter 13, if a comment is needed you may need to refactor your code to more clearly communicate its meaning. In *Extreme Programming Applied*, Ken Auer describes Role Model Software's coding standard. He advises that when "you do something unconventional with reason, you should (only after determining there isn't a better way to do it) document why in a comment." This is echoed in Misconceptions about XP when Jeffries explains that if programmers need documentation they can be expected to recognize this need and provide the required documentation. The documentation may not be formal or distributable. Jeffries points out that "much of the documentation they'll do will be lightweight, [and] ephemeral. Whiteboards and scraps of paper are very common tools for this purpose."

You've seen your share of documentation that provides no more information than is already contained in the code. Remember this is documentation targeting developers who are expected to be able to read code. This is not documentation intended for a nontechnical audience. Java provides the javadoc tool. It takes your code and produces easy to read hyperlinked documentation. Although the tool has gotten quite powerful, you don't need to take advantage of the more subtle features to produce the documentation that helps navigate code quickly. For projects with powerful IDEs, you will have access to tools that can trace through code pretty quickly. If you are using a text editor and command line tools, JavaDocs can be quite helpful.

Over the years, the javadoc tool and associated APIs has gotten much more powerful. You can create your own tags or a different doclet that is used to customize the output of the generated documentation. With the SDK 1.4 you can now instruct the tool to generate documents for a directory and all of its subdirectories. You can exclude directories if you like. If you have set your project files as directed in this chapter, you'll want to generate documentation for the entire contents of the `src` directory and save these generated files in the docs directory. This is easily done by navigating inside of the `src` directory and typing this:

```
javadoc -subpackages example ../docs
```

For your application, just replace `example` with your top-level package. You will see a screen full of information that indicates the files being generated and where they are being placed. Open up a web browser and open up index.html inside of the `docs` directory. If you have a reason to, you can also generate documentation for the `tests` directory.

THE VARIOUS BUILDS

You and your partner are working on code on your machine. You write your tests, write your code, compile, and pass all of your tests. At some point you decide you have done enough that you need to update the current build. XP stresses continuous integration. Some of the biggest headaches come when you and your partner are working on code and another pair is working on code and each pair has made changes to the same method. The longer you wait to integrate, the more differences there will be that need to be reconciled. If you integrate after making a small but important change and announce to everyone that you have, then everybody gets your modifications and can work from this new common code base. Conversely, when you are told that new code has been integrated, you need to update your local version as quickly as possible. You'll have fewer adjustments to make (possibly none). If there are adjustments to be made, you want to make them quickly and move on. You soon see that there are benefits of integrating often. That way, others are adjusting to your changes.

Integrating Code

It is often good to have an integration machine. This is a machine that holds the latest version of the project. Each person can get code from it and send code to it. It is the host for whatever versioning system you're running. If you don't actually have an integration machine, pretend that you do. Send your code, perhaps as a zip file, somewhere that everyone on the team can access it.

The steps in integrating code are basic but important.

1. Make sure that you have the latest version of the integration machine's code. It won't do you any good to have incorporated your changes in an old version of the code and try to integrate them on the integration machine.
2. Make sure that your code compiles and all the tests run.
3. Notify your team that you are integrating.
4. Go to the integration machine and run the tests on the existing code. They should all pass. The last group to integrate should have checked this. You check anyway.
5. Send your revised code to the integration machine.
6. Compile your code on that machine and run all of the tests. You may need to clean out the old class files by hand.
7. If all of the tests run, notify your team that they need to update their code. If the files don't all run then you need to back out your changes and take a look at your code. Make sure that you really are working with the latest version of the code on your home machine.
8. Remember, never leave the code on the integration machine in a state where it doesn't compile and pass all of the tests.

Many IDEs support CVS or some other Source Control Management (SCM) system. You should investigate whether one of these would be easy to set up. It is convenient to let the automatic system take care of numbering the different versions and keeping track of which files have been updated since you last looked. You can easily spot the differences between your file and the repository file and accept or reject changes. Having such software makes integration much easier—so long as you are integrating all the time. Before you upload your changes, these systems make it clear which files need to be reconciled; therefore, you can't ignore step 1. If you don't have an application that assists with SCM, then your group needs to agree on numbering conventions and other practices for integrating so that it is clear to all what the most recent version of the files is.

Distribution Checklist

Before you send your code to the client, you can strip out the source code, but this isn't enough. You have probably generated many `TestCase` classes for executing your suite of unit tests. You don't need to jar these up and submit them to the client. You also don't want to keep class files around that belong to source files that no longer exist. If you have files a.java and b.java and compile them, you'll end up with a.class and b.class. Now if you decide to eliminate a.java and modify b.java,. when you recompile you'll end up with the old a.class and the new b.class. Nothing indicates that a.class is no longer needed. Regularly clean out old and unused classes. If you have separated the source files and class files into two separate directories, this is easy to do. Just eliminate all of the contents of the `classes` directory.

In any case, before you release your code, clean out your `classes` directory and recompile all of the classes other than those that are test related. This should be easy if you've taken the time to keep your test hierarchy separate from the other source files. Create a jar file for your distribution and an easy way for the client to execute your application. As a final check you may want to send your candidate to at least one other machine and test that the application works there.

One of the biggest concerns is that your application depends on files or a special configuration that you've set up on your machine. All dependencies should be documented so that you can make sure the client machine is configured correctly. Then the client can ensure that the eventual target machines are also configured correctly. You can avoid many of these problems by not adding files to your classpath in the system settings. Explicitly add them with the `-classpath flag` when compiling or running your Java applications. You did this when you compiled your tests in the previous example. You explicitly added junit.jar to the classpath.

Similarly, note the version of the JVM that your application is using and the JVM available to your client. What have you placed in your `jre/lib/ext` directory that is being automatically added to your classpath without your even remembering? These are all questions you'll need to answer to assure yourself that you're prepared to install. The good news is that very early in the project you will have worked these issues out. You shouldn't be fiddling with the client machine trying to get something to work during the final delivery of the software.

Automating the Build

There are tools available for automating the build process. One of the more popular is the open source offering called ANT available at http://jakarta.apache.org. There's no point in providing examples of ANT scripts, as it is in the process of being revised in a way that will break the old scripts. You can specify targets in ANT that allow you to perform different tasks easily. For example you can clean out the classes directory. You can compile your source code and run all of the unit tests. You can also produce your release build that doesn't include the source code or the unit test classes. The documentation that accompanies the ANT release is clear and complete and can be used to simplify and automate your different builds. Another goal of the ANT project is to provide a GUI front end. It has already been integrated in several popular IDEs.

Appendix A

Experience in the Trenches—

Sharing User Stories

This appendix is a collection of frequently asked questions (FAQ) expressed by students while taking the XP course, along with a solution or an answer to each question as it arose during the course. Some of the entries present potential pitfalls in the course: how they came about and how they were resolved. Others shed light on the benefits of some XP processes or illustrate potential problems caused by not following them. Feel free to contact us at stories@extremeteaching.com with stories from your introduction to XP.

1. "Do we have to follow all of the XP practices all of the time?"

   Initially, this should be your goal. There are synergies in the XP practices that you can't appreciate unless you follow them all simultaneously. When you begin, you won't be following all of the practices because you will be learning them. That isn't the time to decide what is and isn't working for you. By midsemester you may have a feel for a practice that needs to be modified or dropped in your particular situation. Talk to your instructor or coach about what you are thinking of doing. Some practices, such as testing first, are core to XP and can't be eliminated.

2. "How do we communicate as a team when there are sessions where only part of the team is present?"

   One recent XP team exchanged over 600 e-mail messages on a group account during the semester. That's an average of over five messages a day for fifteen weeks. Not only did this provide a good, open forum for planning and debating, but it also provided the instructor and the coach an up-to-the-minute reading on the pulse of the project. It also proved to be a simple but effective way of archiving of the group's debates and resolutions. Being able to go back and recreate the thought processes that led to a particular action benefited the team. Especially if the action did not turn out the way the team had hoped and the argument had to be revisited.

3. "How do we do continuous integration without a source control system like CVS?"

Teams that use a group e-mail provider should choose one that allows them to upload files. For the team in the previous entry, this proved to be quite helpful by supporting collective code ownership and continuous integration. Whenever a pair finished working, they'd upload the current system to the group site and whenever the next pair got together, they'd start by downloading the most recent system. Subsequent groups have chosen other communication options, including a wiki, and web-based education software packages, like Blackboard.

4. "Who is in charge of our team?"

No one. This creates a more fluid environment while programming but can cause organizational difficulties. When no one is in charge, everyone must become more responsible. Individuals can't reason that they aren't that important so it won't matter if they miss a particular meeting. On two different occasions during the early stages of the semester, pair programming sessions were scheduled, but only one person attended. There were also group meetings for which everyone showed up except the person who had access to the meeting room, and there were teams that failed to decide on a suitable location for a meeting before the meeting started. A typical e-mail to the group would read, "I'm available to meet at 3:00 on Tuesday, let me know where." Then either no one would respond or many people would respond with different time and place suggestions. Tuesday would come and go and no meeting would take place. The resolution was that the team member who wanted to schedule the meeting had to propose a time, a location, and a topic. If the location of a meeting required a specific person to be involved (say if the meeting was in a student's dorm room) and that person couldn't make the meeting, it was his or her responsibility to arrange an alternate location and inform everyone of the change.

5. "How important is it that we all work together?"

Very. The more time you can find during the week when the entire group can work together at the same location, the better. On the other hand, it is hard to coordinate the schedules of your group members. The ideal industry XP project consists of a colocated team so that the pairings are fluid and the team members are able to take advantage of synergies. At the least, schedule a regular time and place for your weekly standup meeting. It doesn't have to be a big block of time—maybe right before or right after class. This allows time for communication when you can settle issues raised in the previous FAQ. During your group meeting you can set the times and places for pairing sessions and resolve issues such as missed meetings from the last week. These times may not be static during the semester, as someone in your group may have to make a big push for another class. You can update each other on the best way to be contacted during the upcoming week if there are any changes.

6. "Why can't we do spikes for the first few weeks and then start delivering code?"

Your goal in this course is to deliver software. You will learn a lot about the problem space you are working in but that is a side benefit. Your goal is not to learn about technology or techniques as it is in other courses; your goal in this course is to learn about the process. Your team may be putting off starting to code to cover any possible technology that might come up in the project. The problem with the use of perpetual spikes is that you are not writing any production code and there is no way to tell which spikes will benefit the final system. Spikes should be done only on an as-needed basis and should be very limited in scope.

7. "What if we need to research a technology to make a design decision?"

Make certain that you have to make the decision. If you do, then perform a spike. One of the bases for eXtreme Programming is that by starting with a simple design and continually improving it, you'll end up with a good design. You don't need to state at the outset, "We need to use hash tables in this project." You may end up with a hash table, you may not, but it can only come about as the result of a hash table being the simplest solution to the current problem. However, because your code is in need of refactoring, the obvious design improvement is to use a hash table. When it becomes clear that a hash table is the right way to go, then such a spike can be useful. On the other hand, there are times when a technology decision does need to be made. If your data is to be stored as XML files that will be parsed and transformed, you need to decide how to parse the data. A couple of hours spent with the Java servlets JAXP and with JDOM might help you choose which of the two is easier to use and better suits your needs. Spikes need to be well understood so that they aren't over- or underutilized.

8. "Why do we have to test first if we're producing working code?"

Testing first has more far-reaching implications than simply working code. Code develops differently under the test-driven approach. On multiple occasions, teams resisted test-driven development. The teams argued that even though they were not testing first, they were pairing, generating code in a timely fashion, and not missing a delivery to the client. In one case, the instructor temporarily required two teams to turn in all the tests they wrote each week. Once the teams were forced to write the tests anyway, they began doing it as a matter of course and saw results. One of the teams was never really pleased with testing first, but the other teams embraced the practice and even carried it over into other programming projects not associated with this course.

9. "How many unit tests are enough?"

Stop writing code once the tests pass. With test-driven development you don't tend to write application code without a failing test. You should always be intent on passing the current test so that you can write the next one. The "Test-Driven Development" cycle includes writing a test, writing the code that passes the test (if any is required), and then refactoring.

There is no unit test per line of code metric to rely on; however, there is generally a large collection of tests per user story. Even for individual methods used in a class, there may be multiple tests. One XP team revealed that they had generated a dozen unit tests for a system that contained twenty-seven classes. Their results should have given them a good indication that their process was not sufficient. This team started out by writing a test and then did the simplest thing to get the test to pass. But then they would keep going. Once they'd written the first code, they tended to keep writing code for a while, without writing any additional tests. By sticking to only writing code when they had a failing test, they ended up with an appropriate number of tests.

10. "Can we work on the tasks as a team?"

A couple of XP teams did not assign weekly tasks to specific individuals. Instead they bid on the tasks as a team and then worked from a communal list of tasks for the iteration. This turned out to be an interesting coping strategy reacting to an aspect of academic XP. Since the team did not have any pairing sessions that overlapped, they recognized that a single development path was feasible. So instead of working on separate tasks, each pair would work on the "current" task. The process made it difficult to develop individual estimation skills, but it turned out to be a workable approach in the beginning of the project. The initial user stories were quite sequential, so until the team completed a core portion of the development, the communal bidding was beneficial. After the initial stories were completed, the team bid individually on tasks and even though they never did parallel pairing sessions, it would have been possible to do so.

11. "Don't we need to see the GUI to make sure it is working?"

Any testing that requires visual inspection of the GUI to perform the test or to determine the outcome cannot be done automatically. Fortunately, this is seldom the case. You can usually automate the manipulation of a GUI and the gathering of results. Humans are visually oriented creatures, so it is natural to want to see what something looks like to get a feel for it. Clearly, the layout, the colors, and the sizes of the graphic components will need to be manually inspected, but virtually every other aspect of the interface can be tested automatically.

12. "How do you write unit tests for GUI software?"

Most testing of a GUI can be done nonvisually. By creating appropriate mouse events and applying them to the correct components, the team can test all of the GUI's interactions without ever bringing a visible component to the screen. The team doesn't have to test that the act of clicking on the JPanel invokes the associated Listener's mouseClicked() method. Instead, the team only needs to test that execution of the mouseClicked() method causes the desired action to take place. Any of the graphical component's characteristics can be queried and compared, again without bringing them to the screen. Another approach is to use JUnit extensions such as JFCUnit. One XP team spent quite a lot of effort setting up Java's Robot class to manipulate the mouse and simulate clicks on different buttons and panels to verify the correct behavior. This approach allowed for semiautomation, but every time the test suite ran, multiple windows would open cluttering the screen and obscuring JUnit's color bar. Even when this approach is done deftly and with aplomb, it is still cumbersome and unnecessary.

13. "How can XP possibly succeed without first designing an overall structure for the program?"

XP projects succeed because you design a little at a time during the entire project. You can't possibly anticipate the problems and alternatives that will arise once you start coding. One XP team did not see how a complex system would develop from a simple design and refactoring. So they felt that the only way to get to a working system was to put all the complexity into the system up front, and then use XP techniques to write the code to fill the gaps. This team was looking at the development process from the top down while XP is a bottom-up process. They (thought) knew that for the system to work, they needed an interactive GUI that was connected to two complex subsystems.

They wanted to start with a simple GUI, stub versions of both subsystems, and define the interfaces through which these three entities would interact. Then they felt that XP might serve as a useful way to complete the different parts of the system. It was a case of not accepting that a succession of "simplest things" and refactorings could lead to an overall working system.

14. "What do we do when we don't quite finish a story?"

You report to the customer that the story is not completed. You may choose to reestimate the story. In XP everything is black or white. A story is either finished or it isn't. The worst thing you can do when you estimate is to figure that you are almost done with a story. It causes your estimations in the next iteration and your reports to your customer to be off. If you finish a story more quickly then estimated, go ask the customer for more work. They will be delighted.

15. "What do you do if you are stuck?"

Do a quick check to make sure you are still doing XP. In particular, are you testing first, doing the simplest thing that could possibly work, and taking small reversible steps? At one point an XP team made no real progress for two development cycles. They were completely stalled on a single line of code. The offensive line of code apparently worked correctly in their spike code, but would not work in their production code. They checked everything. What went wrong? In the simplest terms, the team stopped doing eXtreme Programming. Because the solution always seemed just around the corner, the efforts to find it remained the same. Something wasn't working. They needed to start writing tests for parts of their program that they were positive worked correctly. They needed to refactor to clean up their code. They needed to return the system to a state in which all of the tests were passing. In this case, since the team felt that the solution was always lingering just out of reach, a tactical retreat was not considered. Weeks went by without progress. Try to keep out of the mindset of "we're almost there."

16. "How can a coach help us get unstuck?"

A coach is not a teammate and has nothing invested in choosing one solution over another. The coach is there to help you with the process. Perhaps the coach will pair with you, but the value in that session is not the code the coach adds but the modeling of XP that the coach displays. While working on a particular user story, a group was attempting to parse an XML input file. As with the situation in the previous FAQ, this group got stuck on a small bit of code and they were stuck outside of XP. They knew they were "almost done" but they refused to return to basic XP practices and couldn't get unstuck. The XP coach met with the team and helped to steer them back to the basics. Step-by-step he asked the following questions: What user story are you currently working on? What task have you carved out of the story? What particular test case are you trying to solve? Why didn't you test these simpler things first? The coach helped bring the team back into the XP process and along the way found that some of the simpler tests uncovered other problems. Eventually the source of the problem proved to be related to the way SAX handled white space. Taking small steps is a key to XP and if you get stuck, the best thing to do is to go back and see where you could have taken a smaller step or seek the help of someone who can guide you there.

17. "Do we need to do estimates and have stand-up meetings after the first few iterations?"

Yes. One of the most important skills you are developing is an awareness of your abilities and pace. A keystone of XP is providing many data points on which to build your estimates. One particular XP team hit their sustainable pace early in their project and stopped refining their estimates. The team got so involved in producing code they didn't keep track of their bids and their subsequent accuracy. Rather than making more and more accurate estimates, the relationship between their estimates and their actual progress continued to be fairly random. It is very important to make the estimates and track their accuracy in a simple, visible, and permanent way. Use "A Big Visible Chart" to track your estimates for various tasks and a record of the actual time it took. Nothing fancy is needed. You should not have to add a lot of difficulty to maintain artifacts to an XP project.

18. "Can we have a couple of extra days for this delivery?"

No. There are no schedule slips in XP, only slips in delivery content. As soon as a team realizes that they are not going to be able to deliver everything they agreed to, they must inform the client. The *client* then decides how the team should apply the rest of their effort in the current iteration. If you think about it, it really makes sense. All other types of service industries work this way. How often would you frequent a restaurant if you were told that they could provide a "much better" dinner for you tomorrow afternoon at 3 o'clock? But we do understand if they tell us that they are out of one of the specials and we decide on something else.

19. "Is there the typical crazy push at the end of an XP project to finish everything?"

No. One semester the class had both traditional and eXtreme Programming teams, the last two weeks of the semester the two methodologies differed rather significantly. Invariably, if a group followed the traditional methodology, then there was a determined push at the end to pull everything together. The traditional group was dealing with estimates that covered several months. Meanwhile, the XP teams were calmly finishing because they were dealing with estimates that covered two weeks as they had all semester. The XP teams had already demonstrated the results of their efforts on a regular basis; they knew that the majority of their system already worked. The traditional software-engineering teams had put lots of effort into their project throughout the semester, and they gave demonstrations to the client along the way, but they hadn't yet delivered anything. In the XP groups, the client had in his possession, installed on his hard drive, the sum total of all the work that the group had done up until the end of the previous two-week delivery cycle. In the last weeks, the traditional team was expected to present a semester's worth of effort and the XP team, only two-weeks' worth. Their stakes were lower, so the XP team was much calmer.

20. "What do we do if our client doesn't want to write acceptance tests?"

Help your client write acceptance tests. These tests let you know that you are done with a user story and let the client know that you are done. The creation of the acceptance tests is a joint project, a tight collaboration between the client and the development team. It is both technically involved and user-driven, requiring the efforts of the client and the development team. One XP client and team did not put the necessary effort into this portion of the process. The team concentrated on writing their unit tests and the client relied on the biweekly deliveries to monitor the progress of the development. However, at the end of the semester, the client was unsure if the system met all of the goals specified in the user stories. One solution is to watch how the user verifies that a user story has been completed at the biweekly releases. Help the client turn those manual tests into acceptance tests that can be automated with a framework such as Fit. Encourage the client to write *and run* the acceptance tests as you go. The client will be happier, the team will be happier, and the system will be better for it.

Appendix B

For Professionals—Customizing the Course

This appendix offers alternative road maps for professional developers who want to use this text to learn XP. Two approaches are discussed: conducting a week-long XP training seminar and a taking a self-paced, self-taught course.

TRAINING WORKSHOP

In a workshop, with its high density of material and intense schedule, the most critical aspect for the presenters is preparation. There is no time to generate on-the-fly examples, so all lecture materials and lab exercises must be detailed and complete. Systems must be set up, working, and double-checked long before the students arrive on the first day of class. Some specific XP issues include having a fully worked out project with which all instructors, clients, and coaches are intimately familiar. They must be ready with an answer for all manner of questions and options. If possible, there should be a client for each separate XP group in the course. Because of the tight schedule, each group needs to have immediate access to their client for feedback. An effective approach is to prepare all client materials in advance. For example, the client should have the user stories and the associated acceptance tests ready to go before the class begins. Another approach is to combine developer training with client training. The developers will need initial stories to prime the pump, but subsequent stories and decisions are made with these clients-in-training with help from the client coaches.

Students in such a course are experienced and directed. Only the central material should be covered, secondary topics can be self-taught by interested participants. In particular, the tutorials in Part III should be assigned to reinforce the material after the participants return to their professional lives. In tight schedules, a good mix of lectures and hands-on experiences is most effective. Lectures present lots of material quickly, but because the students only have a few days to assimilate the practices, it is more important that they have lots of time at the keyboard to code in pairs as part of a group working on a project with a real client. This is a situation in which having the instructor act as the client can work, although, the instructor is most often the coach.

The proposed structuring of the material from this text for a weeklong short course is to cover some of the material about the XP spike on the first day by alternating hour-long lectures and hour-long exercises. The exercises on the first day should help the students get comfortable with the environment and some of the initial XP practices. The second day of the workshop should begin with the "real" project. The remainder of the class is spent working on this project as an XP team. After the introductory material on the first day, the lectures should be minimal, focusing on anticipating and answering student questions that arise from the projects.

The Compressed Spike

During a time-compressed version of the XP spike, students will focus on those aspects of eXtreme Programming that can be done with only two practitioners. Specifically, during the lab sessions on the first day, students will not form into XP teams. The practices covered: pair programming, test-driven design, simple design, and refactoring can be learned and performed in pairs. At each lab session, students will pair off with a different partner and work through the corresponding exercises.

The first afternoon lecture is on refactoring and the lab will give the students a chance to practice the technique. At the end of the day, there will be a demonstration–lecture and a lab session on interacting with the client to develop user stories.

Week-long Training Workshop for XP Teams

DAY 1:

Session 1: (~1 hour)

An introduction to the course and XP, including an overview of the principles and practices of XP.

Session 2: (~2 hours)

~1-hour demonstration–lecture on pair programming, test-driven design, and simple design. Instructor-led demonstration encompassing all three practices. Tasks broken down from user stories should drive the activity.
~1 hour of lab time: Students pair off and implement another task using pair programming, test-driven design, and simple design practices.

Session 3: (~2 hours)

~1-hour demonstration–lecture on refactoring, including an example refactoring of code written by students during previous lab time.
~1 hour of lab time: students pair and refactor code written earlier.

Session 4: (~1 hour)

~1-hour demonstration–lecture on getting user stories from the client

By the end of the first day participants should be able to write code in an XP way and begin to learn about interacting with an XP client.

Week-long Training Workshop for XP Teams

DAY 2: MORNING

Session 1: (~2 hours)

~1-hour demonstration–lecture on the planning game. Take the user stories from the closing session on day one and break them down, estimate them, and prepare them for a pairing session.
~1 hour of lab time: Students break off into four- to five-person teams and work through the planning game process with supplied user stories

Session 2: (~1 hour)

~1 hour lecture introducing the project. Also introduce the coding standards, collective code-ownership, and continuous integration techniques to be used.

A Three-day Project

The projects begin no later than the afternoon of the second day. It is often easier to have all groups working on the same project and enough people playing the role of client that each group can get quick access to their client. The raw user stories should be created ahead of time and presented to the teams in the second session of the second day. Because of the short nature of both the course and the iterations, the collection of features cannot be overly complex or involved. The planning game begins and the teams should use about a half-day as their XP development cycle time. This way they can have two stand-up meetings per day with enough time left over for a group discussion at the end of each cycle. Here the instructor and the clients highlight issues that arise, answer questions, and make suggestions for improving the effectiveness of the teams.

The participants will get to experience six iterations and three releases. You may prefer to have releases after each iteration. Each iteration will build upon the previous one, so problems encountered and issues resolved will be different. If a team gets completely off-track during one iteration, it may or may not be useful for the team to continue working on the same code in the next iteration. Sometimes working through a self-inflicted problem and finding a solution is more important than experiencing a different aspect of the project. At other times, when the source of the problem is easily identifiable and avoidable in the future, but correcting the resulting code is tedious and time-consuming, the best approach is to move on.

Throughout each iteration, teams should interact with the client as necessary to resolve issues, ask questions, and reevaluate priorities. Coaches and instructors are also available to answer XP questions, make suggestions, and resolve any issues or problems that occur.

Week-long Training Workshop for XP Teams (continued)

PROJECT DAYS: THREE CYCLES, FROM AFTERNOON OF DAY 2 TO MORNING OF DAY 5

Afternoon Session: ~3 hours

Day 2: Meet with client, get user stories
Days 3 and 4: ~One-half hour question and answer session as a class
Stand-up meeting
One Iteration

Next Morning Session: ~3 hours

Stand-up Meeting
Second Iteration
Delivery to client, get new user stories and priorities

Week-long Training Workshop for XP Teams (continued)

DAY 5: XP POSTMORTEM DISCUSSION

Afternoon Session

The entire class comes together and each group presents the highlights of their team's experience. In particular, they discuss specific problems that their group encountered and what resolution they arrived at. The rest of the class asks questions and discusses the different approaches used by different teams.

The instructor summarizes the course, comparing and contrasting the experiences of the students to similar experiences on professional XP development efforts.

The variety of different experiences also emphasizes the benefits of a class-wide discussion on the final day of the workshop. Sharing the experiences and problems encountered by different groups multiplies the value of the course for all participants.

A Postmortem Discussion

Many more issues will be generated by the five-day project than can be adequately addressed in the allotted time. Different implementation approaches and different backgrounds of the participants will give rise to a wide range of experiences within the same workshop. Hearing about the problems and resolutions of others increases the diversity of experience. In this course, the final day is a full one, with the morning session consisting of the last iteration of the project and the afternoon session a post-mortem discussion and summary of the course.

The final session also provides an opportunity for the instructors, coaches, and clients to summarize the course. They can point out issues that have caused problems in the past that the current class managed to avoid. They can also present the best results from previous classes—particularly clever solutions to the same problems faced by the current participants. This is also a good time to make a strong point about the sustainable pace practice. It simply would not be possible to keep up the level of learning and doing that that has taken place in the previous four days. Most likely, students have already begun to show effects of the intensity of the course. And finally, now that the participants have experienced XP, the instructor can discuss issues related to using XP in the professional setting. They can talk about different types of customizations organizations have tried, and what the participants might take away from the course to apply in their own work environments.

SELF-PACED, SELF-TAUGHT PRACTICUM

Ideally, you should to find a partner who is also interested in learning extreme programming. XP is fundamentally a social activity that centers on interaction, communication and feedback. You should also look for someone locally or an on-line resource where you can address XP questions. With at least two people, you can alternate playing the roles of all the other participants. The quality of the experience and extent of the material that can be covered for two self-paced students dramatically outweighs what one student can do independently. A group of three or more is even better. You should strongly consider finding a partner before deciding to go it alone. In either case, this section will address both scenarios: at least two participants and a single individual.

Learning with a Partner

Finding an XP compatriot is definitely the preferred way to go. With a partner, you can experience and practice most of the features of eXtreme Programming. You'll have to take turns playing the role of the client if you can't recruit an outsider, but for the sake of learning, that can work quite well. If you pair all of the time, then one problem with a two-member team is that you will both be involved in every step. Neither person will be surprised by refactorings, because both will be present for all code changes. In fact, there won't be any issues stemming from collective code ownership at all. In particular, version control and propagation of coding techniques are nonissues. While this will provide a smoother transition into extreme programming it paints a skewed picture. When either of you joins a multiperson XP team you will experience another learning curve and an adjustment phase. Other than that, the XP learning experience in terms of order of material and corresponding chapter and exercises from the book mirrors that of the XP spike. Without time pressure, the duration of the spike can expand to fit whatever constraints are in place. In fact, you may decide that an extended spike serves your purposes in learning XP.

Self-paced, Self-taught Course for Two: Phase I, Improving your Coding Techniques

1. Read the Introduction and Chapter 1, *The Metaphor—Developing a Sense of Where We're Headed.*
2. Read Chapter 2, *Getting Started—Introducing the Core XP Practices*
3. Read Chapter 3, *Pair Programming—Learning to Work Together*, and do the exercises at the end of the chapter.
4. Read Chapter 4, *Test First, Then Code—Understanding Why We Test First.*
5. Do the test-driven tutorial in Chapter 10, *Test First—Learning a New Way of Life.*
6. Do the refactoring tutorial in Chapter 13, Refactoring—Sharpening Your Knife.

For the next phase, one person will be the client and the other will represent the interests of the development team. The most important aspect of this stage is to create a realistic level of earnestness in the client. Simulating a client does no good if the role-player has no vested interest in the client's point of view. If the developer playing the role of the client makes all the client decisions based on his or her developer's persona, then the process breaks down. For example, if you are using a computer version of hangman as your driving problem to learn the planning game, try to imagine that the program would be your only entertainment on a trans-Atlantic flight. After several hours of use, you might care deeply about the size of the database, the format of the "used" letters list, and whether you could change the number of allowable wrong guesses.

Self-paced, Self-taught Course for Two: Phase II, Improving Client Interactions

7. Read Chapter 5, *The Client—Meeting Another Team Member.*
8. Do the Chapter 11 tutorial, *User Stories—Exploring with the Customer.*
9. Do the Chapter 12 tutorial, *The Planning Game—Negotiating the Future.*
10. Read the rest of Part II, *The Iteration—Shaping the Development Process* (Chapters 6–9).
11. Do the Chapter 14 tutorial, *Customer Written Tests—Automating the Acceptance Process.*
12. Read Chapter 15, *Development Mechanics—Organizing Your Project.*

At this point, you've been exposed to the material and practices you need to do extreme programming. You need to exercise this knowledge and try it out in a more realistic setting. If you can find someone with a real programming problem for you to solve, that would be the best way to gain experience. If that is not an option, again have one person act as the client and pick a project that that person really wants done. Use one of the projects at the end of Chapter 3, if neither partner has such a project. Before starting the project, have the "client" flesh out their ideas enough so that when it comes time for a decision to be made, it goes quickly.

Self-paced, Self-taught Course for Two: Phase III, Putting it into Practice

13. Select a client and a project to gain hands-on XP experience.
14. Read Appendix A, *Experience in the Trenches—Sharing User Stories*.
15. Implement the project following the XP methodology.

If you found an outside client or picked a project that at least one of you really cares about, then the amount of time you put into the development is driven from outside, as it should be. If you are doing the project strictly as a learning process, then the criteria for continuing obviously corresponds to the level of continued learning.

An Individualized Approach

Learning XP by yourself is a less-than-ideal prospect from the outset. It's like training alone to play baseball. You can definitely work on your running, your throwing, and your swing, but alone, it's just not possible to react to "real" pitching, practice turning a double-play, or tracking down fly balls. Like baseball, XP is fundamentally a team activity, but its use requires individual skills. Learning these individual aspects makes sense from a self-improvement perspective and/or for the subsequent benefit of the team. If you are planning ahead and laying a foundation prior to initiating or joining an XP development effort, then you can focus on the individual skills and acquire the team aspects later. If you have no plans of joining an XP team in the foreseeable future, then you can still improve personal programming competence.

The best strategy for the self-taught student is to first focus on learning and experiencing the practices of test-driven development, simple design, and refactoring. These are the skills that will most directly improve individual software development abilities whether or not you eventually apply them to an actual XP development. This approach will capture a lot of the flavor of XP and improve your programming.

If you are preparing for an XP development effort, then it is worthwhile to work through the steps of the planning game, just to learn the procedure. Playing both the client and the developer simplifies the process, but it can also provide some insight to subsequent, multiple-participant efforts.

Self-paced, Self-taught Course for One: Phase I, Improving Individual Skills

1. Read the Introduction, Chapter 1, *The Metaphor—Developing a Sense of Where We're Headed,* and Chapter 2, *Getting Started—Introducing the Core XP Practices.*
2. Read Chapter 4, *First Test, Then Code—Understanding Why We Test First.*
3. Do the tutorial in Chapter 10, *Testing First—Learning a New Way of Life.*
4. Work through the exercises for both chapters.
5. Do the tutorial in Chapter 13, *Refactoring—Sharpening Your Knife.*

If you are preparing for an XP development, go through these four steps in detail, providing yourself with as much feeling for the process as possible without having a partner. If you are not getting ready for an XP development, but you expect to be writing code for someone else (if you're a contractor or freelancer), see if you can get a potential client to work through this process with you. If you're just writing code for yourself, then pick and choose from these ideas for the ones that work best for you. Even if you find none of them helpful, the readings and tutorials will give you an idea of what information XP developers expect to have when they start coding.

Self-paced, Self-taught Course for One: Phase II, Laying the Communication Groundwork

6. Read Chapter 5, *The Client—Meeting Another Team Member.*
7. Do the tutorial in Chapter 11, *User Stories—Exploring with the Customer.*
8. Do the tutorial in Chapter 12, *The Planning Game—Negotiating the Future.*
9. Do the tutorial in Chapter 14, *Customer Written Tests—Automating the Acceptance Process.*
10. Read Chapter 15, *Development Mechanics—Organizing Your Project.*

Pick one of the (smaller) projects at the end of Chapter 3 or select a project of your own. Depending on your interest level and the potential use of your programming skills, you may or may not want to develop user stories. If not, start working on your project using the techniques of testing first and refactoring. In lieu of user stories and derived tasks, you must decide what to work on next. However you do this, write a test first, satisfy that test as simply as possible, and refactor when appropriate. Even this limited approach will give rise to a very different development experience.

Even if you don't have an outside client, it makes sense to go through the steps of creating user stories and going through the planning game to generate tasks. This will add rigor not only to the test-driven development, but the overall process as well. Either play the part of the client yourself or enlist a surrogate's help. Work through the planning game to create a set of tasks to do on the first iteration. Then program those tasks using the techniques of testing first and refactoring. As you work on the project, read Chapter 3 and the rest of Part II to contrast your experience with that of a group XP effort.

References

Note that all websites references were accessed to verify that the resources are still in place as of August, 2003.

The Ant homepage. http://ant.apache.org

Auer, Ken, and Roy Miller, 2001. *Extreme Programming Applied: Playing to Win*. Addison-Wesley.

Beck, Kent. 1999. *Extreme Programming Explained.* Addison-Wesley.

Brooks, Frederick P. 1995. *The Mythical Man-Month: Essays on Software Engineering, Anniversary Edition.* 2d ed. Addison-Wesley.

Brooks, Frederick P. "No Silver Bullet." in *The Mythical Man-Month* (see above).

Cockburn, and Williams. *The Costs and Benefits of Pair Programming.* http://collaboration.csc.ncsu.edu/laurie/ Papers/XPSardinia.PDF

Cunningham, Ward, et al. "The Big Wiki." http://c2.com/cgi/wiki.

Cunningham, Ward, et al. "The Fit Wiki." http://fit.c2.com.

deMarco, Tom. 2002 *Slack: Getting Past Burnout, Busywork, and the Myth of Total Efficiency*. Broadway Books.

Fowler, Martin, et al. 1999. *Refactoring: Improving the Design of Existing Code*. Addison-Wesley.

Gamma, Erich, et al. 1995. *Design Patterns.* Addison-Wesley.

Hendrickson, Chet. "When Is it Not XP." http://www.xprogramming.com/xpmag/ NotXP.htm.

Hunt, Andrew, and David Thomas. 1999. *The Pragmatic Programmer: From Journeyman to Master.* Addison-Wesley.

Jeffries, Ron. "Essential XP: Documentation." http://www.xprogramming.com/xpmag/expDocumentationInXP.htm.

Jeffries, Ron. "Misconceptions about XP." http://www.xprogramming.com/xpmag/Misconceptions.htm.

Jeffries, Ron, Ann Anderson, and Chet Hendrickson. 2000. *Extreme Programming Installed.* Addison Wesley.

Johnson, Steven. 2002. *Emergence: The Connected Lives of Ants, Brains, Cities, and Software.* Touchstone Books.

The JUnit homepage. http://www.junit.org.

Kerievsky, Joshua. *Refactoring to Patterns.* http://industriallogic.com.

Martin, Robert Cecil. 2002. *Agile Software Development, Principles, Patterns, and Practices.* Prentice Hall.

Martin, Robert C., Micah Martin, et al. "The Fitnesse Wiki." http://www.fitnesse.org.

Martin, Robert C., and Robert S. Koss. "Engineer Notebook: An Extreme Programming Episode." http://www.objectmentor.com/resources/articles/xpepisode.htm.

McConnell, Steve. 1993. *Code Complete: A Practical Handbook of Software Construction.* Microsoft Press.

Moore, Chris. 2002. *Shooting Is Hard.* http://projectgreenlight.liveplanet.com/productions/byline.jsp?storynumber=546.

Palmer, David R. 1984. *Emergence.* Bantam Books.

Royce, Winston. 1970. "Waterfall Method."

Steinberg, Daniel H., et al., "Resources." http://www.extremeteaching.com.

Williams, Laurie, and Robert Kessler. 2002. *Pair Programming Illuminated.* Addison Wesley.

Index